ROLE

REVERSAL

ROLE REVERSAL

MAYNARD TAIT

ISBN, paperback: 978-1-80227-338-0
ISBN, ebook: 978-1-80227-339-7

This book is typeset in Garamond Premier Pro

For my wonderful, hard-working,
agreeable, and gorgeous wife, Jessica.

CONTENTS

Tom Farrow stepped into the corridor, turned, and pulled the heavy mahogany door into its frame behind him, as he left the musty, cigar smoke-filled boardroom of Thornes Paper Manufacturer and Distributors.

He swung around on his heels, lifted his head a little, and took a light hold of his Windsor knot to check that his striped navy and white silk tie was still neatly tucked up against his crisp shirt collar, before starting the two-minute walk back to his office on the second floor. He drew in a deep breath and let it out with a soothing 'Aaagh' as he began his return to the Customer Service department via Accounting, the Secretarial pool and Administration, catching the odd glance from some of the typists as he went, before reaching the stairwell that took him downstairs. A broad, tight-lipped smile covered his face as he walked, his teeth only showing as he smiled politely to people he passed on his way. At the top of the stairs, two women from the typing pool were returning to their desks after their coffee break, and both caught Tom's eyes and he stepped back to allow them room to pass.

'Tom Farrow – always the gentleman,' said the petite blonde-haired woman, throwing Tom a flirty glance.

'There's not many like you nowadays, Tom,' said the tall and slender redhead. 'You're a rare breed.'

Tom smiled awkwardly showing a little embarrassment.

'Afternoon ladies,' was all he could manage before trotting down the two flights of stairs.

On reaching the second floor, Tom entered the Customer Service department to the sound of phones ringing, endless chatter, and the incessant tapping of fingers on computer keyboards. He noticed several of the staff tidying up their desks and hurriedly putting away paperwork. He overheard some arranging to meet up in the pub next door in a few minutes, while others sat motionless on their chairs, coats on, bags and brollies in hand, staring up the clock, as the final working minutes of the week counted down. It was Friday afternoon. Two minutes to five and everyone was preparing for the mass exit, each one wanting to be ahead of the other. Tom quickened his pace as he walked through the chicane of work pods and reached his office with one minute to go before the department would spew its personnel towards the exit. He threw himself into his reclining chair, still grinning. He glanced down at a photograph of his family. His wife, Scarlett, looked stunning as ever in her black evening dress, and Alex, his six-month-old son, toothless and gormless, with a tuft of hair standing to attention on the top of his head.

'Life is great,' Tom whispered to himself, that smile widening as he spoke.

St John's church clock announced five pm by its dull and resonating bongs. Tom switched off his laptop, jumped to his feet, grabbed his backpack, and literally skipped towards the door of his office, not letting his dopey grin drop in the slightest. He opened the door, waited and watched as people across the department switched off their computers, put on their coats, and made their way to the doors. Just like every afternoon that had gone before, a bunch of people clogged together in the doorway, promptly followed by the customary apologies by everyone to everyone. They all had the same agenda, to get out of the office as fast as possible. After all, it was Friday and nobody wants to stay at work any longer than he or she has to, especially on a Friday.

Bidding farewell to Sylvia, his devoted secretary who was always the last person to leave the office, Tom slowly weaved his way to the exit. He stood well back from the fast disappearing crowd as he did every afternoon. He had been working at Thornes Printing Ltd for seven years and after some time he learnt how to deal with certain situations. Leaving the building on a Friday afternoon was one of those situations. He'd learnt to let the mass exit take place before him, to be patient, and then walk out without anyone stepping on his toes or shoving an umbrella up his backside. It happened once and he never fancied it happening again.

Once safely outside and on the pavement Tom took a long breath of the cool, crisp, early evening summer air and practically danced across the road to begin his walk home.

Tom was feeling very pleased with himself, not smug, simply pleased. Earlier in the day, after weeks of presenting stats and more stats, pie charts, graphs, etc., he had finally managed to convince the Board of Directors that job-sharing and flexible working hours were a viable option for the Customer Service department. They had agreed to start this new strategy the following week. Tom then spent the latter part of the day telling the staff the good news and advising them of their new shift patterns, before ending the day by confirming to the Board that everything was in place for the following week. It was a small win in the world of business and commerce, but trying to drag Thornes into the twenty-first century's way of doing business was like trying to tie shoelaces while wearing boxing gloves. It's not impossible, but blooming hard work. The company's owners and the majority of the Board were old school and disliked change. It may be the start of a new millennium, but they seemed stuck in the nineteen thirties. It always took something or someone special to convince them to make the smallest of advances. Tom was one of those people.

Months earlier a lot of the female employees, and one or two of the males, had voiced their opinions about wanting to working part-time or more flexible hours so they could spend more time at home with their children, or at least make it easier to arrange for childcare. Tom had agreed as Head of Department to bring the matter to the attention of the Board of Directors. He did so and came up trumps.

The staff at Thornes felt able to approach Tom. He's a good bloke. He's one of them. He's not a lofty, self-important kind of guy. He's kind, considerate, and a man of integrity. He has a handsome and dependable face, and a head full of well-coiffured brown hair. He stands an inch short of six feet tall; not muscular, but lean and trim, and although he is thirty years old, the ladies say that he doesn't look a day over twenty-five. Some of the blokes say he looks at least thirty-five but that's just envy talking. Tom prides himself on being a hard worker, a constant in times of trouble. He consistently breaks targets set by his bosses and always produces a high standard of work; often well in advance of deadlines. In short, he's the company's golden boy.

At least, he used to be.

Tom began to whistle as he walked home through the park. It wasn't anything recognisable, just a pleasant melody he had composed himself. He could hear the birds singing in the trees, the laughter of children as they played in the sandpit, the playful barking of dogs as they frolicked across the grass chasing someone's ball. Yes, life was grand today.

A pop-up flower stall at the park exit was selling bunches of carnations and he bought two for Scarlett, one yellow, the other blue.

Tom walked home after work every day and usually passed by the same people. He didn't necessarily know them all, but he'd recognise many of the same faces. He'd lived in Frankfield all his life, and as it wasn't a large town, it was inevitable he'd see some people regularly.

On Frant Street, to the north side of the park, was Harry's Butchers, owned, and run by his good friend George. No, not Harry, as you might expect. Harry was his grandfather who established the business almost fifty years earlier. He passed it on to George's dad, also called Harry, who then passed it on to his son, George, before passing away a few years ago following a vicious attack from a very reluctant turkey a few days before Christmas. George turned vegetarian soon after his father's demise, but wanted to honour his father's life and the family business, so decided to keep the name 'Harry' above the shop window. For a while, he considered changing his own name to Harry by deed poll, but he thought that would be extreme. He actually only stayed a vegetarian for four days. After his father's funeral, he reopened the butcher's for business and he found a tray of pork pies that were one day out of date, so he ate the lot, putting it down to grief, and the fact that he absolutely loved his shop-made pork pies and hates food waste.

Today, as Tom walked past, George was demonstrating how to stuff a goose to two female customers, while a couple of men, presumably their other halves, stood behind with their hands in their pockets chewing their bottom lips.

George liked the women and was a well-established flirt. He'd spend ages at the counter enticing them with all sorts of cuts of British beef and Welsh lamb, often offering tips on how to cook them and serve them. Tom chuckled as he watched the master at work before proceeding onward.

A couple of streets later Sam, Tom's local postman and old school friend, was collecting the five fifteen post from a pillar-box. He stood rock steady next to the post box looking down at his watch, while swinging the box key on a chain with his other hand.

Tom checked his watch. It was fourteen minutes past five. Sam would never empty the post boxes any earlier than they had to be. As soon as it was time, Sam would launch the key into the box and rapidly spill its contents into an empty grey bag, close the door with a clang and withdraw the key with a flick of his wrist, the key landing neatly into his trouser pocket. He'd toss the bag over his shoulder, walk to his van, and set the bag down carefully inside against all the other mailbags, before shutting the door and then standing for a few seconds, waiting for the inevitable call from a late poster. Today was no exception.

'Hang on a minute!' Tom could hear.

The skinny office-junior from Woods Estate Agents was running toward Sam with two A4 envelopes clutched in each hand, his pencil necktie swinging loosely around his neck. Sam yanked on his key chain and the key flew out of his pocket. He grabbed the key with his other hand and forced it into the door lock, turned the handle and opened the door swiftly, dropped the key chain and pulled the opening of the postbag nice and wide. The boy came to a stop and dumped the envelopes into the bag.

'Thanks again!' he puffed as he turned and ran back the way he came.

Sam closed the van door and noticed Tom walking by on the other side of the street.

'Oi-oi, Tom! Y'know, sometimes I wonder what repercussions there would be across the world of business if I didn't wait for him every day,' he shouted.

'You're too kind, Sam. That's your problem,' replied Tom as he carried on walking.

As he turned into Firefly Crescent, he caught the scent of wisteria. It was always a pleasant daily experience at this time of year. The plant completely covered the front of Maud's house so much so you could barely see the windows on the first floor and just about see through into the ground floor sitting room, and there she was. This constant in Tom's life smiling out through the thin white voile curtains waving furiously at him.

As far as Tom was concerned, Maud was the oldest woman alive. According to his calculations, Maud must be at least six hundred and twenty-five by now. Tom's Dad first introduced him to her when he was only five. Back then, he had told him that 'she was as old as the hills'. Tom, being five and not having much knowledge about the geology of the earth, guessed that the hills around Frankfield had been in existence for about six hundred years, or thereabouts, so considering he's now thirty...

Maud, without fail, would manage a wave as he passed by her front window every day and she would always have a baby perched on a hip. Maud had been a nanny for as long as Tom could remember, but despite her age, whatever it may be, she still holds down a full-time job. She loves children and there is no one else you could trust to leave your kids with at short notice.

This is just as well, because soon enough Tom would be making full use of Maud.

Tom arrived home at five twenty, just as usual. He walked up the garden path, passed the family saloon, skipped up the two steps to the door under the porch, inserted his front door key in the lock, and entered.

'Hello Darling' was on the tip of his tongue before it all went dark, moist, and smelly. Just as Tom recognised the stench of urine, a soiled nappy fell from his face and flopped to the ground. Tom opened his mouth to yell something ungodly when a sudden pain arrived in his groin and brought him crashing to the ground, landing on his knees with a thud. He doubled over in agony and he thought he could hear giggling. Through squinted-eyes, he could just make out the shape of a little boy, laughing uproariously. The boy picked up the nappy and plopped it onto Tom's head, before turning and running away, his chubby, bare behind wobbling as he ran. Tom managed to suck in enough air to excrete a weak and high-pitched scream of pain just as he heard a low rumbling sound coming from the other end of the hallway. It increased in volume and he could feel the vibrations through his knees as he rested on the oak flooring. Lifting his head slightly he saw a baby encompassed by a plastic-frame on wheels hurtling down the hallway at full pelt, a blood-curdling squeal emanating from its mouth, and then...contact.

Tom took the blow full on his forehead and forced backwards, his head crashing into the front door. Then it went quiet.

Tom woke up lying on the sofa in the sitting room with a cold compress on his crown and a wet flannel covering his thumping, hot forehead. He was delirious. Scarlett hovered over him and removed the flannel to check for any lasting damage.

'What happened?' he groaned. 'Did I trip on the front step again? I had such a horrible nightmare. How long have I been out?'

'Only five minutes,' replied Scarlett softly. 'You took quite a wallop on your forehead, but it was the knock on the door that put you to sleep. It could have been much worse. I'd say the nappy cushioned the blow.'

'And what is that smell?' he asked, poking his nose into his armpit.

'The flowers you bought perhaps? Thanks for those by the way.'

'No...no...'

'Oh, it'll be the smelling salts,' Scarlett responded. 'You were really out of it.'

'No, no. It's...' Tom sniffed. 'It's definitely not that. More of a...' He sniffed again. 'More like a wet nappy sort of smell.'

Scarlett leaned over Tom and sniffed the top of his head.

'Eugh, you're right,' she said. 'You need a shower.'

Tom swivelled and sat upright.

'No, it's definitely a nappy stench.' He tilted his head to the left a little, his memory returning. 'A nappy, yes, now I remember. I came in and a nappy landed in my face, and then, and then...'

'Darling, I need to tell you...' Scarlett interjected.

'...something hit me. I fell to the floor and then...'

'Sweetheart, let me explain.'

'...a baby-walker came toward me and then pain, and then darkness.'

'Tom!' Scarlett snapped.

Just then, Tom heard the same low rumbling sound he heard before passing out and into the room came the rolling contraption, badly driven by...

'A baby!' said Tom matter-of-factly.

'Now, sweetheart, don't get upset. There's something I need to tell you.'

'It's a baby,' Tom offered. 'And it's not ours!'

'Yes, it's a baby,' said Scarlett. 'Well done. At least your observational skills haven't been affected.'

A crashing sound came from the kitchen.

'What was that?' Tom shouted. 'Alex?'

'Oh no! Look, it's not Alex. He's fast asleep upstairs. Um, that'll be the other two,' replied Scarlett, rather cautiously.

'Other two?' asked Tom. 'What other two?'

'Polly and Ralph, they're twins.'

With both hands holding his fragile head, Tom forced himself to his feet and stormed into the kitchen to find two semi-naked children lying on the floor, waving their legs and arms back and forth, covered in baking flour, surrounded by empty cake tins and saucepans.

'Snow angels!' shouted one of them.

'Oops!' said the other before chuckling.

Tom turned to his wife. 'Scarlett. Please can I have a word, in the front room?'

He left the kitchen and Scarlett followed him back into the sitting room where Jasper, the eleven-month-old terror, had somehow escaped the clutches of the plastic-framed walker, found and unzipped Tom's backpack and stuck his head into it. He got to his feet and then toppled forward into the sofa, knocking himself back down again. He giggled, then farted, and then giggled again.

'Okay, here goes,' said Scarlett, followed by a brief pause and a deep breath.

'Do you remember Jackie, from my Tupperware party? The one married to the naval officer?'

'Yes, I think so. What about her?' he snorted.

'Well, she's been going through quite a rough patch recently and she's been admitted to Montague clinic, and I said we could look after the kids for a while, you know, until she gets back on her feet again.'

'What's Montague clinic?' Tom growled. 'A psychiatric unit, perhaps? Because I've only been home ten minutes and already these kids have used me as a punch bag, crash barrier, and waste disposal unit! It's enough to drive anyone nuts.'

Tom was actually being uncharacteristically sarcastic when mentioning the clinic, but the disappointed look Scarlett gave him confirmed he was right.

'Oh,' he mumbled apologetically. 'What's the matter with her?'

'She's clinically depressed and she needs to sort herself out. Nick, her husband, won't quit the navy despite saying he would after he'd served for ten years. It's been fourteen now. Having the three kids, and not knowing if or when she'd have Nick back home again, just got on top of her and it all got too much. All her family live in Ireland and she doesn't want to move back there. She's finding life very hard now, having to cope on her own, Tom. Her consultant hopes she'll be out in a couple of months.' Scarlett spat that one out without any warning.

'Two months,' Tom yelled. 'Did you say two months?'

'Well, it's a private clinic, so there's no rush. If it were the NHS, she'd probably be out in a day or two with a bag of pills and told to fend for herself. Scratch that, if it were the NHS she'd still be on a two year waiting list before she'd even get seen.'

'I hope you didn't agree to look after the spawn of Satan for the whole two months. Did you?'

She nodded.

'Oh, Tom, I'm sorry,' she said. 'And the spawn of Satan is a bit harsh, they're not that bad. Look, Jackie needed someone she could trust, and with a large enough home, and she thought of us. She was desperate. It was either us or their grandmother in Cork - we seemed the obvious choice. I couldn't say no, Tom. She's a friend and friends help each other out. That's what you're always telling me, isn't it?'

'Yes, but how are you going to cope with three kids you know very little about, look after Alex, and run the house at the same time? You tell me you can't even manage to run the vacuum cleaner around the house once a week sometimes. Although you do seem to fit in yoga, swimming, coffee with friends, and a book club during the week. Moreover, what about washing, clothing, and feeding three extra children? It'll be too much for you.'

'Well, I was hoping you would help out a little too,' she said.

'Me?' Tom asked in surprise. He was sort of hoping she was trying to make light of the situation by cracking a joke but her facial expression proved otherwise.

'Scarlett, I have my hands full at work as it is, and you want me to come home and change nappies, clean spilt porridge off the kitchen floor, not just by Alex but three other kids. I'll be exhausted enough without all the extra hassle. Uh-uh, no way. You can't drag me into this.'

Tom dropped himself onto the sofa and closed his eyes in the hope that he was actually still unconscious and dreaming, and when he opened them, all he would see was Scarlett handing him a tumbler of whisky and the evening paper. No such luck. Scarlett sat down on the sofa and snuggled against him.

'Darling?' she said

'What?' Tom barked.

'Did you get the go ahead for job-sharing at work?'

'Yes, thank goodness. Why?'

'Well, I was kind of thinking that maybe we could job-share.'

'WHAT!'

Tom rose from the sofa again and glared, wide-eyed at Scarlett, as if she was insane. Perhaps she was. Maybe temporary insanity had set in and that's how this had all come about. The idea of looking after four children filled Tom with dread. One was hard enough.

'Tom, you agreed to job-sharing at work because you said you believed that parents need to spend more time with their families,' reminded Scarlett.

'I meant mothers, not parents. Anyway these aren't my children,' he replied in defence.

'You did mean parents, I read your notes for the Board meeting,' Scarlett said flatly. 'Imagine how everyone at work could see how you are reacting right now. They think you can cope with anything. That the sun shines out of your backside. Mr Perfect, my foot, more like Mr Two-Face.'

Scarlett began to change tactics very quickly and Tom sensed it. Her tone of voice became more intimidating and it got louder. He knew where she was going but he couldn't interrupt – he knew better than that. After all, they had worked side by side at Thornes for three years before getting married and he knew how she operated. Scarlett took maternity leave one month before Alex was born with every intention of returning once they had found a suitable nursery for him. They hadn't found one yet. When Scarlett had an agenda, she wouldn't let anyone get in her path. She knew her opponents weak spots and she used them to her advantage every time. As she spoke and walked towards Tom slowly, she gauged his reaction to her taunting.

'If they saw you now,' she said, 'they would see a scared, weak, gutless little pip-squeak who can't practice what he preaches. The truth of the matter is you're not up to the task. You couldn't cope!'

Scarlett threw down the gauntlet, and those last three words hurt, especially as she poked Tom's chest with her index finger while spitting them out. Tom wanted to defend himself, but couldn't. She was right and he knew it. Four children against one adult just isn't fair. What was he to do? She also used her words as a challenge and Tom never turned down a challenge. He was Tom Farrow. A man you could depend upon to fulfil an obligation, someone who saw things through to the end. The winner in all things. At least he was at work!

He lifted his head to the ceiling, turned away from her, rested both out-stretched arms against the fireplace, and considered her challenge.

'So you don't think I could cope?' he said quietly. 'You don't think I'm up to the challenge of feeding, washing, and playing with four delightful little cherubs?'

He paused for dramatic effect, took a deep breath, before turning towards

Scarlett.

'Well you're wrong. I could do it as well as you, if...not...better.' Those last three words he delivered individually with force. If she could attack then Tom could retaliate. She wasn't going to win this argument and he would prove it. 'I mean, how hard could it be looking after children anyway? Millions of people do it every day. If you want to job-share,' Tom hesitated slightly, 'then we'll do it. I accept your challenge.'

'Oh, Tom, do you mean it?' asked Scarlett. 'You won't regret it.

It'll be like a trial period if we finally decide to have more children of our own. Oh, thank-you,' she said, wrapping herself around him. 'It'll be such fun!'

Not how Tom would have put it!

'On one condition!' he said.

Scarlett pulled back a little and looked at him nervously.

'What condition?' she asked.

'That I work at the office in the mornings and you do the afternoons. Deal?'

'Deal.'

Scarlett called for Polly & Ralph to join them in the sitting room. They came charging in both with sheepish looks on their four-year-old faces, wisps of flour floating behind them. Scarlett introduced Tom to them as 'Uncle Tom'. He suddenly felt old and over-dressed. He doesn't sport a moustache or own a tweed jacket, never mind a pipe or slippers! He felt too young to be an uncle.

Tom bent over toward the children.

'Hi. I'm Tom,' he said flatly.

'We know that, silly,' chuckled Ralph.

'She just said that,' laughed Polly, pointing at Scarlett.

'Yes, yes, she did. So, are you looking forward to living with us for a while?' he asked.

Silence.

Tom waited for an answer to come from their blank faces, but it wasn't forthcoming. They stared at him with a fixed gaze as if he had spoken in a language they didn't understand.

'Right, well, what do you like to do?' he asked. 'Do you like to play in the park? There's a nice one nearby, perhaps we could go there tomorrow, after breakfast.'

More silence.

'Okay, ah...rugby, do you like rugby? I could take you to a match tomorrow?'

Even more silence.

Tom was struggling to communicate. The king of communication had been dethroned. What was he doing wrong? Why wouldn't they answer?

Scarlett squatted down beside them and with widened eyes, gave them a big grin. 'I know. Why don't you both run upstairs and see who can get undressed first and then I'll give you a bubble bath, yeah?'

'YEAH!' they screamed in unison.

They bumped into each other as they quickly turned to race each other up the stairs.

'I'm the winner, I'm the winner!' shouted Ralph.

'No you're not, I'm going to win!' responded Polly.

'You can't win, you're a girl!' snapped Ralph as he reached the top of the stairs, just behind Polly.

'Girls can win too.'

'No they can't.'

'Yes they can.'

'No they can't.

Tom sighed heavily as he walked to the bottom of the stairs and watched the two children undress at the top of the landing, throwing socks and tops left, right and centre.

'What have you gotten us into,' he said desperately.

Scarlett hugged Tom with a glint of satisfaction in her eyes.

'I'm not sure, but we're the Farrows. We'll cope.'

Maynard Tait

2

Over the course of the weekend, Tom had mastered the art of dodging flying nappies and had managed to sort out with his line manager, Gilbert, the job-sharing details for himself and Scarlett. Tom would leave work at one pm and Scarlett would go in as soon as he returned home; she would take over any work that he had started that day and he would take over at home. At least that was the plan.

On Monday morning, Tom arrived at the office five minutes late. This was the first time he had been late in over six years. As he sat down at his desk, Sylvia came rushing in to his office to see if everything was all right.

'Tom! Tom! What happened? Are you hurt? You don't look hurt!' she said. Her half-mooned glasses fell off her nose but stopped from crashing to the floor by the thick, gold chain from which they hung.

'I'm fine, Sylvia,' said Tom. 'Why are you so panicky? I'm only five minutes late for goodness sake. As unusual as it may be it's not the end of the world.'

'Oh, I'm sorry. Maureen in accounts just told me that she saw a man fitting your description get knocked down by a bicycle in the park a short while ago and there was an ambulance and policemen and...'

'Sylvia, it wasn't me and the young man who was knocked over is fine. Just a broken wrist, that's all. I saw the whole thing and called the emergency services from my mobile. But that's not why I was late,' he added.

'Oh! Then why are you late?' enquired Sylvia.

'Well, it's a long story, but basically, as of today I shall be working part-time, mornings only, for the next couple of months, with Scarlett taking over from me in the afternoons. We have temporarily adopted three children from a manic-depress...er...a friend in need, whose husband is refusing to quit sailing the high seas. And lastly,' he said taking out an unused nappy from his briefcase and holding it up. 'Do you know how to keep these on?'

Sylvia's mouth dropped and she gave Tom a stern look.

'Oh, Mr Farrow. Really!' She turned on her five-inch heels and tutted the whole way back to her desk.

Just as Tom took a rather large bite out of a Danish pastry, Sir Wilfred, the Chief Executive and owner of Thornes, came into Tom's office. He dropped the pastry immediately and grabbed a tissue to mop crumbs from his lips. Sir Wilfred's visits to various departments were scarce and always unannounced. Tom just wished he'd at least knock.

'Morning, Farrow, old boy! How's the wife? Tickety-boo, one hopes,' he boomed.

'Er...yes, Sir Wilf...' mumbled Tom as he stood up from behind his desk.

'Good, good. Always helps to have a good woman to keep a good man in order. Any little Farrows running around the home yet, Farrow?' he asked.

'Yes. Four of them...' Tom answered with flecks of pastry flying through his pursed lips.

'Good heavens, man. You have been busy, haven't you? I'm surprised you don't struggle to get up in the mornings. I certainly do. Something to do with my age the quack keeps telling me.'

Tom smiled awkwardly as he swallowed his mouthful.

'I see what you mean, sir, very witty. No, only one of them is...'

He cut Tom off again. Sir Wilfred is renowned for never letting anyone finish his or her sentences. Instead, he finishes them for them in the hope he can crack a joke or two at their expense or else he'll just ignore them and carry on talking. Very rude, but no one would dare complain about it. He walked behind Tom and wrapped his wealthy frame around him.

'Got to show these women whose boss, you know. Take control. Their place is in the home, Farrow. They are the caretakers of all that we possess. We provide the money; they provide the heirs. We must be the king of our castle, Farrow. If we're not careful, one day they'll stand up and rebel, and then where would we be, eh Farrow?'

'Well, I'm not sure...'

'Well, mustn't dally. I have a business to run. Just thought I'd pop in to congratulate you on this job-share project. It's marvellous, Farrow. First class.'

'Why, thank-you, Sir Wilf...' Tom managed to utter.

'Good to show the women that we care once in a while. It gives them a sense of pride in what they do. Also means that their men get a hot meal at the end of every day, eh Farrow?' he snorted.

'Well, I guess so, sir. Mind you, we men could do more around the house to help out occasion...'

'Quite right, quite right.' He stood bolt upright, walked to the door, and opened it. 'I mean, you wouldn't want a woman pruning your prize orchids, now would you?' he said, leaving the office. 'Keep up the good work, Farrow,' he bellowed after him.

'Thank you, sir,' Tom whispered.

It was almost midday, when Tom had a text from Scarlett asking him to buy some milk on the way home for the children. Apparently, Polly thought it would be a good idea to give her dollies a milk bath because 'it was good for their skin'! She had been watching an educational programme on the television about ancient Egyptians, and it described how Cleopatra used to bathe in milk. Tom thought it just as well they didn't tell the story of baby Moses. He had visions of seeing baby Alex floating across the park pond in a plastic flowerpot.

Tom was disturbed from his daydream by Edward Thorne, Sir Wilfred's nephew, and Scarlett's replacement when she went on maternity leave, hence, Tom's fellow Head of Department. Sir Wilfred gave Edward a job at Thornes to keep him from gallivanting around the world, spending his trust funds in wild abandon, and Monte Carlo, his favourite haunt.

Edward was twenty-four and ruggedly good-looking. His limited brain obviously lay somewhere between his glutei and his knees because every time he had an idea – a word used very loosely with Edward – instead of following the usual practice of scratching one's head, he would scratch his backside. He was a man Tom had no faith in and the last person anyone would trust with a project, which was why his next words took Tom by surprise.

'Uncle Wilfred has given me a project,' he said with complacency.

'What! You!' Tom was genuinely surprised. 'And what exactly have you been asked to do? Find out how many of the female employees wear suspenders and how many wear tights?' Sarcasm may be the lowest form of wit but it was all he could muster for Edward.

Most people spoke to Edward with care and respect. After all, he was the boss's nephew – he could get you fired. At least Edward led everyone to believe. Tom knew otherwise. Sir Wilfred had employed Edward at the request of his late father as stipulated in his last Will and Testament, but had wanted to sack him at the earliest opportunity. Despite Edward's incompetency, Sir Wilfred hadn't yet found a solid and valid reason to get rid of him. However, Sir Percy's will stated, that if Edward should lose his job without good reason, he could contest in court for fifty per cent of the company, which was his rightful inheritance. Sir Percy was fully aware of his son's lack of business acumen, which is why before he died he passed his half of the company to his brother, Sir Wilfred. Edward was just another employee, but in his eyes, he was the heir to the throne.

'Very droll, Tom. No, it's nothing so inviting as that but it may give me the chance of promotion.'

'Promotion?' Tom replied in amazement. 'What do you mean promotion? If anyone is in line for a promotion around here, it's me. I hardly think Sir Wilfred wants you any closer to him than you already are. He can hardly bear to have you in the same with him building never mind on the same floor.'

Edward knew of his uncle's feelings toward him but he also knew that Sir Wilfred was the key to fifty per cent of the company and Edward would do anything to get it. The problem was he didn't have the brains to figure out how, or so Tom thought.

'I overheard Uncle Wilf on the phone this morning and it seems that old buzzard, Crinshaw, intends to retire in a couple of months' time, which means they will be looking for a new Customer Service Dictator,' he said.

Edward's use of the English language leaves a lot to be desired, and often makes Tom wonder how he ever managed to complete even a simple application form for anything, if indeed he ever had. Tom could imagine the opening few lines:

NAME: Edward Thorne

ADDRESS: same as Uncle Wilfred

DATE OF BIRTH: 1976

SEX: Looking forward to it!

Tom regathered his thoughts. 'Gilbert Crinshaw is retiring?' he asked. 'But he's not even sixty yet. And I believe you mean Customer Service Director, not dictator, Edward.'

'I know what I mean,' he barked. 'Seems the old boy has a breast condition and the stress of the job isn't very good for him, so his wife wants him to stop work early. When I first heard of it I thought it meant he would leave at four every day instead of five,' he giggled. 'But I'm not that daft. I soon got the right end of the twig.'

'Chest condition, Edward,' Tom corrected. 'Poor bloke's got angina. I never realised it was that bad.'

'Yes, right, well, as I was saying someone is going to have to fill his slippers and I'm going to be the one.' Edward's tone was defiant.

Tom got up from his chair and slowly walked over to Edward and put his arm around his shoulders.

'Dear Edward. I have been with this firm for seven years now and if anyone is going to get the job, it'll be me. I have the experience, the knowledge, and the tenacity, and above all the Board of Directors actually like me. I've been waiting for this opportunity for three years and I'll prove to the Board over the next two months that I am the right person for the job. Not you or anyone else and there's nothing you will be able to do about it.'

Edward shrugged off his arm and shuffled over to the door and after opening it, he turned to display a smug grin.

'Ah, that's where you are mistaken, Tom. You see, I've got a head start,' he said. 'Thanks to my position in the family and because I move within the right social circles, I have been able to discover what makes each Board member tick and what turns them on. So, over the next couple of months I'll be making sure that their, how shall I put it, hearts desires are met, if you get my meaning?'

'Oh, I think I do. You're going to bribe them with whatever they want, within reason of course.'

'Of course,' said Edward. 'Wouldn't want to spoil them too much, would I? It always worked with the Masters at school. No reason why it won't work here.'

'Sir Wilfred will see right through your scheming little plan and fire you immediately. It'll never work. You may as well not bother,' Tom warned him.

'Already another step ahead of you, old chum,' he scoffed.

Tom was beginning to realise Edward wasn't always as stupid as he made out. Perhaps he had a helper who gave him ideas like the elves help Santa Claus at Christmas time. Whatever was going on in his devilish mind he gave Tom the impression that he had thought it all through carefully.

'Uncle Wilfred has been eyeing up one of the young fillies in the typing pool and it just so happens that she's willing to play games with him for a while, at least until I become the new Director, of course.'

'And what does she get at the end of the game?'

'Just to be my Personal Assistant, and a huge bonus, naturally,' said Edward as he turned to leave. 'Bon chintz, as they say in France.'

Tom sat down and immediately began to think about what he was going to do to secure the job of Customer Service Director. He had been working towards this job for a long time. It was his goal. He certainly wasn't going to let Edward Thorne stand in his way. Just as he was about to make some notes, Sylvia rushed in.

'Tom, Scarlett has just called and she wanted to know why you haven't left yet! She's ready to leave and wants you back home.'

Tom looked at his watch. It was one thirty pm.

'Fiddle!'

He grabbed his coat and ran out of the office brushing past Sylvia.

'See you tomorrow!'

Tom arrived home at one forty pm after running the whole way. He was shattered and sweating profusely. Scarlett glared at him as he staggered through the door.

'Great start, Tom. My first day back to the office and I'm late,' she snarled. 'Alex and Jasper are both asleep upstairs and should be for another hour or so. Polly and Ralph are in the sitting room watching 'Scooby Doo'.'

She looked down at his hands. 'Where's the milk?'

'Milk? What Milk?'

'Tom! I texted you earlier.'

'Ah, yes, sorry. I got distracted. Anyway, if I did stop to buy some I wouldn't even be back yet,' he replied.

'Then you're going to have to go out and get some. I promised the twins banana custard for pudding this evening and they have their hearts set on it. Now, what do I have to look forward to at the office this afternoon?'

Tom filled Scarlett in on the morning's happenings and after giving him a kiss on the cheek, she headed off to work. While he would be playing with the kids, she would be drafting a plan to make sure he got the job of Customer Service Director.

Tom went into the kitchen to make himself a sandwich. Scarlett had left notes on the refrigerator door about each child. They were quite comprehensive, but fool proof. Scarlett obviously wanted to make this new job as easy as possible for Tom. He had just sat down to eat his lunch when he had a feeling he was being watched. Out of the corner of his left eye, he could see Polly and Ralph standing side by side in the hallway, staring straight at him. He felt like Jack Nicholson must have done in 'The Shining'. He didn't know if they were going to come and stab him or tickle him to death. He had no idea what was going on in their limited minds. Ralph turned his head and whispered something to Polly. She looked back at him and nodded slowly. Ralph took two small steps towards Tom and stopped. He continued to stare up at him. Polly coughed lightly which caused Ralph to look round at her. She nodded at him again and he turned back to Tom and walked to the side of his chair. He raised his arm and gently tugged at Tom's shirtsleeve.

'Yes, Ralph?' Tom asked nervously.

Ralph looked deep into Tom's eyes and said, 'Are you our daddy?'

Tom was flabbergasted.

'Pardon?'

He knew their father was in the Navy, but surely, he came home occasionally! Had he really been gone that long they had forgotten what he looks like? Tom tried to be tactful.

'Don't be daft! Of course I'm not your dad,' he said with a laugh.

Ralph's facial expression didn't change. Perhaps Tom was a bit abrupt. Maybe he didn't understand the question.

'Ralph? Why did you ask me that?'

'Well, if you're not our dad, then you can't tell us off like our real dad, can you?'

'What do you mean, Ralph?' Tom asked.

'Well, when we do something wrong, Dad always shouts at us and he makes us cry. You wouldn't make us cry, would you?'

All of a sudden, Ralph's face turned into that of a puppy dog. The edges of his mouth turned downwards and pouted; his sad eyes almost doubled in size. Tom could almost hear him whimper. How could anyone shout at such an angelic little face? Sure, children play up a little, but that's what they do. There's no point in losing the rag just because they've been a little bit silly. After all, they don't know any better.

Tom put his hands on Ralph's shoulders. 'Ralph,' he said, 'I won't make you or Polly cry as long as you are both living here. I promise.'

Polly walked forward and asked, 'What's a promise?'

'A promise is when someone says they'll do something or keep from doing something, and then they stick to it. Like when I said I promise never to make you cry, means I'll never make you cry.'

'Even if we do something really bad?' asked Ralph.

'Er...well, yes, I guess so. If you do something very bad then we'll sit down and have a chat about it, like adults. Scarlett or I will explain why you shouldn't have done what you did and then you will know not to do it again. That's the way grown-ups do things, well, they're supposed to anyway.'

'But what if we break things?' said Polly.

Tom was beginning to feel sorry for the children. Their father must have been a real ogre. It sounded as if he was always angry and shouting at them. Tom didn't want their stay with him to be horrible, so he thought the passive approach would be the best one.

'Polly, people don't break things on purpose. That's what's called an accident.' He thought he'd make it personal just to reassure them. 'When I was your age, I remember I was riding my bicycle along my parents' driveway and I tried to pull the brakes to stop, but they didn't work. I kept going and going until I rode into one of my mum's flowerpots. The bicycle knocked over the pot and it smashed into bits. My mum came rushing out of the house to see what had happened. I told her and she looked at me and said, 'Don't worry, son. It was an accident,' and everything was all right.'

'Didn't she shout at you?' asked Ralph.

'No, not at all. In fact she gave me a hug and said I could help her put the plant into a new pot.'

Polly and Ralph looked at each other and smiled. As Tom rose from his chair, they both wrapped their arms around his legs and said, 'We love you, Uncle Tom.'

He was overwhelmed. They were lovely kids, really. He just had them figured out wrong, that's all.

'I...er...quite like you too,' he told them.

'And you promise never to make us cry?' asked Ralph.

'Never,' he replied honestly.

'Good,' said Polly curtly as they both let go of Tom. 'Coz we had an accident in the sitting room.'

The almost tearful smile on Tom's face fell.

'What kind of accident?'

'Come and see,' said Ralph, with excitement in his voice, as he ran back into the sitting room with Polly.

The palms of Tom's hands became sweaty. He swallowed hard and walked into the sitting room then screamed.

'AAAAAAAGGHHHH! What have you done?' he shrieked rhetorically.

He stared at the sofa in disbelief. It was a mess. Cushion's had various colours of felt tip pen scrawled all over them like a Jackson Pollock painting.

'Ralph was standing on the sofa, trying to draw some men on your picture, but the pen broke,' explained Polly. 'He nearly fell off the sofa so he grabbed the picture, but it fell off the wall and landed on the table.'

Tom looked from the ink-stained sofa to the corner of the coffee table.

'My Lowrie! That's an original Lowrie print,' he cried. 'It's ruined!'

The picture had been punctured on the corner of the table, and hung down, swinging gently.

'It was an accident,' said Ralph, 'so everything's okay.'

'No Ralph, everything is not okay.' Tom's voice rose in harmony with his blood pressure. 'We bought this only last week. Do you know how much this cost? Do you? This cost me two months' salary. That's how much it cost and now it's ruined. And just look at the sofa. It's covered in ink. That'll never come out.'

Tom picked up the picture and almost wept, but anger kept him from doing so.

'Why don't you just buy another one?' asked Polly.

Suddenly, he snapped.

'Another one? You can't just buy another one!' he yelled. 'How stupid are you? Some of these are rare and very expensive. You have just cost me thousands of pounds. Do you know how much that is? And that doesn't include the sofa. You stupid, stupid little brats.'

Polly and Ralph started to cry.

'Oh, that's just great,' Tom said, 'I should be the one crying, not you.'

The crying turned into wailing. Just then, he could hear more crying. It was from upstairs. Jasper had woken up.

'No, not now.'

Tom ran up the stairs to find Jasper sitting on the floor and rubbing his head. He looked around to find a makeshift ladder, made from cuddly toys, in the corner of the cot. Jasper had obviously climbed over the top of the cot and fallen out onto his head. Tom picked him up and carried him downstairs to find Polly and Ralph still standing in the same place and crying louder than ever.

'Oh, come on you two, knock it off.'

'You promised,' wailed Polly.

'Promised what?' Tom asked.

'Not to make us cry,' spat Ralph.

Tom collapsed into the armchair and stared at Jasper's wet and snotty face.

'Please Lord,' he prayed earnestly. 'Give me strength.'

3

The telephone rang at four thirty pm and the insistent chirping woke Tom from a deep sleep. He groped for the receiver and inadvertently knocked an empty tumbler of the bedside table.

'Hello!'

'Hi, it's me,' said Scarlett. 'How are things going?' There was a pause. 'It sounds very quiet.'

'Jush fine, jush fine.'

'Tom. Have you been drinking?' she asked.

'Jush a lirl bit.'

'Tom, you shouldn't be drinking with the children in the house.'

'Oh, it's fine,' he told her. 'They're not here. I took them to see Maud.'

'Tom, you can't just fob the children off onto Maud whenever you feel like it. She already has two children to look after, full-time, and on your first day with them. I can't believe you, Tom.'

'She said she didn't mind. She also said she could give them their tea, so it's worked out okay. She said she'd give them custard for pudding. Anyway, they annoyed me. I had to get rid of them so I could calm down.'

'What did they do?'

'They only went and ruined the Lowrie, and the sofa.'

'What! Oh-no!' said Scarlett, 'I hope you didn't go too hard on them. We can replace the sofa and get money for the print back from the insurance company anyway, can't we?'

Tom gulped heavily before answering.

'For the sofa, yes,' he winced, knowing what was about to come.

'And what about the print?' asked Scarlett.

There was another pause.

'You did add it to the policy, didn't you?'

More dead air.

'Didn't you?'

'I forgot,' mumbled Tom.

'You forgot!' she yelled, before launching into a verbal attack on Tom's intelligence.

Tom had been so busy at work, what with the job-share project, that he had honestly forgotten to call the insurance company. Somehow, he didn't think they would see it that way, nor did Scarlett. Scarlett hung up the phone after warning Tom that she would be late home, as Sylvia had dumped some customer complaint letters on her desk that needed urgent attention, and telling him to tidy up the house before she got back. Tom dropped the phone onto the floor, slumped back onto his pillows, and relaxed into another deep sleep. Too much whisky has that effect on him!

Tom woke at five thirty pm and the house was silent. He didn't know what time Scarlett would be back but he had to make sure that he had collected the children from Maud's before she got back. His body and heart had other plans, however. He lay completely still and stared at a small speck of blue paint on the bedroom ceiling. It made him think of how he constantly tried to cover up who he really was and where he came from. He had painted the ceiling with white emulsion but even after three thick coats, there was still evidence of what went before. It may have taken a long, hard stare, but he could see it. It made him think of his life so far. When Alex was born, instead of embracing fatherhood naturally, Tom fought against it, viciously. He would spend a lot of late evenings at the office, telling Scarlett he had to meet important deadlines, when in fact he would be sitting at his computer terminal playing Solitaire. Other times he would join the office gang in the pub after work and then go home quite merry. It was Tom's way of avoiding the responsibilities that a child brought into his life. Scarlett suffered his period of insecurity silently. She didn't react as the average new mother would be expected to. She knew Tom would come around sooner rather than later. She knew he wanted to be a good father to Alex; it was just that he was scared of failing. Failure was something Tom had issues with in the past and he never wanted to go there again.

When Tom was sixteen, he left school with very few qualifications and a bad report from the Headmaster. The report had stated that after five years at the school he had wasted teachers' time and his own; that he had a high risk of failure in the real world and even the smallest challenge would prove too much for such an incompetent and unreliable person. In was a damning summary of his time at secondary school, but quite correct. Over the following seven years, he tried his hand at several apprenticeships, but nothing became of any of them. Tom never stayed long enough to gain any experience and any knowledge he did gain he usually forgot about after a weekend of heavy drinking and gambling. It was only when he turned twenty-three and had been unemployed for nine months that his situation improved. Tom's life was drifting away. No matter how many times his parents tried to 'cheer him up' by saying things like 'you should have worked harder at school' or 'by the time I was your age I had been working for ten years', he just couldn't motivate himself, until one day he got a phone call from the job agency. The woman caller told Tom about a company called Thornes and that they needed a new mail boy and they had rung and asked about him specifically. Without even an interview, Tom was offered the job, and he started the next day. He couldn't believe his luck. The job went well for the first couple of weeks. He managed to make it on time every day and he even made a few friends. The work, however, was very mundane and it certainly didn't tax the brain. Tom guessed it was perfect for him; at least it was until he found out the reason behind his employment.

One Friday afternoon, Tom was asked to deliver the internal mail to the team managers in the Customer Service department. He asked Bill, his manager, why his route had been changed, as he usually did the finance department run. Bill told him one of the managers instructed him to make the change and it wasn't his place to ask questions. Tom collected his post, wheeled his trolley up to the second floor from the basement, and started to deliver the mail. He handed out all the mail packages and each time he did so the person he gave it to would slap him gently on the back. Tom thought this a bit peculiar and he was on his way to deliver the last one when he noticed the name of the addressee on the envelope. It was for Raymond Thorne. Tom stopped the trolley dead just before entering the last office.

'It couldn't be!' he thought.

Tom slowly walked to the doorway and peered into the open office. Just then, he heard giggling from behind him. He turned around to find a group of people laughing in his direction and Tom caught some of their eyes just before they turned their heads away. Tom was trying to figure out why they were laughing when suddenly a tall, bear-like man walked up to him, grabbed both his cheeks, and kissed him on the forehead.

'Get off me, you idiot,' Tom shouted.

'Why, I was only giving you what you wanted,' the man laughed back.

Everyone burst out laughing and Tom felt extremely vulnerable and very embarrassed.

'What! I didn't ask for that, you pillock.'

'Oh yes you did, sweetie! It's all across your back. Look!'

Tom reached over his shoulder and ripped of a piece of paper that had been stuck with tape. It read 'KISS ME PLEASE'. Tom was livid. He grabbed the walking armchair in front of him by his shirt collar and was about to punch him when he heard someone shout, 'Don't even think about it, Farrow!'

Tom turned to find Raymond Thorne standing behind him with a massive grin across his face. Tom couldn't believe it. The once skinny, be-spectacled, spotty little runt, who he used to bully at school, now stood in front of him and for the first time in his life, it looked as though he had the upper hand.

'In here, Farrow,' said Raymond as he walked into his office.

Tom didn't know whether to follow him or spit in his eye. He decided against the spitting, followed him into the office, and then he noticed the sign on the door. It read 'Raymond Thorne - Head of

Department'. Tom was about to sit down when Raymond said, 'Please stay standing, Farrow.'

He had never spoken to Tom like that when they were at school. If he had, Tom would have given him a wedgie followed by a few slaps with a hockey stick.

'So, how does it feel to be publicly humiliated, Farrow?' asked Raymond as he slowly sat into his chair. 'Not very nice, I would say. I've been waiting for that since your first day here,' he said smugly.

'How did you know I was working here?' Tom asked bluntly.

'Because, Farrow, I was the one who gave you the job,' he smiled. 'How are the rats getting on down in the mailroom?'

'What do you mean you gave me the job?'

'One morning I saw you come out of the social security office and I assumed, quite correctly, that you were collecting your unemployment benefit. After a couple of telephone calls I organised it for you to work here, so that I could have the satisfaction of seeing you push a trolley around delivering my mail.'

'Why?' Tom asked.

'Because, it's all you're fit for,' hissed Raymond. 'When we were at school you made my life a misery. Now I've got my chance to get my own back.'

'A bit immature, don't you think?' Tom said. 'A little boy like you playing the bully. Get a life, Thorne.'

It was only then that Tom realised it.

'Thorne. Raymond Thorne. Well, well, well. You're the owner's son. How stupid of me not to notice.'

'Stupid indeed,' said Raymond. 'That's exactly what you are, a stupid little brat with no chance of success in anything. Always were, always will be.' He stood up to give himself a sense of superiority, which, as much as Tom hated to admit it, he did have.

'As long as you work for Thornes you will never leave the mailroom because that's where vermin belong - in the basement. Now get out of my office, Farrow, and get back to work,' he ordered.

Tom glared at him with hatred in his eyes. He turned and began to walk out of the office when Raymond called him back.

'Oh, Farrow, sorry about my little prank earlier,' he said. 'Just a touch of humour. No hard feelings, eh?'

Tom turned, walked away, and said nothing. As he was getting into the lift with his trolley, he saw Raymond walk to the door of his office. He looked in Tom's direction and shouted.

'You'll never amount to anything, Farrow. You're a born loser!'

As the doors closed and the lift descended Tom looked at his reflection in the polished steel walls and swore that he would never let a Thorne get the best of him, especially Raymond. He would amount to something and he would prove him wrong.

Tom had never worked as hard as he did over the following four years. After only three months in the mailroom, he managed to secure a job in the Customer Service department as an Administration Assistant. This job gave him an insight as to how the department worked and what he would need to do to become a Customer Service Telephone Advisor. If he were able to become an Advisor, he would be in a better position to work his way up to Head of Department, which was Tom's ultimate goal, and to usurp Raymond. He wanted to show Raymond Thorne, and everyone else, that he was as good as he was, if not better. Tom wanted to prove to himself that he was more than a poorly educated, useless drunk.

Tom had been with Thornes for just over one year before being promoted to Customer Service Advisor, and as he began to prove himself in that position, he befriended one of the Team Managers. Dick Rose had been with Thornes for eight years by this time and joined the same year he left school at the age of sixteen. Dick was a lot like Tom. He left school with very few qualifications and was unsure about what he wanted to do in life. Initially employed as an Advisor, within a very short time he managed to work his way up to Senior Advisor, and seven months after that took up a Team Manager position. He had reached his goal. When he joined Thornes, Dick set out in his mind what he wanted to achieve and then worked towards it. 'Anyone can do anything,' he used to say. 'If you just put your mind to it. It doesn't take qualifications to do a job; it just takes common sense and initiative. If you've got those two things then you'll make it.' Dick and Tom became good friends, and he used to give Tom private tuition about the role of Team Manager; and what it took to get results from a group of unenthusiastic people. They spent hours in the pub after work discussing daily work plans, drawing up rotas, team dynamics, ownership of work, about commitment to excellence. Dick was a Godsend. Without him, Tom wouldn't be where he is today.

It was on Tom's twenty-fifth birthday when things changed. Tom wished he could say it was a momentous occasion in his career; however, the circumstances of his premature promotion make it a sad one to recall. It had just gone nine am and Dick had not arrived at work. This was unusual, and didn't go unnoticed by other members of staff, especially his team. At nine thirty, the rest of the Managers asked their teams to switch off their telephones and make their way to the conference room. Sir Wilfred Thorne had an important announcement to make. The look on the Managers' faces was far from content. Everyone crammed into the large room and as soon as the doors were being shut, Raymond Thorne stood and leaned on a long walnut table and confirmed to us all that the meeting would be very brief. Just then, Sir Wilfred entered the room from a door directly behind Raymond before telling him to sit down. This was the first time Tom had seen Sir Wilfred and he was more intimidating than he had imagined. His large body seemed to quiver as he began to speak.

'I will be as brief, but as tactful as I can be with what I have to say to you all.'

This already sounded ominous. The room was silent except for the odd cough.

Sir Wilfred continued, 'It is with great sadness and a heavy heart that I must say that Dick Rose died late last night. On his way home from work, Dick was savagely attacked and robbed. He died later in hospital from head injuries.'

The words echoed around the room as people tried to take on board what they had just heard. Some people cried, others swore. Tom wept. His birthday celebrations were forgotten about that day. Instead, a small gathering met in the pub after work to drink a toast to Dick, as boss, colleague, and friend.

One week after the funeral, Tom received an internal memo from Sir Wilfred. He asked Tom to meet him and the two Heads of the Customer Service department in the conference room 'to discuss his future'. Tom had no idea what this meant, but it did mean that he would be in the same office as Raymond Thorne for the first time in over a year. Raymond had been on his holidays when Tom was offered the job as an Advisor, but on his return he had made it quite clear to him that had he been around Tom would still be collating documents in a side room somewhere. It was his co-Head, Scarlett Robins, who had offered Tom the job in his absence and the decision put a large divide between them. So much so Raymond once moaned to the Board of Directors that Scarlett wasn't pulling her weight and that he was carrying the department. It was the wrong move, as Scarlett, only two days earlier had gone through the next six months projected figures with the Board and they were very impressed. Raymond was now in their bad books and had to redeem himself.

Tom entered the room with fear and keen interest. What was going to happen? Had he done something wrong that Raymond knew about and he'd forgotten?

Sir Wilfred asked Tom to sit down in the chair opposite them. He casually introduced himself and then Scarlett and Raymond as a matter of course. He proceeded to tell Tom of his long-standing friendship with Dick Rose's father and that he had known Dick ever since he was a baby. Once a month Sir Wilfred and Dick would meet at a country club and discuss old times as well as the business. Dick's father had died when he was eight and Sir Wilfred had promised Dick that he would look after him as though he were one of his own. Sir Wilfred made it clear, however, that everything Dick achieved at Thornes was through his own hard work and nothing to do with him. He then spoke of how Dick used to tell him about Tom. Of how Tom was learning so much about the business and how they would spend many hours playing 'work games'.

'He admired you, Farrow,' said Sir Wilfred. 'I know you were good friends and I'm sure you are finding this time quite difficult, as am I, so I'll cut to the chase. Before Dick died in hospital he asked if he could choose his replacement here at Thornes.' Sir Wilfred sniffed. 'Always the worker, eh Farrow?'

'Er...yes, Sir Wilf...'

'I said 'yes' and he wanted you. What do you say, Farrow?'

Tom was stunned.

'Me?'

'Yes, Tom,' said Scarlett. 'You've progressed very well in your current role and all the knowledge you've gained from Dick shouldn't go to waste. You're the obvious choice, Tom, and I'm not saying that just because you were Dick's friend.'

Her smile and tone of voice were both warm and comforting. Tom had obviously seen Scarlett around the department regularly but never had the opportunity to talk directly to her before now or even make eye contact. Tom noticed how dimples appeared in her cheeks as she smiled. She was very pretty. Little did he know then that the same smile would greet him every morning after they were married.

Raymond's face was sour. He glared at Tom without blinking once and his mouth was tightly creased shut. It was obvious he didn't get any say in Tom's new promotion. Tom just smiled at him, then at Scarlett, and finally at Sir Wilfred and said plainly, 'Thank-you, sir. I accept the offer.'

Within a week, Tom was sitting at Dick's old desk taking his place. He vowed then to work as hard and as close to the staff as Dick had done. To be their 'rock' as Dick would put it. He did that and after two years as Team Manager Tom was put forward as Raymond's replacement and Scarlett's partner. Ever since Raymond's faux pas with the Board of Directors, he continued to put his foot in it, by making false allegations against Tom to try to get him fired. One morning, staff arrived at work to find photocopies of a bare bottom plastered all over the office walls. Raymond told the Board it was Tom who done it, but the security guard who had watched the culprit do it the previous evening on one of his security monitors had hard evidence to prove otherwise. The company nurse confirmed the duck-shaped mole on the left buttock in the picture was that of Raymond Thorne. She remembered noticing the mole on a previous occasion when she had to give him two stitches on his bottom after he sat on an open box of staples by accident. Sir Wilfred dismissed Raymond, his own son, from the company, and was deeply ashamed of his son's behaviour. Tom got the job and has been Head of Department for the past three years.

Tom noticed the speck of blue paint suddenly move and then fly away out the open window. It was a bluebottle.

'Looks like I didn't miss a spot after all,' he smiled.

4

Maud looked radiant as ever as she opened her front door. How she managed to look so casual and worry-free was an eternal mystery to Tom. She glided down the hall as if she were a freshly fallen leaf caught on the ripple of a lake and led Tom to the sitting room. Both babies were gurgling away at each other in a playpen set in the corner of the room and Tom could hear the twins playing outside in the back garden. Everything seemed peaceful. How did she manage it?

It had just gone six fifteen and it was a beautiful summer's evening. Tom went to the kitchen and could see Polly through the patio doors sitting in a Wendy house talking to a dolly. Goodness knows were Ralph was or what he was up to but no doubt with Maud around he wouldn't be up to any mischief.

'Thanks ever so much, Maud, you're a real star. I am sorry I dumped this lot on you at such short notice.'

'Not at all, Tom. You know me, I'm always ready and willing when it comes to God's little children. They keep me young and they give me such pleasure.'

'Yes, well, next time I'll give you more than ten minutes warning before bringing them round.'

Tom really didn't have to apologise to Maud, but it was only polite. She would drop whatever she was doing to help someone in need. The most memorable occasion was when she didn't even turn up to her own husband's funeral because she was asked, at the last minute, to mind her neighbour's new-born baby. The mother had tripped and fallen down the stairs and broken her ankle, and as she had to go to hospital, she asked if Maud could take the baby with her to the funeral and ask another friend to mind it during the service.

'Nonsense,' she said. 'A funeral is no place for a baby. I'll stay right here at home.'

'But Stan was your husband. You have to go to his funeral!' said the mother.

'Listen, my dear! I can help you. I cannot help Stan. Anyway, he's not going anywhere after today. I can pop over and say goodbye to him tomorrow. Now off you go,' replied Maud.

If the truth were told Tom could easily have asked Maud to keep the children overnight and she would have said 'yes' too, but Scarlett would never have forgiven him.

'So, Tom, how are you finding fatherhood? We haven't spoken much since Alex was born.'

Oh,-oh! Could she sense how Tom was really feeling or was she just being curious? Better to be positive and lie than tell the truth. Tom didn't want to end up crying in her lap like he used to when he was a little boy.

'It's terrific! Couldn't be better. Scarlett says I'm a natural. In fact, it was my idea to look after Jasper and the twins. They're just adorable, aren't they?' he said looking tenderly at the babies.

'Don't lie to me, Tom.'

Oh-no! She's caught him. He should have known better.

'It's not in you to lie,' she continued. 'I hope you ask God to forgive you for that before you go to bed tonight,' she scolded.

'Sorry Maud.'

'So! Tell me how you are feeling. What are you scared off, Tom?'

Maud never tiptoed around an issue. She believed in getting straight to the point. Tom knew he couldn't hide how he really felt from Maud. From Scarlett, yes he could, sometimes, but not for long. From his parents, no problem. From Maud, no way!

'Maud, I'd love to sit and chat, but I do need to get these kids back home to bed. It's getting rather late and I've taken up too much of your time already.'

Tom rose from the chair and called for the twins to come inside.

'You shouldn't bottle things up, Tom. You can only face fear if you talk about it, you know. God can help you,' she said. 'When was the last time you went to church?'

Tom was more than expecting that one. Maud was a Christian of the highest calibre and to get out of her house without her mentioning God or church would be inconceivable. Perhaps she was an actual angel. That would explain things a bit better. She may not be a saint yet, but no doubt, St Peter will fling wide the heavenly gates for her when the time comes.

'Well, just before Alex was born, I guess. We haven't been able to get there on time, what with one thing or another.'

Tom's own faith in God was still strong, but finding the time to go and see him every Sunday morning was almost impossible now.

At least that was his excuse. The real reason they didn't want to go to church with Alex was the noise. As a teenager Tom would sit in church every Sunday trying to listen to the sermon, but it was nigh on impossible for the noise of crying babies and screaming toddlers. Even though the Vicar always indicated that the services were child friendly, the rest of the congregation wasn't. He used to feel sorry for the parents who were stared at throughout the service by the 'holier than thou' people in the front pews. It was a quiet way of registering their annoyance and asking parents to take the children out to the crèche or Sunday school. He remembered, vividly, the look on the face of the churchwarden one Sunday when the Vicar announced the death of one of the parishioners. As soon as the Vicar mentioned the name of the deceased, a little toddler, who sat behind the warden, blew a rather loud raspberry. The warden swivelled around on his polished pew and glared at the child's mother. His face turned bright purple and his eyebrows almost knitted themselves together as he frowned the deepest of frowns. The mother, deeply embarrassed, not by her baby, but by the warden, picked up the child and ran out of the church. The warden calmed down just as the name of another deceased member of the congregation was announced. Tom never saw that family again.

'Tom, people won't mind if you bring Alex to church. It's a lot more relaxed than it used to be, you know that. Last Sunday the Vicar shared his pulpit with two toddlers as he delivered his sermon, but carried on nonetheless. He even referred to them throughout the talk and it helped to put the parents at ease.'

'Yes, well, perhaps we'll make it this weekend. But remember, we have four of the little bugg...er...darlings to look after, not just Alex.' he said.

'Others will help, Tom, you'll see,' said Maud.

Tom rounded up all the children and thanked Maud for her help. She gave the twins a sticky lollipop each and the babies' kisses on their heads before Tom wheeled them outside in the double buggy. He was opening the gate at the bottom of the path when Maud called for him.

'Tom! Remember what I said. Don't bottle it all up. Talk about it. If not to God then to Scarlett, it'll help.'

He knew she was right, but for now, he'd soldier on.

'Goodnight, Maud,' he replied.

'Na-night,' shouted the twins in perfect harmony.

'Sleep tight, little ones,' said Maud.

Both twins sat at the front of the buggy and Tom pushed them home. They managed to arrive home before Scarlett, but only just. Tom was taking Ralph's shoes off when she came in the door. He could tell that she was tired and needed the loo. She dropped her briefcase and her coat on the floor just in front of the door and started doing what Tom described as a jig. When Tom needed the toilet, he didn't usually announce it. Scarlett not only announces it, she dances about it too!

'Hello, darlings!' she said as she hopped about.

The twins started to laugh while Jasper just stared at her with mild amusement. Alex had fallen asleep on the way home, so missed out on the frivolity.

'I'm just popping to the loo then I'll be back down,' she said in a tone of desperation.

Polly and Ralph thought Scarlett was playing some kind of game and began to jump up and down too, laughing as they did so. Tom began to chuckle.

'I'm going to the loo, too,' giggled Ralph.

Tom giggled along until he realised by the growing dark patch on the front of Ralph's trousers that he was actually going to the loo, in his pants.

'NO!' Tom yelled, as if that would stop him from peeing. 'You can't do that here.'

But, he did. Polly thought this was even funnier than seeing Scarlett doing her Michael Flatley impression and fell on the floor in hysterics. Tom lifted Ralph up, who was still laughing, and began to carry him up the stairs.

'I'm going to wet myself,' screamed Polly.

'Don't even think about it,' Tom yelled. 'Scarlett. Hurry up!'

'I'm doing a number two,' she shouted from the bathroom.

'So am I,' tittered Ralph.

'What! You can't do that now.' Tom shouted.

He was still holding Ralph up in the air when his face began to go blue and his eyes bulged.

'Ralph! Stop it! You have to wait.'

'Can't!'

'Well, try harder!'

His face turned blue again.

'Not pooh harder!'

However, it was too late. Tom heard the toilet flush and Scarlett quickly opened the bathroom door.

'Finished!' she said.

'Me too,' said Ralph.

'And me,' chuckled Polly.

Just when Tom thought it was all over, Alex broke wind in his sleep and the laughter started once more. Except, this time, Tom wasn't laughing.

It was almost nine o'clock before there was complete silence upstairs. Polly and Ralph decided to play hide and seek as soon as Scarlett turned out their bedroom light. She left them to it hoping that they would calm down quicker on their own than if she was in the room with them. It worked.

'Right!' she said, flopping onto the floor beside Tom. 'What are we going to do with this mess?' She was looking at the blue stained sofa and the remnants of the Lowrie.

'Perhaps we could sell the sofa to the Tate as a piece of modern art and call it '*With Love, from the kids!*' That way we could cover the cost of the Lowrie and replace the sofa,' Tom said sardonically.

They both sighed heavily. Scarlett opened a bottle of white wine and offered Tom a glass. Dinner was still cooking in the oven, but neither of them felt capable of eating it; they were exhausted.

'I am shattered,' Tom said.

'Me too. At least you get a rest-bite in the morning. I have to wait until the afternoon for some relaxation,' said Scarlett.

'Not if I can help it.'

'What do you mean?'

'I thought I'd try and make a start on next month's projections for the Board. If Edward is to be believed, he will be too busy trying to woo the Directors with wine, women, and song, at every opportunity. He'll completely forget about real work for the next couple of months and I want to make sure that I have everything under control. I'm not going to let him beat me to this promotion.'

'Tom, I hope you're not going to do anything underhand.'

'Me?' he asked in sarcastic amazement. 'I wouldn't know how to. How dare you insinuate such a thing?'

'Just because Edward's not playing by the rules, it doesn't mean you have to stoop to his level as well. You're a changed man now, and for the better.'

'Don't you worry, darling. I have everything under control.'

The oven-timer beeped to signal that dinner was ready so they retreated to the kitchen to eat. They ate the main course in relative silence and it was during pudding that Tom approached the subject of Alex's Christening.

'Seeing Maud today reminded me that we haven't had Alex christened. I think we should have him dunked, don't you?'

'What's brought this on?' asked Scarlett. 'The last time we talked about this, you said you weren't sure if you believed in God anymore, never mind in infant baptism. You're so fickle! Anyway, there's no dunking if it's a christening.'

'Scarlett. Ask anyone the same day a plane falls from the sky and kills over two hundred innocent people and they'll all say there's no God. It was a heat of the moment thing. I have my doubts now and again, doesn't everybody? Anyway, back to the subject in hand. I just think it would be a good way of slowly easing ourselves back into church. Plus, it's a good reason to have a good old knees-up.'

'Hmm, so which is the most important, I wonder?' replied Scarlett with a wry smile.

'Well. What do you think?' Tom asked.

'Tom, you know I want to. I'll give the Vicar a ring after dinner to arrange a date.'

'Excellent.'

Tom lifted up his glass of wine and made a toast.

'To the unsuspecting congregation at St Paul and St James's.'

'Cheers!'

The next morning Ralph woke Tom and Scarlett up by bursting into their bedroom singing 'Bob the Builder'. Tom wouldn't have minded but those three words were all Ralph knew and hearing them repeated over and over and over again first thing in the morning was worse than waking up to the sound of the diggers working on the building site on the other side of the street. His incessant chanting woke everyone else up too and for the fourth morning in a row, Tom found Jasper sitting in the middle of his cot with a damp nappy on his head. Alex was still adjusting to sharing his bedroom and he stared bewilderingly at Jasper's antics.

It was six am when the family's day began, and it took almost two hours to get the children out of bed, washed, clothed, and fed, before Tom left for work. By the time he reached the office, he was ready for his mid-morning coffee and another Danish bun.

'How was the rest of your day, yesterday?' asked Sylvia.

'Oh, just marvellous,' he mused.

Tom could just manage to see evidence of a smile on her face. Sylvia was never one for smiles, she was too busy to smile, but if pleasure did overcome her, you could see the left hand corner of her mouth turn upwards with a slight wrinkle on top of her lip. This indicated happiness for Sylvia.

'What are your plans for this morning?' she asked.

'I need all the call log stats for last month. I also want a full head count for the whole department, i.e. whose part-time, full-time, temporary. I need to know the exact figures for outstanding work and I need to see all the team mangers before eleven o'clock this morning. Last, but by no means least, I need a cup of coffee.'

'Give me two minutes for the coffee and half an hour for everything else,' she responded.

Tom looked at her with pride.

'Sylvia?'

'Yes, Tom?'

'You know if you were a building, you'd be the cornerstone.'

'Why, thank-you, Tom. I think.'

Throughout the rest of the morning, Tom forecast the amount of work that would be outstanding when Gilbert Crinshaw would leave the company. He wanted to have a plan in place for that time which would show the Board of Directors that the Customer Service department could run efficiently with the same amount of people and with less work outstanding come November. It was now the beginning of July and he envisaged that this would be his busiest summer ever at Thornes.

How wrong he would be. He had no idea then of what lay before him.

5

It took twelve minutes for all the Team Managers to arrive for the eleven o'clock meeting, the first only arriving at five minutes past. Tom loathed latecomers, but the fact that they were all late put a hold on his reprimanding; plus the fact that they were too old for a telling off anyway. Brenda Savage was the last to enter the meeting room and she brought with her a large tray of fresh cream cakes.

'We can't have a meeting without cakes, now can we?' she giggled.

''Course not,' shouted Phillip Kramer, the departments' living food waste bin. Before Brenda had set the tray on the table, Phillip wrestled his bulky body out of his seat, stretched past everyone, and grabbed three cakes.

'Cor!' he mumbled. 'And the teams think we come in here and do nothing.' Everyone laughed.

'Okay, settle down please,' Tom said firmly but calmly. 'We've a lot to discuss today and from now on these weekly meetings are going to be more constructive instead of slagging off team members, eating cream buns and criticising the other departments. The next two months are going to be tough for all of us, but it will be worth it in the end.'

They all looked at each other, bewildered.

'You do know what I mean don't you?' Tom asked.

'I think I speak for all of us when I say 'no' we don't know what you mean,' replied Brenda.

Tom was not surprised. Edward had told him that he had emailed all the Managers about Gilbert Crinshaw leaving, but clearly, he had not.

'Well, Gilbert is retiring at the end of next month which means that the Board will be looking to choose his replacement.'

'Which will be you, naturally,' said Howard Sprat confidently. Howard was Tom's deputy and they'd been friends ever since they began working at Thornes.

'Thanks for your vote of confidence Howard, but Edward is also in with a chance.'

Tom had barely taken in a breath when the room convulsed with hysterical laughter. He was glad to see that he was not the only one who believed Edward to be the last person the Board would offer the position to.

'Oh come on,' chuckled Craig Spanner. 'Even Sir Wilfred wouldn't be bonkers enough to vote Edward in as a Director. The man's a bona fide cretin, moron, and dunderhead all in one package.'

'Say what you think, why don't you, Craig!' said Howard.

'Okay, the guy's a real dozy sh...'

'Alright, thank you,' Tom quickly interrupted. 'Let's just calm down and concentrate on making sure that Edward doesn't get the job.'

'I don't think you need worry,' said Howard.

'Well, I'm not going to leave anything to chance. Edward has his plan on how to get the job, but I have mine. The problem is, it will mean longer hours for you for a while and more work, and I need to know that you'll all support me. If I get the job then I'll make sure you are all well rewarded for your hard work and commitment over the next couple of months. So, who's with me?'

Tom paused to let them cheer and applaud him. Nothing. He immediately thought that Edward had gotten to them.

'Well don't just sit there staring at me, say something!'

Craig reached over and put his hand on his shoulder. 'Sorry, mate!' he said solemnly.

'Eh!' Tom muttered in disbelief.

'Of course we'll back you, you big Jessie!'

They all began to cheer, clap, and throw paper at him. For a moment, Tom thought he was sunk. Thank goodness for friends!

The meeting finished at midday and Howard and Craig invited Tom along to the pub for lunch to celebrate his impending victory over Edward.

'The race is only beginning boys,' he said as he rested his elbows on the bar.

'Yeah, but it's already won, Tom,' said Howard.

'Three lagers and three sausage, egg and chips, please,' shouted Craig at the barman before turning towards them. 'Too right it is, Tom. You're the dog's wotsits, mate. Doesn't matter what Edward gets up to over the next two months, you've got it in the bag. Ever since you replaced Raymond, morale has risen and everyone loves you. If you left, the whole department would fall apart.'

'I'm not sure that's true, but thanks for the vote of confidence.'

Howard and Craig looked at each other. They had just realised something important.

'Just a slight detail,' said Howard. 'But if you do get the job, and believe me you will, who'll replace you as Head of Department?'

They both stared at Tom through narrowed eyes in anticipation. This was one question he didn't want to answer. He knew whichever answer he gave, someone was going to be disappointed.

'Let's just hope I don't get it then. I mean I wouldn't want the department to fall apart, now would I?'

He rose from his seat and headed off before they could speak.

'But!' they said in unison.

'Sorry! Gotta pee!'

As it was almost one pm Tom thought he'd call Scarlett to say he'd be home a few minutes late, but when he called he didn't get any reply. He called her mobile number as well in case they were all out in the garden and couldn't hear the phone. Still no reply. Tom ran back to Howard and Craig and told them he was going home and not to expect Scarlett until later on in the afternoon. He grabbed his coat and left, running most of the way home. Tom opened the front door of the house hoping to find everyone sitting in the kitchen having lunch. No such luck. He ran around the house, upstairs and down, but nobody was home. Now he had cause to panic. Just as he was about to call Maud the front door opened and in charged Polly and Ralph, knocking over Tom's briefcase and the umbrella stand as they went. Scarlett came in next with the two babies fast asleep in each of her arms.

'I'm sorry I'm late home,' she said softly. 'I went to the surgery to pick up my next prescription, but the GP hadn't signed it, so I had to wait and there was a huge queue.'

She sounded exhausted.

'That's alright. I told Howard and Craig not to expect you for a while so you can stay here and have your lunch before going in.'

'Oh, thanks. I'll just pop up to the loo and get changed after putting these two down in their cots.'

'Okay. Scrambled egg on toast alright for you,' Tom whispered.

'Fine.'

Tom walked into the sitting room to find the twins already lying down in front of the television watching a video about a talking cow dressed in a kimono.

'Well, that's novel,' he muttered.

The kitchen looked as though a bomb had hit it. Empty milk cartons lay all over the floor and the pile of dishes in the sink almost blocked out the window behind it. It looked as though Tom had his work cut out for him this afternoon. He opened the fridge to get some eggs and milk to find that there were no eggs or milk, or butter, cheese, yoghurts, beer or orange juice. In fact, the fridge was completely empty except for a half-eaten tin of tuna, which smelt worse than it would ever have down when it was alive. The cupboards were well stocked with enough Farley's Rusks and rice cakes to feed the biblical five thousand, had they all been babies. He was about to give up hope of finding something that passed for proper food when he found a tin of soup hidden behind the jars of pulverised banana and chicken casserole. The '*use by*' date was one month earlier, but things in tins are usually okay for years after the end date. This information came from Tom's brother who as a student used to stock his larder once a year with tins of economy baked beans and fruit cocktail. Tom wanted to trust this information, for Scarlett's sake. He opened the tin at arm's length and was pleasantly surprised to find nothing wriggling inside. He turned on the electric hob just as the phone rang.

'I'll get it,' he shouted.

It was Scarlett's mother wanting to know if he still had her videotape of '*Lady and The Tramp*'. Apparently, she had lent it to them over three years ago and she 'desperately' needed it back that afternoon 'for research'. Tom had no idea what that was supposed to mean, and just as she was waffling on about how Disney films are no longer the classics they used to be he looked out of the kitchen window and saw that all his roses had been beheaded.

'Sorry, Isidora, must go. I'll call round later.'

He hung up the phone and walked over to the window to view the damage more closely when he inadvertently put his right hand on the hob for balance.

'YEEEAAAHHOOOO!' he screamed.

The pain seared through his flesh as he clenched his wrist with his left hand.

'What happened?' shouted Scarlett from the bathroom.

'I've burnt my flamin' hand.'

As Tom turned on the sink tap, he threw pots and pans over his left shoulder in haste to make some room for his hand. Scarlett rushed downstairs and entered the kitchen just as a rolling pin landed in front of her. She didn't notice and as she stood on it, the pin rolled from under her and she crashed to the floor.

'Scarlett! Are you alright?' Tom cried.

Why is it whenever we see someone who is in obvious pain, do we ask the most obvious of questions?

'Does it hurt?' Tom was referring to her left leg, which seemed twisted at a funny angle just below her knee.

'It's killing me. I think it's broken.'

'I'll phone for an ambulance.'

It was only as Tom picked up the phone again that he realised his hand was throbbing and he too was in agony. He quickly wrapped some cling film around his right hand and then called for an ambulance with his left. In the fifteen minutes that they waited for the ambulance to arrive neither of the twins had moved an inch from the television to see what the matter was. Curiosity may have killed the cat, but it sure as heck wouldn't get the better of a toddler who was in the middle of watching '*Tweenies*'.

'I'll be along as soon as I can get someone to watch the children,' Tom told Scarlett, as she was being stretchered into the ambulance.

'I'm afraid you're going to have to come along with us too, sir,' said one of the paramedics. 'Those fingers of yours look awful, they need seeing too right away.'

'Oh, okay, just a minute. I need to make a call.'

Within five minutes of ringing, Maud arrived with two more toddlers in tow.

'Don't you worry yourself, Tom. Everything will be fine here. Just you get going and take care of Scarlett.'

'Thanks Maud. You're a star.' Tom gave her a kiss on the cheek and then leapt into the back of the ambulance.

As they drove off Maud closed the front door of the house and went into the kitchen. There she found Ralph with a dirty colander on his head and a mop between his legs pretending to be a knight.

'Come on, Auntie Maud. Come and fight with me,' he said.

'All right then,' she said as she put an unwashed pot on her head and grabbed a dripping pair of tongs. 'But bags I get to be the king.'

'Okay,' said Ralph thrusting out a wooden spoon. 'Enguard!'

'Enguard!' shouted Maud.

Luckily, for Scarlett and Tom, the casualty ward was almost empty when they arrived and medics attended to them very promptly. X-rays confirmed Scarlett had suffered a broken fibula while Tom had grade one burns to the fingertips and palm of his right hand. After a couple of lengthy phone calls to their insurance company, Tom managed to get Scarlett transferred to a private room. She would only have to stay for one night, but at least this way she would be able to get a proper night's sleep.

'The room's very comfortable,' she said as she hobbled from a wheelchair to the bed. 'A television with all the digital channels, a coffee and tea maker, private bathroom, fresh flowers, and a three course dinner this evening. Can I stay more than one night, please?'

'No chance,' said Tom. What's the bed like?'

'Lovely and soft. It would be much nicer without this thing on his leg though.' She gave her plastered leg a wrap with her knuckles.

'Yes, I know. This is my entire fault. I should be more careful.' Tom snuggled up beside her on the bed.

'Yes, you should.' Scarlett gave him a kiss on his forehead. 'How are your fingers feeling?'

'To be honest I can't feel a thing. The specialist has given me painkillers and my word they're working.' Tom kicked off his shoes and slid under the bedclothes.

'So, what were you doing in the kitchen anyway when this all happened?'

'I was looking out of the kitchen window and I noticed that all my roses had been beheaded. Would you happen to know anything about that, Mrs Farrow?'

'Ah, I was going to tell you, honest. This morning Polly asked if she could play in the garden. It was a lovely day so I said 'yes'. Ten minutes later, she walked into the house and handed me a box. I opened it to find it full with the rose heads. I was just about to tell her off when she said she had seen an advert on telly were people gave other people a box of roses to say thank you and that's what she was doing. She was thanking us for looking after her and Ralph. You should have seen her face, Tom it was so sweet. I couldn't tell her off after that.'

'No. I guess you couldn't,' said Tom, but he still needed convincing.

'They are lovely sometimes, Tom,' reminded Scarlett. 'It must be hard for them living with people they don't really know, sharing all the attention with Alex. They must be missing their mum terribly.'

'Yeah. You're right. It's not their fault things have turned out like this. Poor kids.'

They lay still for a while, thinking quietly.

'I'm going to miss you tonight,' Tom said.

'Me too.'

'What do you say we...er, you know?'

'Tom! I can hardly move. What if a nurse comes in?'

Tom fumbled with the buttons on Scarlett's nightie.

'Can't. I've locked the door. Don't worry, I'll do all the work.'

'Well that would make a change,' Scarlett said knocking Tom's hands away. 'Come on, don't be silly. I'm not in the mood. Go on. You need to get home.'

'Oh, alright, I'm going.'

Tom swung his legs off the bed and struggled with the sleeves of his coat as he tried to put it on. Suddenly their current predicament struck him.

'What are we going to do?' he cried.

'About what?' asked Scarlett.

'What do you mean 'about what'?' About everything. The kids for a start. And work.'

In all the commotion of the afternoon, they had both completely ignored their situation. How were two temporarily handicapped people going to look after, care for four children, and run a busy Customer Service department at the same time?

'Oh dear!' said Scarlett.

'Oh dear!' repeated Tom. 'That's all you can say? Scarlett, can't you see? How am I going to be able to work without my right hand? Who is going to do all my reports, letters, and stats? I can barely hold a cotton bud in my right hand never mind use it to write and type with.' Tom was beginning to panic. 'Oh, why did this all have to happen now? I'm not going to get this promotion after all.'

'Now, now. Don't get all silly on me. There must be a solution to this.'

They sat for a few seconds trying to figure out what to do and then it finally hit them.

'Maud,' they said in unison.

'We'll employ her as nanny to Alex and Jasper and we can manage the twins,' offered Scarlett.

'Excellent idea, but that doesn't help me out, does it? I still can't work with my hand like this.'

Tom could tell Scarlett was cooking up something spectacular in her brain from the intense look she had on her face. However, the way she was holding back a smile told Tom he wasn't going to like it much.

'I've got it.'

'Got what? And give it to me gently. I don't think I can take many more shocks.'

'Why don't I take over from you for the next few weeks and you stay at home and look after Polly and Ralph? That way I can keep my leg out of harm's way and sort out your imminent promotion at the same time. Sylvia won't mind bringing me to and from the office. Then, when my cast is taken off and I'm back on two feet again we can reverse roles. You can finish off what needs doing at work before Gilbert leaves and I'll look after the twins. How does that sound?'

Tom stared off into the distance. If it weren't for the fact that what Scarlett had just said made sense, Tom would have thought that her painkillers were getting the better of her. She knew she was onto a winner and Tom couldn't come back with a plan B. Tom couldn't help but envisage himself tied up on a railway line with Polly and Ralph at the controls of an oncoming train, yelling and laughing as they ended his life.

'Tom? Tom!'

'Yes. You're right. I know you're right. At least I won't have nappies to change or worry about buttoning up romper suits. Are you sure you can cope with everything at the office? Edward will do anything to get that job.'

'I'll manage. Anyway, if there are any problems we can work on them together in the evenings. I'll arrange for Gilbert to sign me out a laptop and then you can check on things yourself.'

'Okay, okay, you win. I'll call Howard and Craig tonight and let them know what's going on and ask them to hold the fort tomorrow. If anyone can help you, they can.'

'OK, that's settled,' said Scarlett.

Just then, there was a knock on the door. Tom managed to run to the door and unlock it before the handle turned and the ward nurse came into the room.

'I believe it's time you went home now, Mr Farrow,' said the nurse.

'You're quite right, nurse. I'm just leaving.'

He kissed Scarlett goodbye and left.

'I'll call you tomorrow when I'm ready to leave,' she said as he closed the door behind him.

The clock in the taxi told Tom it was only five thirty pm. For some strange reason he thought it was much later than it actually was. He stopped at a kebab shop to pick up something for his tea before going home. He arrived home at six pm and when he went in all he could hear was Maud's soft, soothing voice. He peered into the sitting room but there was no one there. He checked the kitchen but it too was empty. He was just walking out again when he looked back into the kitchen. It was spotless.

'Maud, you are a star,' he whispered.

Tom crept upstairs expecting to find toys everywhere. Instead, Maud had put Alex and Jasper to sleep and she was sitting on the edge of Ralph's bed reading the twins a story. In a strange way, Tom was envious. He suddenly felt the urge to want to read them a story. He didn't read to Alex because he believed Alex was too young, so what would be the point. From watching Maud, he couldn't have been more wrong. Polly's eyes had closed and Ralph's were barely open. It wasn't the content of the story that kept them quiet; it was the way it was read. Maud had a knack of making anything sound fascinating and this story was no exception. Tom smiled when he noticed the cover of the book she was holding. When Tom was younger, Maud used to send him to sleep by reading things like '*Hansel and Gretel*' or '*The Three Little Pigs*'. Tonight she was reading '*The BFG*' by Roald Dahl, another one of Tom's childhood favourites. It certainly did the trick then and it did it now.

When Ralph finally nodded off Maud joined Tom in the kitchen.

'I see you're still eating healthily,' she said sarcastically.

'Kebabs have all the nutritional values of any home cooked meal.' He opened the kebab up and showed her. 'See, there's fresh lettuce, cabbage, tomato, chilli, served up with the most tender lamb you can imagine, all served in a delicious warm pitta bread.'

'Not the same as my home-made Irish stew though, is it?'

'You're not wrong there.'

She picked up the kettle and began to fill it.

'Tea?'

'Yes, please,' Tom replied.

Tom finished every scrap of the kebab before asking Maud if she would be willing to look after Alex and Jasper.

'Tom, you know I will. I finish looking after the current ones this weekend anyway.'

'Thanks, Maud. We'll pay you at the end of each week if that's okay.'

'Of course it is.'

There was an unnerving silence. It wasn't abnormal for Maud to have her quiet periods. She was usually thinking about how to approach a subject with the person she was with, which was why Tom was feeling nervous.

'So, Tom. I know I've asked you before, but how are you coping, really?'

'I assume you're referring to me being a father?' he asked.

'You know I am. Before Alex was born, you threw yourself into your work and now he's here you're still making your job your highest priority. Why?'

'Maud, Alex is very important to me, of course he is, but this promotion is more than what I was hoping to achieve at Thornes. It may not be the greatest leap in other people's careers, but it's mine. I never thought I'd have the job I do now and the idea of being a Company Director, well, it's fantastic. More than I could have dreamed. In addition, if I get the job of Director it will be good for us as a family. It'll mean extra security. Alex will get everything he needs and so will Scarlett. I'm only thinking of them.'

'Are you?' she asked. 'Come on, Tom. You can't fool me. I know you love Alex, but there's something more to it than that.'

She put her hand on his forearm and he didn't know where to look. She was right. Tom wasn't scared for himself, he was scared for Alex.

'I guess I just don't want him to grow up believing he's a failure, like I did. I want to provide for him so he can get the best education, get the best opportunities in life. I've had to work so hard to get where I am today and the chance of furthering my career is something I can't turn away from.'

'Tom, Alex is only a baby. He doesn't know about dry nappies yet never mind career advancements. It may not seem like it, but these are crucial months for him. He needs to know that you'll be there for him whenever he needs you, not just the odd fifteen minutes in the evening or for a couple of hours on a Sunday afternoon.' She sighed. 'If you spend time with him now it'll be second nature to take time out with him as he gets older. Spend more time at work now and you'll find it increasingly difficult to come away from it as Alex grows up. He'll want to know why you spent so much time away from him. He won't see that you're providing for him, that won't be important to him, time with you will.'

'When I grew up, my father never gave me any chances. If I did badly at something, he wouldn't encourage me; he'd blame me. It was always my fault. Teachers never helped me; they just thought I was stupid and lazy. Alex is not going to be treated like that.'

'Then encourage him even now. Contrary to what you're thinking, he's never too young, Tom.'

Maud got up, kissed Tom on his head, and said goodbye.

'I'll pop over in the morning at eight to collect the babies. Think about what I've said, Tom.'

'I will, Maud. I will.'

She left Tom alone to ponder her words. So, he did.

After phoning Howard and Craig, Tom poured himself a tumbler of whisky and fell into an armchair. Craig thought it hilarious that Tom was going to be a 'housewife' for the next few weeks. He wanted to know if Tom would be wearing a pinny while doing the dusting with a napkin tied around his head.

'Anymore wise cracks like that and I'll show you where I can stick my feather duster,' Tom told him. Still, he could see the funny side of it. In a matter of hours, he'd gone from an aspiring Customer Service Director to a one-handed Domestic Technician. He switched the telly on and caught up with the world news. After a couple more glasses of whisky, he finally caught up with his sleep too. He never knew an armchair could be so comfortable.

6

The rising sun pushed its way through the sitting room blinds and through Tom's eyelids. Tom didn't have any option other than get up to hide from the unfriendly wake-up call. He shuffled into the downstairs toilet and relieved himself of half a bottle of whisky, a small one thankfully. As he stared at his saliva-encrusted mouth in the mirror, he realised that it was ridiculously quiet. He stood perfectly still and waited for the sound of a falling baby or the screams of a demented toddler, but there was nothing. Just perfect silence. It only took two steps from the toilet door to notice why. The hour hand on the hall clock just reached five am. He crept up the stairs and went into his bedroom to try to get another hour of sleep. He had just gotten comfortable when Alex started to cry.

'Thanks a bunch,' he said looking skywards.

Tom rolled out of bed and shuffled into Alex's room as quickly as he could. He managed to get him out of his cot before his crying woke up Jasper.

'Good morning, my little man. How are you this beautiful sunny morn?'

Alex rested his head on Tom's shoulder and closed his eyes. By the time Tom had walked down the stairs he had fallen back to sleep. They sat down in the armchair and Tom pulled an old throw over them. For a moment, Tom nearly took this time for granted as he had done over the past few weeks, but he remembered Maud's words. He looked down at Alex's face and kissed his soft cheek. For the very first time since he was born Tom just stared at him. He hadn't noticed that the shape of his mouth was the same as his and his ears, poor kid. The almost oriental slant at the outside of his eyes was practically identical to Scarlett's. It had never occurred to Tom that this little baby could be so obviously his. When Alex was born everyone, especially the older folk, commented on how he looked; that he had his mother's eyes and his father's mouth. Tom used to laugh at them and think they were bonkers. He guessed he wasn't looking as closely as they were. Why hadn't he noticed this before? Tom began to think of all the other things he'd probably missed over the past months, like Alex's first giggle. He remembered plenty of smiles when he was a few weeks old, but then Tom realised that was just wind from down below. For the life of him, he could not remember when Alex first giggled, or when he had his first bath. Was he actually there? Probably not. He was probably in the pub with the boys, more than likely. Exactly how many nappies had he changed? If he was honest, he could have counted the number on one hand. And he couldn't remember bottle-feeding him either, not once. This small bundle of life hardly knew him, yet here he was fast asleep in his arms without a care in the world. He was secure in the fact that there was always someone there for him whenever he needed him or her; more secure than Tom was about being a good father. What he would give to be a child again. Free from worry or anxiety. Innocent. Content.

'I'm sorry, Alex,' he whispered. 'Daddy does love you, you know. I've just a funny way of showing it. But, we'll have such fun over the next couple of months. We're going to see a lot of each other. Auntie

Maud will look after you while Mummy's at work and I'll pop in to see you loads and you can play with Polly and Ralph.' Tom thought about that for a second. 'Or maybe just Jasper!'

Tom gave him another kiss and got a whiff of baby-powder.

'I'm going to be a proper daddy from now on. The one you deserve.'

Polly and Ralph didn't wake up until seven thirty, shortly followed by Jasper. Whatever Maud did to them last night it certainly did the trick, except for Alex of course, but Tom certainly didn't mind. As soon as he had all the kids dressed and washed, he headed off to Maud's hoping to get to hers before she made her way to his. It was a beautiful, warm summer's morning and everything felt good, apart from his right hand. It was still throbbing slightly and he found dressing the children quite an ordeal.

Maud was standing at her front door when he arrived just about to pull it closed.

'My, my! This is a turn up for the books. I wasn't expecting to see you so early. Did you sleep well?' she asked.

'Like a log,' said Tom. 'And waking up to the sound of the birds instead of a crying baby does wonders for you. I feel terrific.'

'Marvellous. So what are your plans for today?'

As Tom answered, Alex and Jasper happily crawled their way to the playroom. Polly and Ralph ran into the drawing room and started to read some books.

'Well, I need to go to the office to sort some things out. With Polly and Ralph in tow I'll need to be brief.'

'Don't worry about them. They can stay here for a while,' offered Maud.

'No, Maud. It's fine. You're doing enough as it is. I'll cope.'

'As long as you're sure.'

'I am. Thanks. I'll come by around four this afternoon to collect the babies.'

Tom called for Polly and Ralph and they came running out of the front door and stood stock still next to him. They said goodbye to Maud and then headed towards town. As they passed by Harry's butchers Tom heard George shouting at the top of his voice. Although Tom was outside in the street and George was at the back of his shop, he still felt he was intruding on a private conversation, as did everyone else who passed by, judging by their expressions. Unsure whether to go in and see what was going on, he asked Polly and Ralph to turn around, walk past the shop window, and have a good look inside. When they had done so they were to come straight back to him and tell him what they saw. He shouldn't have been too surprised when they walked past the window and went inside. Now he didn't have any choice, he had to go in. There were no customers around except for an elderly Spanish man called Juan, who came in every day for his free fish pieces. Tom smiled an acknowledgment toward Juan and now knew why George was shouting. Juan was completely deaf, but George felt if he yelled at him that he would somehow make a breakthrough. He hadn't in fourteen years of serving Juan, but he continued shouting anyway.

Both Polly and Ralph stood against the glass-panelled cabinet and pressed their faces into it as if to try to get a better look at what was going on. Tom was about to usher the children out when George came out of his back office and stopped them in their tracks.

'Tom, Tom, the pipers son,' he sang badly. 'It's been quite a while since you came to visit. Mind you, I'd still prefer the company of that pretty wife of yours.'

He put his large purple hands on his hips and looked out of the window with a glazed look in his eyes. 'Yes, she sure is a beautiful young thing, your Scarlett. I seem to have missed out there, haven't I Tom?'

'Ah, well, you can't have 'em all, George. But my word, you've certainly tried!'

George was well in his early sixties, had countless romantic relationships over the years, and sired eight children, but he still had an eye for the women. 'It's not the only thing I have for them,' he always joked. The last time Tom had spoken to George he told him he was 'between women'. Knowing George as he did he wasn't sure if that meant he was single or enjoying the benefits of a ménage-a-trois relationship.

'Sorry George. I didn't come in for anything. It was Polly and Ralph here. They ran off on me and came in. We were just on our way to the park via the office.'

George leant over the counter and smiled a huge soppy grin. He suddenly remembered Juan. 'Oh, excuse me for a minute, kids,' he said.

He scooped a pile of fish bits from a large blue bucket and put them into a plastic bag before giving them to Juan. He bent down and practically chewed Juan's ear off as he shouted, 'Here you go, Juan. Enjoy. When you come in tomorrow I'll give you something for your cats as well.'

Juan left with a content look on his well-tanned and pruned-up face.

'Now then,' said George to Polly and Ralph. 'Where did you two come from?'

'From our mummy's tummy,' answered Ralph.

'No we didn't,' scolded Polly. 'We came from her uterus. I saw it on the television.'

'You watch too much TV,' Tom said.

'Well, wherever you came from it's still nice to meet you.' George opened his shirt pocket and bent down to Polly. 'There's something in here I think you two would like.'

Polly and Ralph looked at each other and them up at me.

'Go on then, Ralph, you first.'

He put his hand in slowly as if he was expecting the contents of the pocket to bite. He pulled out his hand and smiled. He held the biggest gobstopper Tom had ever seen.

'Wow,' he said, and shoved the large ball in his mouth.

'Well, little lady? What about you?' asked George.

Polly stretched out her arm and just as she was about to put her hand in the pocket, George growled at her like a bear and almost frightened the life out of her.

She jumped behind Tom as Ralph burst out laughing, but only for a second. Suddenly his face went purple and Tom realised the gobstopper had gone down his throat and stuck. Tom slapped Ralph's back forcefully a few times, but nothing happened. George ran to the front of the counter and grabbed Ralph by the waist with both arms, picked him up and heaved. Ralph's body crumpled as the sweet forced its way forwards out of his mouth and into the ample cleavage of an unsuspecting customer. Judging by the low-cut top that she was wearing Tom had no doubt she was hoping to get something down there, but clearly, a gobstopper was not what she had in mind. George saw a damsel in distress. He dropped Ralph to the floor and offered his apologies to the woman before offering to retrieve the sticky candy. She accepted the first but declined the second and left the shop twice as fast as she had entered. George turned with a rejected look on his face.

'Looks like you were right, Tom. You can't have 'em all.'

He hadn't noticed Ralph was crying, so Polly went up to him and told him off.

'You made Ralph cry,' she said, before blowing him a raspberry.

'Why, I'm sorry, little fella,' said George. 'Tell you what, come give me a big hug and I'll see if there's something else in my pocket for you, eh?'

'No!' shouted Ralph, before releasing an even louder raspberry.

George looked positively hurt. Tom thought it was time to show his feelings too.

'Well, what do you expect, George? You shouldn't give little kids things like that; he could have choked to death. How would I have explained that to Scarlett?'

'It wasn't the gobstopper that caused the problem; it was when I growled at Polly that made him choke. So you tell me, Tom, which was the worst evil; giving Ralph the gobstopper or giving Polly a fright?'

'If you ask me, you shouldn't have given either of them anything. Not only has Ralph lost his sweet but you've also made Polly scared of you and you've managed all this in a matter of seconds.' Tom was getting angry now. 'I wish we'd never come in in the first place.'

'Well done, Tom.'

'Well done? What do you mean 'well done'?' he asked.

'It's all a matter of consequences, isn't it?'

'You've lost me, George?'

He walked behind the counter and leant against it with his arms on top.

'Well, if I had given Polly a sweet instead of a fright, the probability of Ralph choking would have been close to nil, as the sweet is what they both would have been expecting. Correct?'

'Perhaps, yes.'

'Therefore, Ralph would not have been surprised, hence, no choking.

'Yes, I get that part, but what are you on about, George?'

'Well, I don't like taking the blame for something that is ultimately your fault, Tom,' bellowed George.

Tom was amazed. 'My fault! How's it my fault?'

'Like I said, it's to do with consequences. If you hadn't come in here in the first place, I wouldn't have given Ralph the gobstopper; he wouldn't have choked and blasted it into the bosom of the most beautiful woman to have come into the shop this morning, and I wouldn't be standing here shouting at you.' The veins pulsed out of his forehead. He was in full flow. 'Instead, I would have come out of my office, had a nice chat with Juan, and then introduced myself to that beautiful woman with the ample bosom, before asking her out for a seductive candle-lit dinner.'

He finally took another breath and composed himself. He then walked back into his office and slammed the door shut. By now the children were both standing behind Tom with all four hands clutching onto his coat. He took their hands in his, wincing as Polly tightly gripped his right hand, and walked them to the door. But Tom needed to have the last word before leaving. He turned and shouted, 'I won't be buying any of your chopped liver again. It's probably got cirrhosis.'

Terry, Thornes' security guard, was the first to congratulate Tom on his new role, as Tom walked into Thornes with Polly and Ralph several feet behind him. 'Good luck for the next couple of months, Mr Farrow. You'll need it!'

'Thanks, Terry. Always one to encourage!' Tom replied.

Before leaving home, Tom gave Polly and Ralph a pep talk about how to behave in the office and a list of things they were not to touch. They seemed to listen and take it all in which made him feel a bit wary, so he asked them to repeat what he had said. Ralph was very quick to point out that he hadn't ever heard of a photocopier or a printer, so how would he know if he were touching one or not.

He had a point.

'Okay. This is what you do. When we get into the office, I want both of you to put both of your hands in your pockets. That way you won't be able to touch anything. Understand?'

They both nodded. As they entered the lift, Ralph asked if he could press the button.

'Sure. See if you can do it with your nose.' Tom answered.

'Which number do I press?'

'Three.'

He shuffled up to the number pad, stood still for a few seconds and before Tom could stop him, he pushed the wrong button.

'No,' Tom shouted. 'I said three, not eight.'

'Oops! Sorry! I get those two mixed up.'

The lift rose to the eighth floor and the doors opened at the magnificent reception of Hubert Maier and Golding. They were a solicitor's office and one of the finest in the building. The woman on reception stared over her walnut desk at the three of them. 'The Child Obedience courses are on the seventh floor with Professor Schnapps,' she growled.

Tom was mystified.

'I beg your pardon,' he said, not understanding her remark.

She looked at the children. Polly was sticking her tongue out while rolling her eyes around her sockets and Ralph was facing backwards with his trousers and pants hanging around his ankles. The lift doors began to shut.

'Ah, no. It's not that,' he shouted back. 'I'm just taking them to the office with me.'

'Believe me,' she bellowed back. 'Take them to the Professor; it'll be better in the long run.'

Tom was too busy pulling Ralph's trousers back up to notice Polly pressing another button. The lift descended the whole way to the basement. The doors opened once again, but this time they were at Thornes mailroom.

'Hey, Tom!' shouted Dexter Flynn. 'Come on in. It's been a while.'

'Come on you two, we'll go in here for a few minutes and then we'll go upstairs, and don't touch anything.'

As they stepped out of the lift, two post trolleys were being wheeled in.

'Hi, Dexter, how are you?'

'Very well,' he replied. 'And who's this young lady?'

'Well, this is Polly, and this is...huh? Where's Ralph gone? Ralph?'

Tom turned around too late to stop the lift doors from closing in front of Ralph's smiling face.

'No. Come back,' yelled Tom.

The lift ascended and stopped at the second floor. The mail boys wheeled out the trolleys and Ralph followed.

Tom stood in the basement and watched the lift indicator stop at two.

'Okay, he's on the second floor. Polly, let's go.'

He grabbed Polly's arm and dragged her to the stairs. They ran up, as fast as Polly would let them, but when they reached the second floor there was no sign of Ralph. Tom asked Janine at the reception desk if she had seen him come out of the lift.

'I did notice something come out after the post trolleys. Maybe it was him, I don't know. I was doing my nails at the time. I can't just look up at things when I'm doing my nails, you know.'

'Janine, you're a receptionist, you're supposed to notice people when they come out of the lifts.' Tom paused and had a scary thought. He realised his nightmare was just beginning as Janine confirmed it.

'Perhaps he got into the other lift.'

The other lift! Why hadn't Tom thought of that? Only one lift went down to the mailroom. The other stopped at the ground floor. The level indicator for the other lift was moving. It was going up. Four. Five. Six. Seven. Eight.

'Oh-no. He's gone back up to Hubert Maier and Golding.' Tom grabbed Polly's arm again and trailed her over to the lifts. He thumped the call button several times, but both lifts were in use. 'Looks like it's the stairs again.'

Polly groaned and muttered something about her shoes, but Tom wasn't really listening. He needed to find Ralph before he caused mayhem. They charged up the stairs as fast as they could. By the time they reached the eighth floor Polly had practically caught up with Tom. He gasped for breath and bent over the handrail as Polly reached him. The embarrassing thing was she still had both her hands in her pockets.

'I need to exercise more,' Tom moaned.

'Excuse me!' It was the same woman as before. 'Can I be of assistance?' she asked curiously. 'You don't look well.'

'I'm okay, I'm okay.'

'You certainly don't look it,' she said sharply handing Tom a small paper funnel with water in it.

'Thanks.'

He stood up properly and regained his composure. Polly just stood beside him waiting patiently for the next instruction.

'So,' began the woman. 'You took my advice, did you?'

'Advice? What advice?'

'You left the boy with Professor Schnapps, like I advised.'

'Ah, well. No.'

'Oh! So where have you left him then?' she asked.

Tom suddenly remembered the feeling he got when he was at school and his English teacher would ask him in front of the rest of the class why he hadn't done his homework, knowing that whatever excuse he was about to give wouldn't be good enough, and that the she was going to get even madder? That was how he was feeling now. His mouth moved as he tried to think of a very plausible answer and his eyes followed that invisible fly one sees during moments like this, but he couldn't think of an answer. Polly did.

'He's lost him,' she snapped.

Tom glared down at her. 'Thanks a bunch.'

The woman raised her eyebrows and removed her glasses. 'You've lost him? How could you lose a boy? What kind of father are you?'

Before he could interrupt and amend her misjudgement, she flew off on one.

'Perhaps you'll think twice before taking your children to work with you again. You can get help, you know. There is such a thing as childcare. Grandparents are a great help as well. Does your wife know what kind of father you are?'

Just as she was trailing off Tom noticed Ralph's head in the midst of the open-plan office ahead of him.

'There he is,' Tom shouted.

Tom took Polly's arm and began to lead her into the office.

'But my shoes!' cried Polly, but Tom carried on regardless.

'I'll wait by the lifts in case he tries to run,' called the woman.

Tom and Polly crept through the office trying not to disturb anyone. Many people were talking on the phones and others were typing furiously on their computers. Tom watched Ralph carefully. He was standing by a water cooler next to a maintenance ladder.

'Come on Polly, there he is.'

'But I'll trip. My shoelaces aren't done up.'

'Right, right, okay! Tie them then, you did it this morning.'

Tom kept looking back at Ralph so he didn't lose him.

'I can't,' said Polly.

'Yes you can. Come on, hurry up,' Tom barked.

'You do them.'

He turned round to face Polly and showed her his right hand. 'I can't do them, can I?'

'Try,' she spat.

After a fleeting glance back to the water cooler where Tom noticed Ralph moving a box, he knelt down in front of Polly and tried to tie her laces as she sat on the floor.

'What is it with you kids? You can do something one minute and lose all knowledge of how to do it the next. Ow!' Tom's right thumb stuck in the knot.

Without him knowing it, someone was walking along the aisle with reams of copier paper. Tom was just finishing off the painful task of tying the laces when he noticed Ralph standing on the box with both his arms clasped round the large water drum.

'Oh-no! No, Ralph.'

Tom jumped up just in front of the man carrying the paper. Polly didn't. The man tripped over her and his load of paper went upwards as he crashed to the floor. Tom turned back to help him and then looked back at Ralph. He was about to lift the water drum of the cooler. Tom ran towards him, but tripped over an uncovered electrical cable and landed on the floor right in front of Ralph. He threw his head up to see Ralph detach the almost empty water bottle from its stand. What water that was left in the bottle gushed out onto the floor all over and around Tom, and a small stream ran down Ralph's trousers. Suddenly the office went dark.

'Hey! Who turned out the lights?' someone roared.

'What's happened?' shouted another.

As Tom lay on the floor, he looked round and saw that his foot had ripped out a plug from its socket. A floorboard had been removed and a sign that read '*Danger – electrical repairs*' rested against the nearest desk. Tom was also too late to notice the water drip down into the open floor. Within seconds, sparks and smoke came up from beneath the desk, and without warning, all the computers went blank.

There was uproar.

People shouted and swore with words that would make even Eddie Murphy blush. Others ran around trying to find the reason for the problem. Tom felt a dark presence above him.

'You found him then!' It was the woman from the reception desk again.

She stood over him between two rather large security guards, which Tom was about out was due to excess muscle, rather than fat.

He glowered at Ralph. 'I told you to keep your hands in your pockets.'

The water drum slipped from his hands and landed on Tom's head.

'Oops!' said Ralph.

Tom stood in another angry woman's office and offered the most sincere apologies that he had ever bestowed on someone. Mrs Hubert was known for her ferocity, and Tom certainly bore the brunt of it as he tried to explain how the disaster came about. She wasn't having any of it. Tom noticed his clothes were dripping over her genuine Persian rug and he slowly backed off it as she continued to hurl abuse at him. Sylvia, who once notified of the morning's events by Mrs Hubert's receptionist, had taken down the children to Tom's office.

'Never in all my life have I experienced such a disgraceful exhibition,' said Mrs Hubert.

'I've said I'm sorry a thousand times, Mrs Hubert. I'll pay for any damage we've caused, I promise.'

'We've?' she yelled. 'Don't you dare blame those innocent little children for your actions. Children are the product of our design, Mr Farrow. How you behave is how they will behave. As far as I'm concerned all expectant parents should go through a rigorous examination to see if they will be fit parents for the child. I am certain that if such an examination existed, you would have failed, hands down.'

Tom stood there for a moment, unsure of what to say.

'Alright, so I made a mistake. Don't we all? I'm not perfect you know.' It was time to stand up for himself. 'Children don't want perfect parents. They just want to be loved and respected.' He turned to walk out of the office. 'I don't have to prove it to you anyway, but I'll be a fit father, one day.'

Mrs Hubert laughed. 'Ha! You'll never be a fit father. You're not even a fit man. Now get out of my sight.'

Tom left her office and slammed the door behind him.

'Snooty old fart.'

Sylvia poured Tom a hot cup of coffee while he removed his wet sweater and shirt. He was cold and angry. Polly and Ralph sat on the couch in the corner of the office staring at the floor. Sylvia sat next to Ralph and put her arm around him. Tom exploded.

'I can't believe you two. No wonder your mother's in a mental hospital and your father doesn't come home.'

'Tom!' reprimanded Sylvia.

'Well, look at them. It's as though butter wouldn't melt in their mouths. It would curdle!'

Polly and Ralph began to sob. Sylvia stood up, grabbed Tom's arm and walked him out of the office.

'Tom, that was pathetic. You sound like a bully. Using words against them won't help at all. They don't understand.'

'I'm angry, Sylvia.'

'Why? Ask yourself why.'

'Because Ralph ran off. He disobeyed me and Polly was just being silly and obnoxious. If Ralph had stayed with me none of this would have happened.'

'Maybe not, but it wasn't his fault he didn't get out of the lift in time. If you want someone to blame then how about the mail boys who were wheeling in the trolleys, or Julia on reception for not doing her job properly.' She took a breath. 'Or perhaps you should not blame anyone. Just go in there, apologise to Polly and Ralph, and give them a big squeeze. As you so delicately put it, their mum, and dad aren't around to do it and at the moment you're the next best thing.'

She was so right. Tom was such an ass. He went back in and they were still sobbing, but they hadn't moved an inch. Tom got down on his knees and rested his hands on theirs.

'I'm very sorry,' he said slowly. 'I didn't mean what I said and if all this was anyone's fault, it was mine. You see you've got a head start on me with all this toddler business because you're already there and I only started learning a few days ago.'

Polly looked at him and wiped her eyes. 'Sorry!' she said.

'It's okay. You've nothing to be sorry about.'

'I tried to tell you about my laces.'

'Yes you did.'

Ralph slid off the couch and gave Tom a huge hug pushing his head under his chin. 'I'm sorry too,' he said. 'I only wanted a little drink.'

Tom sighed.

'I'm sorry too, little buddy.' He pulled Polly into him too. 'Tell you what. When I've finished here how about we go get some pizza and milkshakes?'

'Oh, yeah!' screamed Ralph.

'Can I have anchovies and banana on mine?' asked Polly.

Tom looked at her. 'You're not pregnant are you, Polly?'

She laughed aloud. 'What's pregnant?'

'Never mind. Yes, you can have whatever you want on it.'

'Hurrah!'

Sylvia smiled through a crack in the door.

Tom left the children in the capable hands of Sylvia as he tied up a few loose ends before calling a quick meeting with Howard and Craig.

'So, have you found anything out about Edward yet?' he asked.

'Well, it's true about the floozy down in the typing pool,' said Craig. 'Sir Wilfred has already had a couple of outings with Miss Charlene Fleck.'

'Oh! How'd you find that out?'

Howard smirked before answering, 'Well, young Craig 'Studley' Spanner here asked her out for himself when she mentioned that she was already seeing another man.'

'Yup,' continued Craig. 'And after a few probing questions I found out the other man was Sir Wilfred. But, I'm sworn to secrecy, of course. Told her I wouldn't tell a soul.'

'Course not. Very gentleman-like. So, he's already got to Sir Wilfred. What about the other Board members?'

Craig and Howard looked at one another. It was Howard who answered.

'Well, you're not going to like this one, but Edward has just bought a sea-shore villa down on the southern coast of Italy and he's allowing old 'Tanned' Taylor to use it at his pleasure. Well, there's no way Sir Tarquin would turn that down. He spends more time in the Mediterranean than a Greek fisherman.'

'Terrific!' Tom responded sarcastically. 'Anything else you need to tell me? If so, please go easy.'

'There is one vote that you're not liable to get,' said Howard.

'Whose?'

'Bertie Flotsam.'

'Why not? He was an absolute certainty. He may not know me from Adam, but he absolutely hates Edward and there's no way he'd vote for him.'

'Hated,' muttered Craig.

'That's what I said.'

'No, you said 'hates' as in present tense. I said 'hated' as in past tense.'

'That's what he is,' said Howard. 'Past tense. He choked to death last night after eating oysters. Apparently he got a pearl lodged in his wind-pipe and they couldn't get it out.'

Tom's heart sank. Bertram Flotsam was a definite 'yes' vote for him and now he'd gone. Selfish old buzzard. Always thinking with his stomach.

'Well, looks like I've got my work cut out for me.'

'You mean Scarlett has,' said Craig.

'Yes, you're right. Scarlett has.' He looked up at the clock. It was twelve twenty.

'Oh no! Scarlett! Sorry guys, got to go!' Tom ran out of the room. 'Please help Scarlett as much as possible. I'll thank you for it in the end!'

'Sure thing, Daddy-o!'

'See you, Pops!'

Tom collected Polly and Ralph from his office and rushed over to Maud's. Before leaving, Tom reassured them that he would be back within an hour to go for the pizza and milkshakes that he had promised them. They seemed happy enough. Tom ran back to the house and found a claims inspector from the insurance company standing on the doorstep. Tom asked to see his identification before tossing him the front door key. Tom told him to go on in, make himself comfortable, and assess the damage over a cup of tea.

'I'll be half an hour at the most,' Tom shouted as he got into his car and started the engine.

The man seemed somewhat bewildered and shouted back that it was against company rules to assess damage when not in the company of the client, or words to that effect. Tom was closing his door window at the time.

Thankfully, there was very little traffic on the roads, so Tom made it to the hospital in good time. Not having been home at all during the morning Tom had no idea what time Scarlett wanted collecting. Tom told her to leave a message on the answering machine if he didn't pick up the phone when she called. Tom only hoped he wasn't too late. When he arrived at her room, Tom was expecting a barrage of abuse. Instead, Tom found an orderly cleaning out the bathroom and the bed was empty.

'Excuse me!' Tom said sticking his head into the bathroom. 'Do you know where the lady who was in this room has gone?'

'Gone?' he repeated, a gormless expression covering his face. Judging by his response and the amount of metal rings protruding from his face and head, Tom thought he'd been pierced once too often. The last one must have clipped his brain severing all relevant nerves that connected to his mouth.

'Yes. Gone,' Tom repeated once again.

At this, the man slumped over his soaking wet mop and stared blankly at the floor. 'Gone,' he repeated, again.

Tom left him to mull over his answer while he went in search of someone with the capability of joining two syllables together. The ward clerk wasn't much use either. After checking her documentation three times she told Tom that his wife had been taken down to the morgue prior to her autopsy. She offered Tom her deepest sympathy with an all-too-realistic sniffle before he decided to go look for her by himself. Twenty minutes later Tom gave up and went to the admissions desk. After a very brief conversation with a receptionist Tom found out that Scarlett had left the hospital and taken a taxi home as her 'sod of a husband' hadn't come to collect her after waiting for over two hours. Oh dear! The drive home was supposed to be as quick as the one to the hospital, but somebody had other plans. Tom was just pulling out of the hospital car park when halfway across the road his car conked out. Tom turned the ignition on half a dozen times, but nothing happened. Drivers beeped their horns incessantly at Tom to get out of the way, so he hopped out and slowly pushed the car over to the pavement. As they passed him, they all thought it fit to shout an obscenity or gave a rude hand gesture, as if that was going to help matters.

'Oh, yes, that's lovely,' Tom shouted back. 'As if the bird will make my car start, you pathetic sack of ...'

A van full of builders stopped in front of him and all the doors opened. Tom began to wish he wasn't so eager to retaliate with useless name-calling.

Tom opened the front door of the house just as the claims inspector was putting on his overcoat.

'Ah, Mr Farrow. I've had a look at the damage. I did wait until your wife arrived home before having a cup of tea though. Don't like to snoop around other people's houses when they're not in it. I'll make my report up over the next few days and you'll hear from us soon.'

'Surely you can tell us now if we can get reimbursed. I mean it's only a sofa for crying out loud.' Tom's temper was slightly frayed and showing.

'Yes, perhaps, but we do need to look at all the facts before coming to a conclusion, Mr Farrow. We need to make sure it was actually accidental damage, don't we?' If he was anymore patronising Tom was going to slap him.

'Of course, it was an accident. A child broke a pen and the ink spilled over the sofa.'

'Yes, perhaps, but as I say, we need to clarify all the details. We need to assess whether or not the third party was acting wittingly or unwittingly.'

'What?' Tom snarled.

He brought his nose to within an inch of Tom's. 'We need to be sure the child wasn't being malicious. If he caused the mess on purpose then we may have to deny your claim.'

Tom grabbed him by his lapels. 'Now listen, you little...'

'Tom! Let Mr Prescott go,' said Scarlett as she limped into the sitting room.

Reluctantly, Tom let him go. 'Sorry,' said Tom. 'I'm not having a great day.'

'That's alright, Mr Farrow. People do lose their patience now and again while undergoing stressful periods, but don't worry, it will... lapse.' He laughed. 'A little insurance joke there...lapse.' He noticed Tom's blank expression. 'Oh dear, perhaps I need to...renew my sense of humour.' Another chuckle. 'Okay, well. I'm all done. I'll let myself out now. Thanks for the tea, Mrs Farrow. Goodbye!'

'Glorified paper pusher,' Tom scowled as he pushed the front door shut.

Tom walked into the sitting room. Scarlett was lying on the sofa on top of a dustsheet, her plastered leg resting up on the coffee table.

'If we can't get rid of it yet then we might as well use it. The ink has all dried in.' She noticed his overly purple forehead. 'What happened to you?'

'Road rage.'

She tutted. 'Did you shout at someone?'

'They shouted at me first and stuck their fingers up at me.'

'They?'

'Four builders. Luckily the driver was the only one who kissed me; the others just got out of the van to watch.'

'Kissed?'

'He was Glaswegian.'

'Ah,' said Scarlett.

Tom took his coat off and dropped it on the floor before pouring himself a drink.

'Oh-no you don't, matey! I've just spoken to Maud. Polly and Ralph are still waiting for the pizzas and milkshakes that you promised them hours ago. Get your coat back on and get over there, pronto. We'll talk about this morning when you get back.'

Without saying a word, Tom picked up his coat and shuffled his way out to the car. When Maud opened her door and saw his forehead, her dentures almost fell out of her gaping mouth.

'Don't say a word!' Tom warned her.

'About what?' she replied innocently.

Polly and Ralph were ready to go and it was the first time Tom noticed them looking almost cute. They were both standing to attention with smiles across their faces. Ralph pointed at Tom's head and was about to speak.

'Ah-ah!' Tom uttered 'Don't ask. Just say thanks to Auntie Maud and go and get in the car.'

'Bye!' they shouted running out the front door.

'They've been positively glowing this afternoon, Tom. What happened this morning?'

'I'll tell you some other time. I don't want to keep them waiting any longer.' Tom got into the car and lowered his window. 'I'll be back for Alex and Jasper around six.'

'Fine. Enjoy yourself.'

Tom drove towards the town centre when Polly saw some swings in a park. Tom didn't want to have another fight so he agreed to let them run around for a half-hour or so. Tom parked, took out a football from the boot, and followed the children as they ran towards the swings. There was an empty bench opposite the play area so Tom sat himself down and tried to relax. His hand was throbbing a bit from driving the car, but it was a beautiful summer's afternoon and nothing was going to stop him from enjoying it. After the morning he had had, he just wanted a few minutes of peace and calm. Polly and Ralph laughed loudly as they swung higher and higher into the sun. Children are so free, Tom thought. Nothing hinders them, except maybe grown-ups.

Tom was about to do some more psychoanalysis on parenting when a young woman sat down next to him. She was very attractive with short brown hair; sort of a bob but not quite. She was wearing a pair of denim shorts that rested closer to her hipbones than her knees. She wore a white cropped top that proudly helped to display a fantastically flat stomach. Not that Tom noticed any of this until she spoke to him, of course.

'Hi! I'm Geri.' Her pearl white teeth glistened in the sun as she smiled the most radiant smile.

'Tom. Tom Farrow,' he responded in an octave even the most renowned alto would be proud of. He realised he was staring at her a bit too long to be comfortable, so he looked away and tried to focus his attention on Polly and Ralph.

'I'm sorry, I didn't mean to startle you,' she laughed.

Startled, yes, that was it. Tom was just startled.

'Oh, that's okay.' Tom kept staring ahead, but felt he ought to carry on the conversation. 'So, here on your own?' he asked.

'No, my little boy is over there on the swing. The one in the yellow dungarees.'

'Oh, right. Cute little fella. Those two beside him are with me.'

'Twins?'

'Yep! And there's another two back at the nanny's,' he added.

She turned toward Tom, crossed her smooth, olive-coloured legs, and smiled at him in wonder. 'Four kids? Wow! You don't look old enough. They must keep you busy!'

'Yes, they do. I've had to give up work to look after them, well, two of them anyway. The nanny looks after the babies during the day.'

Tom didn't notice but Geri gave him a pitiful look before looking back towards the children.

'So, are you on your own?' she asked.

He took a deep breath. 'Yeah. My wife's out of the loop. She's left me to look after the kids while she recovers and gets stuck into her work.'

'I think it's you who needs to recover, not her.' Geri said angrily. Tom wasn't sure what she meant and then he remembered his hand.

'Oh, this...oh...I'll be fine. A few days discomfort and then everything will be as good as new.'

'Not for those poor kids,' she whispered.

'Yeah, well, they've been passed around from pillar to post over the last few days, but they'll have me from now on. They'll be sick of the sight of me in no time,' Tom joked.

'Somehow I don't think they will,' said Geri, her deep brown eyes staring back at Tom.

Tom began to feel sweat run down his spine. 'Phew, it's hot today. At least you're dressed for it,' he said smiling awkwardly and nodding towards her long, perfectly tanned legs. 'Look at me. Still in my suit; tie choking my throat.'

'You look very smart...and handsome. I guess I am quite hot too,' she said as she slowly pulled her right hand across the top of her chest forcing a bead of sweat to roll downwards.

'Yes you are,' said Tom aloud, a little too enthusiastically. 'Er...I mean, of course you must be. In heat like this why would I be the only one getting all hot and bothered? Anyway, enough about me. Do you have a partner?' Tom asked that question slowly and nervously. In today's society, it's always a hard question to ask in case you cause embarrassment.

'No,' she smiled. 'Stephen left when he found out I was pregnant. He got frightened at the prospect of losing his social life. Hated the idea of being responsible for someone else's life.'

Tom was about to feel sorry for her when she told him not to be.

'It was my fault really. Stephen and I had been married for two years and we'd never talked about having children. One week I didn't take the pill for the simple reason that I ran out and I didn't get around to renewing my prescription. It just happened to be that week that Stephen took me away for a romantic holiday to the south of France and, lo and behold, I became pregnant. He got scared and ran off.'

'What a dirt bag!' Tom said thoughtlessly. 'Oh, I'm sorry.'

'Don't be. I think I'm better off without him and so is Alex.' She nodded in the direction of her son.

'Alex? Your son is called Alex?'

'Yes, why?'

'That's the name of my youngest.'

'Wow! What a coincidence.'

They both laughed together for a while and swapped some kiddie stories. She roared with laughter when Tom told her about the painting and the sofa. It had almost turned five pm when Tom asked Geri if she and Alex would join them for pizza.

'Well, seeing as we're both on our own, why not?' she answered with a smile.

They collected the children and left the park just as the warden was closing the gates. They went to a large family owned pizzeria and the food was terrific. The waiter who took their order didn't even bat an eyelid when Polly asked for a pizza with anchovies and banana. Geri's little Alex was the same age as Tom's little Alex. In fact, they were only four days apart and the twins were very good with him. They had a lovely time and when it was time to leave Geri asked if they could meet up again. She said she didn't have any friends with children in the area and it was nice to meet someone with whom she had a lot in common. Tom did mull it over for a second thinking how Scarlett would react, but Tom knew that if she were here with Geri she'd do the same thing, so Tom said 'yes'. Out in the car park Tom offered them a lift home but Geri said she'd rather walk, as it wasn't very far to her flat. Tom wrote down her phone number and promised to call her in the next few days. They said goodbye and as they did, Geri gave Tom a lingering peck on the cheek and thanked him for a fun afternoon. Tom blushed, aware that the kiss was a little longer than he was expecting. She smiled and wheeled Alex away in his pushchair.

Maynard Tait

8

Heavy rain clouds covered the evening sun quickly and what was a beautiful summer's day had turned into a grey and miserable evening. Tom had been looking forward to reading Alex a bedtime story for the first time, but he was out for the count as soon as his precious little head touched the mattress in his cot. Polly and Ralph also crashed out in record time leaving Jasper the last one to conk out just before seven pm. Scarlett looked as though she hadn't moved an inch since Tom left her earlier in the afternoon. However, the box of chocolates and the bottle of wine sitting on the floor beside the sofa gave the game away.

'Sheila from two doors down popped over with them. She felt sorry for me and thought I'd need some cheering up. I only got up to open the door before hobbling back to collapse here again.'

'How did she know you'd need cheering up?'

'Tom, why would people just sit in their armchairs and watch '*Neighbours*' when they could get up for a few minutes and watch their real ones getting carted off in an ambulance. It's a lot more interesting seeing it happen in real life. I'd be very surprised if anyone in the street missed all the commotion yesterday.'

Tom picked up the bottle to pour himself a glass.

'Ah-ah!' snapped Scarlett. ''Tis mine. Get a beer from the fridge if you want a drink.'

'Charming! I've been running around like a blue...'

'Tom,' she interrupted. 'I don't like that phrase. Choose another one.'

'Like a demented single parent and all I want is a soothing drink.' Tom plopped into an armchair. 'I suppose you would like me to make you some dinner.'

'No thanks. I'm stuffed after eating all these chocolates.'

Scarlett reached down to the floor and picked up a piece of paper. Before she spoke, Tom realised that it was the piece of paper with Geri's phone number on it. It must have dropped from his pocket when he leaned over and kissed Scarlett when he arrived home.

'What's this? Looks like a phone number.'

Tom was blasé and took the paper from Scarlett.

'Oh that. I met another lone parent in the park this afternoon. I said I'd call them and arrange to meet up with the kids again.'

'Quite the socialite, aren't you? So what's the name of this lone parent?'

'Geri. And would you believe it, their little boy is called Alex too.'

'No!' said Scarlett in genuine surprise.

'Yup! And he's only four days younger than our Alex.'

'Isn't that funny? So what does Jerry do then?'

'Nothing. Looks after Alex full-time. They haven't got many friends in the area, so I said we could meet up again seeing as the kids got on so well,' Tom said in honest innocence.

'That's good of you. At least it'll help to get the children out of the house and away from the telly. They'll end up with square eyes soon.'

Scarlett picked up the TV remote and flicked through all the channels. 'Why is there never anything good on when you decide to spend an evening in front of the box?'

'They plan it like that. The programmers think that by changing the start times of your favourite programmes every week, you will watch telly more often to find out when your favourite programmes actually start. There must be logic in there somewhere, but I'll be darned if I can find it. It just makes me want to switch it off altogether and read a book.'

Scarlett looked at Tom with raised eyebrows. 'You read a book! The last book you read was the manual for the car and you gave up on that after the introduction.'

'I've read books,' Tom said. 'There was that one about the countries of eastern Asia. That was interesting.'

'Tom, a travel brochure does not fall into the same category as a book.'

'I still read it the whole way through.'

'Only to ogle at the bikini-clad sunbathers in it. Why don't you go down to the library tomorrow with the twins and see if you can borrow a real book? There's a children's section which will keep Polly and Ralph amused until you've made your choice.'

Tom wished for a decent excuse not to go to the library but the thought of being stuck inside the house all day with two toddlers made him think otherwise. He'd rather sit in a quiet library and read '*War and Peace*' than lie on the sitting room floor pretending to be a train station platform with passengers walking up and down on him. Reading a book, however, was not his idea of relaxation. More like torture. When Tom was at school, he had to study the moralistic reasoning behind Iago's ruination of Othello's life. Tom was only thirteen at the time and it was enough to put him off books for life. Tom spent the next few years thinking that people like William Shakespeare wrote all books and written in a language only the middle and upper classes could understand. Books were evil. Tom grew up a little bit and realised, gladly, that his thoughts were incorrect, but to this day Tom has never read anything longer than the Film Guide for 1992. What put him off the most about reading a book was the time it would take up. Tom remembered sitting on a bus one time and overheard a woman tell her friend that it had taken her three months to finish reading a novel. Just think of the amount of telly that she had missed during that period. And what about keeping track of current affairs? Did she put everything else on hold while reading this book? How long could the book have been? Of course, Tom wasn't thinking logically at the time. Scarlett put him straight and said the woman probably only read for fifteen or twenty minutes a day when she found some spare time. 'Some books can be read in an instant, some take longer because of the content and some are fun just to pick at whenever the mood takes you,' she told him. Still, Tom was a responsible adult now. If Tom was to broaden his knowledge then he guessed there was more to brain gain than just Teletext news and GMTV.

'I suppose I could give it a go,' Tom said to Scarlett.

'Good boy, Tom.' Patronisation was only one of Scarlett's endearing qualities, especially after a few glasses of Shiraz.

'Thanks for your support. I'll go down to the library first thing tomorrow and who knows, I may even come home with more than one book.'

'Steady on, Mr Bookworm. You don't want to use up all your brain cells at once.'

'Well at least I've got some.' Childish and futile, Tom knew, but it made him feel better!

They both went to bed relatively early, both extremely exhausted. Tom lay awake for a while, however, trying to get Geri out of his mind. Tom wasn't having impure thoughts, at least he wasn't trying too; they just rather popped up. Tom was trying to figure out if he was doing wrong by meeting with her and Alex. If he was honest he was only being friendly, but there was something in the way Geri behaved that made it seem she was after more than friendship. Perhaps Tom should see what happens. After all, they're only meeting up because of the children, right?

The last thing Tom noticed was the time on his bedside clock. It was two twenty-three am.

Sylvia collected Scarlett bang on eight thirty and it was the first time she had seen Scarlett in her pyjamas. It took some time to get all the kids up and ready again and Sylvia blushed as she stood waiting in the hallway for Scarlett as she got to grips with her crutches.

Road works at the main road into town hampered the drive to the library for Tom. He decided to keep his cool with the other car users today as he was aware they were only as annoyed as he was. While the bruising on his forehead wasn't obvious, the throbbing reminded him he didn't want another 'kiss' from an angry Scotsman. The library was bigger than Tom had imagined and busier. After taking the twins to the children's section, where they sat in front a TV of all things to watch '*Willy Wonka and the Chocolate Factory*', Tom wandered off in search of the ideal beginner's book. He couldn't get over how many different sections there were. Students brushed past some senior citizens at the history section. Two teenage boys began to fight over a book about World War 2 and within seconds, one of the elderly men grabbed them both by their ears and told them to sit down and share the book before they started World War 3. They did so and the man turned back to the shelf and continued his search for whatever he was looking for. Tom came across the fiction section and gaped in awe at the sheer volume of books. If anyone had seen him, they'd have thought he'd just had his sight given back to him after years of blindness. His mouth was wide open and Tom began to feel shaky.

He stood in the same spot for over five minutes just taking in the names of all the authors from Aardmann to Zelech. How on earth was anyone supposed to choose a book from all this lot? Another five minutes had passed when a timid looking old lady approached him and asked if Tom needed any help. She stood with both hands clasped together and Tom could smell the pungent odour of mothballs coming from her khaki coloured cardigan. Her watery eyes sunk deep into their sockets and her brown velvet skirt rested on the floor over dusty black plimsolls.

'I need a book,' was all Tom could think to say.

'What kind of book?' she squeaked.

He gave her a puzzled look. 'Preferably a small one, to start with.'

She continued to look up at him. Maybe Tom gave her the wrong answer.

'Is it fiction that you want?'

'Yes, yes. It is.'

'Which type? Action and adventure, thriller, horror, humorous, straight or perhaps,' She gave a deep sigh. 'An erotic novel.'

Tom couldn't tell from the way that she said 'erotic' if she was recommending it or if she had just had a pleasant memory from a wartime romance with a Yank. What Tom was hoping she would do was grab one book from a shelf and say 'here you go – get stuck in', but no such luck. Instead, she continued to gaze into his eyes with a look that said 'I knew someone young and virile like you once!' To be rid of the sorry sight Tom spat out 'Thriller, please.' She then listed times in which the thrillers were set and as fast as she recited them Tom asked for a modern day story. She walked a few feet away from him and removed a huge, black covered book that resembled the encyclopaedia's that used to be pushed in his face on his doorstep by some jumped-up little school-leaver trying to make a living. It was a Tom Clancy novel.

'It looks a little fatter than what I was hoping for,' Tom sneered.

Without moving a muscle in her mouth, she replaced the literary doorstep back to its position and lifted out a book that looked small enough to fit into his jacket pocket.

'How about this one?' she grumbled. 'It's set in the eighties. A disgruntled British marine employed by a group of Japanese terrorists has to blow up the Houses of Parliament after the British government placed a rice embargo on their country. The Japanese President is very angry and wants his revenge, only, in the process of setting his detonators, the ex-marine is found out by a beautiful, sexy, long-legged, big-busted blonde cabinet official who happens to fall haplessly in love with the ex-marine, all within the same page. The marine suddenly has a change of heart, but remembers the threat from the Japanese samurai that they will kill him and all his family if he does not carry out his task for which they are paying him one million dollars. What will he do? Leave and go and have lots of funs with blondie or carry out his mission and receive his reward? It's up to you, there's a choice of three endings.'

Tom raised an eyebrow.

'Sorry. I think I've read it.'

Tom excused himself faster than a polystyrene pellet from a Nerf gun and rescued the twins from '*Noddy*' on the telly before taking their leave from the library. Before leaving however Tom grabbed the first book his fingers touched and rented it out. Tom couldn't wait to show it to Scarlet, she'd be so proud. But that would have to wait. Over the last few days they had been living off the dregs of what was in the kitchen cupboards and the fridge-freezer. It was time for the grocery shop. Tom had been putting this off because usually he and Scarlett would do it together and with only one little baby. This time Tom was on his own with two troublesome toddlers. Mind you, since the office incident they had been behaving much better. With that thought in mind, Tom headed to the supermarket.

As soon as Tom had parked the car and lifted the twins out, they both rushed over to the trolleys and began to climb into them.

'I want pushed,' shouted Ralph.

'Me too,' yelled Polly.

Here they go, thought Tom.

'Listen, I can't push two trolleys, can I? You're going to have to take it in turns to help me push the trolley while the other sits in the seat.'

'I want to push first,' cried Polly.

'I want to sit here first,' said Ralph.

'Fine. Polly you help me with the trolley and remember to go slowly.'

They went through the sliding door three times just to keep Ralph happy. Tom wanted to oblige the children a little instead of getting himself all worked up, as he always seemed to be doing of late. The longer Tom was patient the easier his life would get, apparently. He laid down the law about not touching anything unless Tom handed them something to put in the trolley. They seemed to accept these terms and Polly helped wheel their way happily into the fruit and veg section. Tom filled up clear plastic bags with potatoes, carrots, onions, bananas and apples. Tom passed then to Polly, one by one, who then handed them to Ralph. As Tom was walking in front of the trolley he didn't always see what the twins were doing, but he just let them get on with it. Little did Tom know that whenever he handed Ralph a bag, he threw it back onto the shelf where it came from. Tom only noticed three aisles later after hearing Ralph exclaim 'Oops!' He had managed to split a one-kilogram bag of rice on the corner of a frozen meat packet and it spilled to the floor and bounced everywhere.

'Oh, Ralph, look what you've done.'

'Sorry. It was an accident,' he responded.

Tom had to take a deep breath and realised that it was indeed an accident.

'I know, Ralph. I'm not mad. I'll get someone to clear it up.'

The assistant Tom asked to help was cheerful enough until Ralph dropped a bag of flour on her back as she bent over to pick up the rice. It, too, split and went everywhere. Well, not everywhere. It mostly went down the assistant's neck. The girl was furious, but kept her cool as the store manager arrived on the scene. Tom told him what had happened and the manager apologised profusely for the bag of rice splitting 'due to the sharpness of the frozen meat packet'. He gave Tom a written note to hand to the cashier when he was paying so that he would get ten pounds taken off his final bill. He waffled on about always wanting to find ways of improving customer satisfaction and he would get the frozen meat packets looked at immediately so that the same thing wouldn't happen again. He half-bowed as he backed away from Tom to reprimand the assistant for her 'angry disposition'.

'Well, Ralph. Seems you've just saved me ten quid. I think you deserve a treat when we're done here.'

'Yippee! Yippee!' he wailed.

'What about me?' asked Polly.

'You'll get something too, Polly. Don't worry.'

'Hurrah, hurrah!'

As they continued down the dairy product section Ralph managed to eat his way through a six-pack of chocolate mousses while Tom pondered over the cheese range. Polly would have normally been the first to tell on him, but she too got stuck into a large tub of Greek yoghurt. Tom wouldn't have known what they had been up to as he put his Gorgonzola into the trolley except for noticing Ralph's brown fingers and Polly's yoghurt moustache.

'Your treat has just gotten smaller,' Tom scolded.

The rest of the shopping trip was rather uneventful until the very end when Ralph leaned out of the trolley and fell into a freezer full of garden peas, ripping about ten bags.

'Guess what?' Tom asked after setting Ralph back in his seat.

'No treat,' said Ralph sadly.

'Correct.'

Luckily for them, Tom was feeling generous and on the drive home they kept quiet by sucking on a lollipop.

Scarlett sat behind her desk with one foot rested upon an upturned bin. Sylvia insisted she have a cushion underneath her foot, but Scarlett gently reminded her that she couldn't even feel her foot, so it wouldn't make a blind bit of difference.

'It's really nice to have you back in the office, Scarlett. I have missed you.'

'That's sweet of you, Sylvia. It's nice to be back. I didn't realise how much I missed this place until I sat down in this chair. It's strange not having Alex around though. I want to phone Maud to check up on him every ten minutes.'

'I'm sure he's fine,' reassured Sylvia. 'It's Tom I worry about.'

'Yes, I do too, if I'm honest. But, he was very adamant that he could cope, so I'm not going to interfere. If he can trust me with making sure he gets this promotion then I should be able to trust him with the safety of the children.'

The driver of the car in front got out and assessed the damage. It all happened so suddenly. One second Tom was driving home, singing along to Aerosmith, the next his car was entwined at the bumpers with the car in front. It only took a small lapse in concentration, but enough time to incur the wrath of the Chief Inspector who Tom had inadvertently rear-ended. He was still in his car gripping the steering wheel, which in effect caused him great pain in his right hand when the uniformed policeman wrapped on his door window. Tom got out of the car and followed him to the front of it as he beckoned him with a curled finger.

'Are you blind, sir?' he asked calmly.

'No,' Tom replied in fear.

'Are you under the influence of alcohol at all, sir?'

'No.'

'Have you taken any illegal or recreational drugs recently, sir?'

'No, definitely no,' Tom answered.

'Then, sir, perhaps you can give me a satisfactory explanation for your idiotic driving.'

Tom rather thought the C.I. was over-egging it a bit, but there was no way he was going to argue. He didn't want to end up in a cell for mouthing off at a policeman. The officer towered over Tom in his steel reinforced boots and the veins in his cheeks seemed to throb as Tom tried very hard to think of a sensible excuse.

'It was the children, Chief Inspector.'

What a coward!

'What?'

'The children...in the car...distracted me...sir.'

In fact, the only distraction they caused was when they both yelled 'look out' in stereo while Tom was head banging along to the music just as he crashed into the back of the large black car. The Chief Inspector stormed back to Tom's car and looked in the rear seats. Polly and Ralph sat straight-faced and stared back at him. He came back to Tom.

'Those children are barely five or six...'

'Four actually,' Tom interrupted.

'...and you have the gall to blame them for your actions? What kind of a father are you?' There was that question again. Was it rhetorical or was Tom supposed to give him an answer? Tom didn't give Mrs Hubert an answer when she asked it, but then again she wasn't about to have him arrested for reckless driving and endangering the lives of others, so Tom obliged him.

'A very poor one, Chief Inspector.'

'Indeed. You're darn lucky I'm in a rush to get to the Town Hall for a charity lunch, otherwise I'd have you arrested for reckless driving and endangering the lives of others.'

'I thought you might.'

'What?'

'Nothing sir.'

He took out a pen and a pad of paper and asked Tom for his insurance details, home phone number, etc. before climbing into the back of his chauffeur-driven car and pulling away at speed. Polly and Ralph just gawked as Tom got back into the car.

'Are you two okay?' They looked at each other and then nodded. 'Thank goodness. Sorry about all that.'

Tom drove the rest of the way home very slowly and in silence.

Edward opened the office door and then knocked before Scarlett could say anything. He was dressed in a tuxedo, and he had his thick, auburn hair slicked back over his head with a handful of Brylcreem.

'Well, well, well. So, Tom couldn't stick the pace he had to send in the little lady. How are you Scarlett?'

'Fine, thanks for asking, Edward. Why are you looking so repulsive?'

Scarlett and Edward had this sort of hate-hate relationship. The first time they met at a company function, Edward thought Scarlett was one of the typists and tried his luck with her by clutching her buttocks from behind and saying, 'My! What a fresh pair of buns. How about coming back to my place so I can butter them up?' The force with which Scarlett landed a punch into Edward's crotch left every man in the room with tears in their eyes. Edward left the room over the shoulder of one of the security guards and spent the rest of the night sitting on a bag of frozen broccoli. Despite this unfortunate event, Edward still hadn't learnt his lesson.

'Well, if you get out of those frumpy rags you're wearing and scrub up a little; perhaps I'll take you with me and show you.'

'Edward, even if you were the only man on earth and I was the only woman, locked in this room with you, wearing nothing more than tassels on our privates, you still wouldn't get anywhere near me.'

'Ooh, what a picture. Can I hold that thought?'

'It's the only thing you'll be holding, so why not!'

He walked to the front of the desk and leaned across it, close enough to give Scarlett a choking breath of his over-powering cologne.

'If you must know I've arranged for the Board members to have an evening of fine wine, fine cigars and most importantly, fine women at the Elgar Hotel in town, all at my expense, of course.'

'You're disgusting, Edward, and so are your ethics.'

He leaned in closer.

'What you say you and I get these sweaty clothes off and get disgusting together?'

Scarlett smiled.

'The only thing that'll have sweat on it in a few seconds is your brow, when I do this.'

'Do what?' asked Edward.

Scarlett pushed her plastered leg off its cushion and it came crashing down on top of Edward's left foot.

'Oh! Sorry, Edward.' Scarlett pushed her chair back far enough to show him her leg in plaster. 'Take a good look if you want,' she laughed. 'This is the closest you'll ever get to them, you creep. You know, one day Edward, women will rise up in unity all across the world against your kind of sexist, bullish behaviour. But until they do, I'll continue to stand up for myself.'

Sylvia came running in. 'What's going on?'

'Edward's plastered again, Sylvia.'

'You little...' groaned Edward.

'Ah-ah. Don't swear at me. There's more where that came from.'

He turned and hopped out of the door shouting expletives in every direction.

'Scarlett, you are terrible,' said Sylvia. 'He could sue you for assault.'

'He could, but he won't. I have more on him than he has on me. Now, what about those staff turnover figures?'

'Coming right up.'

✳

Tom had just sat down in the sitting room about to drink a cup of coffee when the doorbell rang. Polly and Ralph didn't even flinch. They were watching some programme about a one legged duck. Tom opened the door to find George standing on the step with arms outstretched holding two bags of cut meat.

'My best venison for you and Scarlett, and a kilo of pork and sage sausages for the kids.' He gave Tom a sideways glance. 'I'm sorry about before, Tom. You know I wasn't angry with you, don't you?'

'Well, I guess you weren't. Okay, apology accepted, you big oaf. Come in for a coffee and let's have a chat. It's been a few days since I've had a decent conversation.'

'Ah, thanks, Tom. You're a real gent. In fact there was something I was hoping I could talk to you about.'

As they walked by the sitting room, George peeked in and smiled. 'Aw, children. Aren't they sweet?'

'Sometimes, they are,' Tom said.

Tom put the kettle on again and put some biscuits on a plate.

'So how's the hand? I heard you and Scarlett had a bit of an accident.'

'I'm afraid so. The hand's okay, but Scarlett has her leg in plaster.'

'Oh dear! So where is she then?' he said looking around.

'Ah, well. Due to the nature of our injuries, we thought it best if I stay at home with the children while Scarlett takes her job back at the office for a while. It's only for a few weeks. Temporary thing. It would drive me bonkers if I had to look after the children full-time. I certainly don't envy single parents, I can tell you.'

Tom had a momentary picture of Geri come into his head and for a second he'd forgotten what he was saying.

'Have I offered you coffee, George?'

'Yes, but I'm still waiting.'

'Sorry, I went blank for a moment there.'

'Thinking of your fancy woman, were you?' said George.

'What? Don't be so stupid. I'm a happily married man.'

Tom didn't realise how strong his reaction was.

'Okay, okay,' laughed George. 'I was only kidding. I thought I'd hit a nerve there for a second.'

What was Tom thinking? Why did he react like that? He hasn't done anything wrong. He didn't even feel guilty, and why should he?

'Sorry George. It's been quite a day, again.' Tom emphasised 'again' hoping George would ask what he meant, so he could unload a little. He did ask and Tom did unload for the next few minutes. And he needed it.

'...and what I can't figure out is why Scarlett didn't ask me beforehand.'

'Maybe because she knew you would only agree to it if she had already said yes to Jackie. Be honest, Tom. If Scarlett had come home and asked you, nice and polite like, if you could have a few kids to live for a few months, what would you have said?'

'No, of course.'

'And would she have argued about it?'

'No.'

'Why not?' pressed George.

'Because…because…'

'Because she knows that once she has made a decision, she has you tied around her little figure and you don't like to upset her, so you go with the flow. Am I right or am I right?'

He was right. If Tom had one weak spot, giving in to Scarlett was it. Tom hated upsetting her, especially when she had her mind made up on something. She knew Tom was a pushover. Seems like George knew it too!

'I mean, Tom, whose idea was it to buy the Lowrie?'

'It was mine,' Tom replied adamantly.

'Yeah, only because Scarlett put down a deposit on it behind your back knowing that if she didn't, she wouldn't have had something to bargain with. She may as well have bought it straight out.' He took a sip of coffee. 'Let's face it, Tom; you're a big girl's blouse when it comes to Scarlett.'

'Am not!' Tom frowned. 'Well, maybe just a little bit.'

'Come of it, Tom. I reckon Scarlett has hers and your future already planned and she knows how to get around you should she come across a hurdle.'

'George, I am my own man. I make the important decisions in this house not Scarlett.' George gave him a wry smile. Perhaps Tom should have been more firm with that sentence then he would have probably believed it himself. 'Okay, it's true. I'm a wimp. I can't stand up to my wife. It's only because I love her and I don't like to see her upset or hurt. If she's set her heart on something, why should I be the one to break it?

'I'll ask you again. Who spent four thousand quid on a picture?'

Tom raised his eyebrows in defeat. 'Scarlett.'

'Who decided on having the children to stay, really?'

'Scarlett.'

'And who decided that you stay at home and be the homemaker while she went to work and make dozens more decisions every week on your behalf?'

Tom gulped. He'd never thought of it like that. For years Tom had been making decisions on his own and the more he thought about it the more he realised that for as long as he'd known Scarlett, all the important decisions had been made by her. She only ever ran them by him for approval, but it was nearly always too late to do anything about things anyway, had Tom disagreed. Here Tom was, at the most crucial point of his career, and it was his wife who was deciding his future.

'What a mug!' Tom declared.

The chair Tom was sitting on squeaked on the lino as he pushed it back and stood up. Lukewarm coffee bounced from his cup as Tom slammed it down on the table. 'She doesn't trust me, George. That's it, isn't it? She doesn't trust me.' Tom was more disturbed than angry.

'Aw, come on now, Tom, don't beat yourself up. You're taking it to the extreme. Look at it another way. She just wants to be sure that the decisions you're going to make are the right ones.'

'Rubbish, George! She thinks I'll mess this whole promotion thing up. That's why she's at the office right now and I'm here molly coddling the children.'

Tom began to perspire. This was getting to him. He began to look at his marriage in a new light.

'I should have known. Why haven't I seen it before? I've been blinkered all this time. Everything seemed too perfect.'

'Tom, Tom, you're reading into it too much.' George began to smile as if to dull the sharpness of the dagger that he had thrust into Tom's heart. 'You're being a little melodramatic, if you don't mind me saying?'

Perhaps Tom was.

'And what about our Honeymoon?' Tom remembered.

'What about it?'

'Scarlett knew I wanted to go to Italy, but before I had a chance to book anything, she went and put a deposit on a safari to Kenya. You see, she was already doing it even before we got married.'

'Tom, what was one your dreams when you were a teenager? '

Tom knew where George was headed. He looked away from him as if he had to think hard about the answer, but he didn't.

'To have a balloon flight at sunrise over the African bush.'

'And did that dream come true on your Honeymoon?'

The swine.

'Yes.'

'Well then.'

'Ah-ha! What about this house? It was me who made the decision to buy this house not Scarlett?'

George looked at Tom as if he had completely lost his marbles, never mind his memory.

'Before you got married, you were very happy living in your town-centre-one-bedroom-studio apartment, and I vividly remember you telling me on your stag night that you resented the fact you had to buy a nice three bedroom semi, with front and rear gardens and detached garage 'just to please the missus.'

The git. Why couldn't he let Tom be right for once? All sorts of thoughts began to run through Tom's head. He felt like a little boy whose mummy would walk him to school in case he lost his way, although he'd been walking there practically every day for years. It was a safety issue. The mother knew he was too young to walk on his own, and the boy, although a little resentful, needed the comfort and guidance of someone he could trust. Tom trusted Scarlett completely with any decision she ever made but it was as if *she* didn't fully trust *him*, so she had to make sure it was she who made the decisions in the first place. Was Tom confusing the issue?

George got up to boil the kettle for another cup of coffee.

'Tom, sit down and let's think this all through methodically.' He got some scones out of the cupboard and cream from the fridge before joining Tom back at the table.

'It's a woman's natural instinct to want stay at home and care for her children, but sometimes they need more. Like any man, they need the company of adults; they need mental stimulation, something more than changing nappies and wiping up puke. We men think they have it easy and we are always relieved to know that it's not us that have to give birth, but being a father means more than bringing home the pay cheque, paying the bills and washing the car. Women need to know that their partners are sharing the parenting equally. I mean look at me; I've got eight great kids but it was only after the third one was born that I realised I was needed more at home than just the odd hour in the evening.' George took a deep breath. 'Tom, Scarlett doesn't want you to be a great parent or father of the year. I think she just needs reassurance that you want to be a dad.'

That made him Tom uneasy, but he knew what he meant.

'You got so caught up with your career that you hard hardly ever saw your family and that's what you've got now, Tom, a family. She's scared, Tom. But she does trust you, implicitly.'

'How do you work that one out?'

'Tom. She's left it to you to look after these children. You're with the twins all day, every day, and you see Alex ten times more now than you would do if you were at work.'

'True.'

'Well, can't you see? If she didn't trust you, the last thing she would ever consider trusting you with is children, right?'

He was right. Tom couldn't believe he could be so blind. The greatest thing Tom could be trusted with was his own child and the children of others.

'You're right. Of course you are. What was I thinking? Thanks for making me see sense, George'

Tom sat back in his chair and smiled. His wife does trust him. How could he ever have doubted her? In fact, what did make him start doubting her?

'Hang on!' Tom glared at George. 'It was you who brought all this up in the first place.'

George reached across the table and grabbed another scone. 'Umm, these are delicious. Wheat and damson, my favourite.'

'George!'

He shoved the scone in his mouth and got up from the table.

'Sorry Tom! Time to go and shut up the shop. I left Patrick in charge and he can never remember the code for the alarm. I'll see myself out.'

He put on his coat and opened the kitchen door.

'Wait! Wasn't there something you wanted to talk about?'

He stopped for a moment and then carried on down the hallway. 'Oh, don't worry,' he mumbled. 'Some other time when it's more convenient.'

'Just pop in anytime,' Tom shouted as he opened the front door.

'Enjoy the steaks!'

'We will. And thanks, I think!'

Maud dropped Alex and Jasper home around five thirty pm just after Scarlett called to say she wouldn't be home for dinner. She said she wanted to spend some time going over the costs involved if the Customer Service department took on a few extra staff for the next few months. Tom was just in the process of boiling some pasta when Alex crawled into the kitchen. At first, Tom was overjoyed to see him and then he remembered that he was supposed to be in the playpen. Tom heard Jasper crying and went to find Polly and Ralph playing babies in the playpen.

'I'm the baby!' shouted Polly.

'I am,' retorted Ralph.

'No, I am!'

'Okay, enough, both of you. Jasper and Alex are the babies and you shouldn't have taken them out of the playpen. They could have hurt themselves and I wasn't in the room. It was naughty.' Tom was about to suggest they watch some telly but realised that that was all he seemed to offer them when they were in the house. His lack of imagination really began to bother him. No matter how hard Tom tried, he couldn't think of anything for them to do. It's so easy to just say 'play' and then watch what happens and not get involved. Deep down Tom knew he did want to get involved. So why couldn't he think of something to do?

Polly must have been reading his mind. 'You play with us then,' she frowned.

'But I'm always playing with you. Yesterday I took you to the park.'

'Yeah, but you just sat on the bench and talked to that lady.'

Valid point.

'True. Well this morning we had fun at the library, didn't we?'

'No!' piped Ralph. 'We're not allowed to play in the library and you had an angry face when we left it.'

Tom wasn't doing very well here. Alex was only six months old and he didn't really need playing with, so Tom was lacking experience. It wasn't his fault. No one advises you to go on a '*Learn How to Play With Toddlers*' course when they find out you're going to be a parent, do they? When Tom was a child, his parents never said 'Now, remember how we're playing with you because you'll need to do this when you're our age'.

Alex continued to dribble on Tom's shirt, as he stood motionless, pushing his brain to the limit, determined to think of a game the kids could play. Tom tried desperately hard to revive memories of his childhood, but he couldn't muster a single picture in his mind. Why was that? People often tell you how they remember the first time they tied their laces or their very first day at school and can give you exact details. Others can recite where they went and what they did for every summer holiday from the age of three. Why couldn't Tom do that? Was his childhood really that uneventful? Tom began to feel sorry for myself. Perhaps it was because it was *so* eventful that there was so much going on that his brain couldn't keep track of it all. Yes, that was it, at least, that's the way Tom wanted to look at it. It still didn't help him in the current situation. By the time Tom had stopped trying to find the path to memory lane the twins had put on yet another video, Alex had fallen asleep on his shoulder, and Jasper sat in the doorway chewing the head of a plastic doll, drooling everywhere.

'The pasta!' Tom shrieked.

As Tom pushed open the kitchen door, he could hear the boiling water sizzle on the electric hob as it bubbled its way out of the overflowing pan. When Tom turned off the hot ring, the water ceased to boil and settled, revealing a pot of limp and congealed penne. He huffed and puffed before taking Alex up to bed. As Tom laid his blankets over him, he silently promised him that he would do his utmost to give him a memorable childhood.

'By the time you reach ten you'll have been to Africa, America, and Asia. You'll go to loads of pantomimes and have fond memories of every Christmas. Not one of your birthday parties will be the same as another and you'll be the Captain of your school rugby team, if you decide to play rugby that is. If you choose football, well, I'll support you, I suppose.'

Tom kissed him on his forehead and whispered a little prayer over him. He looked so peaceful.

'I love you,' Tom said.

Scarlett arrived home just after eight o'clock. Tom had called her earlier and asked her to pick up a couple of pizzas because he didn't have the patience to stand in the kitchen and cook yet another meal. After only a couple of days of househusbanding Tom knew it wasn't for him, full-time anyway. His admiration for the women who spend all day, every day at home with the children, cooking, cleaning, washing, ironing, driving, teaching, playing, buying, increased by the power of ten just over two days. They all deserve medals as far as he was concerned. How do they survive? In the past week, Tom has been punched, wee'd on, soaked, yelled at, and burnt. No housewife Tom knows grumbles about these sorts of things. It's as if they know there's no getting away from it. Life with children is hard, but as they all say, 'it's worth it in the end'. Tom flippin' well hoped so! His own mother is a prime example. If any woman deserves a medal for motherhood, it's her. Every day, for as long as Tom could remember, she cooked, scrubbed, ironed, and all of the above things, without ever complaining except when as a teenager Tom would use the house as a hotel and take everything for granted, then she complained, but rightly so! For a few years, she had a part-time job working in a supermarket, and so his Dad, bless him, had to cook, or reheat, which was often the case, dinner for one day of the week. His burnt custard had that sort of sharpness to it that set it apart from his mum's custard, but Tom ate it just the same. Wouldn't want to knock his ego now would he? Thinking of how his mum behaved gave him hope. Grin and bear it. 'Have a little faith in yourself and the good Lord above, and everything will work out fine'.

'Meat feast or three cheeses?'

Scarlett de-railed his train of thought.

'Huh? What?'

'You heard. Which one?' She held both pizzas in her hands, weighing them up and down.

'Um, hard choice,' Tom said cheekily.

She dumped the spicy hot pizza down on the table in front of him.

'Don't be so cheeky! I've had enough from Edward today. The last thing I need is pathetic, childish behaviour from my husband, thank you very much.'

And she thinks she's had a hard day. Wait until she hears about Tom's. She didn't wait. She rattled on about the office and somewhere in the middle, Tom switched off. For the first time in seven years Tom didn't really care about the office, well, that's not true, he did, it just didn't seem as important as it used to. He let her talk about her day and then she let him talk about his. It was a healthy dinnertime arrangement that they have which helps them to get things off their chests without ruining the rest of the evening.

'Wow!' she gasped. 'And I thought I had a bad day.'

See.

'Yeah, well, I was lucky not to get arrested. Then again, a night or two in a quiet cell would be bliss. No kids, no screaming, nothing. Absolute peace. Perhaps I should get down on my knees tonight and thank the Lord the officer was very forgiving.'

'Oh, praying again are you? Very Christian of you, Tom.'

'I'm just getting myself psyched-up for meeting with the Vicar tomorrow night. His assistant called to confirm it was still on.'

The meeting was to see the Vicar about Alex's christening. It was to be a very informal meeting, but if Tom knew the Vicar, that wouldn't stop him from overpowering them with his theological knowledge. He's a very quiet man. At least that's the impression you get upon meeting him. He stands no taller than five feet four inches, but looks smaller due to his stooping posture. His collar length grey hair adds a further ten years to his age of which Tom guessed to about eighty. His personal assistant, a term that should not be used for clergy staff in case of misinterpretation, invited them to join the Vicar at the vicarage tomorrow evening at five minutes past eight. On asking why couldn't they just make it eight o'clock she proceeded to tell Tom of the Vicar's need for his daily constitutional after watching the Channel 4 news.

Tom then joked and asked if they could join him for it after which the lady replied laughing, 'I don't think the Vicar would appreciate you all squashing into the downstairs cloakroom together. He might spill his drink and you don't want that to happen'. The mind boggles.

Tom had been chewing on his pizza crust for some time in silence when Scarlett asked Tom what he was thinking.

'I was just trying to remember what games I played with my parents when I was a kid. I can't think of any. Can you remember much from when you were a toddler?'

'You mean like the twins age?'

'Yes.'

Scarlett pondered for a moment and then took another mouthful of pizza. She frowned. She looked very pensive.

'It's funny, I can't remember playing with my parents, but I do remember playing games with the other children in our street. We must have been about four or five when we used to play bulldog in someone's back garden. We'd take turns in asking our mum's if we could have it at our houses. If it were raining then we'd all hide in Naomi Wilkins dad's garage. She was always very particular that we hid in her dad's garage and not someone else's.' Scarlett began to laugh as she remembered it all. 'I remember once, when it was Judy's seventh birthday, some people didn't turn up for her party, so she went to all of their houses and demanded they come to her house. When everyone was collected they all stomped back to Judy's to watch her win all the party games. They had to; she was a real winge-bag. And her mum thought it best for everyone if Judy won everything. 'Anything for an easy life' they used to hear her say.' Scarlett grinned and stared into thin air. 'It's funny the things you remember when you think back, isn't it?'

Tom glared back at her. 'No, it's not funny. That's why I asked. I can barely remember a thing. I've been racking my brain for the past three hours trying to think of something and the only memory I have is of my first day at school.'

'Well that's good, isn't it?'

'I meant grammar school, not primary,' Tom sulked.

'Why do you remember that one then?'

Tom raised his eyebrows and looked at the floor. Tom hadn't ever told anyone what he was about to say and he just knew Scarlett would burst out laughing after she heard it. It took him over six years to come to terms with it and it'll haunt him to his dying day.

'Well, come on,' she insisted.

'I don't want to tell you.'

'Don't be silly,' she teased. 'If it's funny I promise not to laugh.'

'Yes, you will.'

'No, I won't.'

'Yes, you will!'

'Oh stop it. Just tell me.'

'Well, I was getting dressed for school and I ripped my underpants and all my other pairs were in the wash basket, so...' Tom stopped.

'Go on, 'So'...'

'So, I took a pair of my mum's knickers and put them on instead. I couldn't find my dad's.'

He knew it. Scarlett folded over in a fit of the giggles.

'That's not the whole story.'

'You mean there's more?' she managed to utter.

'Well, when I arrived at the school I was accosted by some Prefects. They pushed me around saying I wasn't wearing the right uniform because I was wearing a white shirt and not a grey one. Trying to stand up for myself, I pushed the biggest one over and he fell into a thorn bush. Not surprisingly, he was pretty mad and he shouted at his mates to grab me. And...'

'And what?' asked Scarlett.

'They dragged me into the middle of the playground and de-bagged me in front of the whole school. Everyone exploded. I was called Frilly Knickers for the next two years.'

Scarlett creased herself. Tears poured out of her eyes as she tried to stop laughing, but she couldn't. Suddenly she sat up straight.

'Oops! I've wet myself,' she laughed.

Honestly.

'Go and change yourself then.'

'I will. And don't worry I won't need to borrow your undies,' she roared. 'I've got a spare pair of my own.'

She hobbled upstairs laughing the whole way.

'Wasn't funny at the time, I can assure you,' Tom grumped.

So much for sharing secrets. Tom wouldn't even share a packet of crisps with her for weeks after that.

10

It **was raining** very hard when they arrived at the vicarage the following evening. The good old British summer was back in full force. Tom wished he had organised a holiday abroad for this time of the year, then he would have had an excuse for not taking the twins and Jasper indoors to live with them. Instead, Scarlett, Alex, and he would be sunning it up in Ibiza or somewhere exotic.

Scarlett said she had an umbrella with her but to his surprise, she had actually forgotten it. Not the Scarlett he knew. Scarlett always dressed in accordance with the early morning weather forecast and if she knew it was going to rain in an evening she would always pack the car boot with two umbrellas, their wellies, and rain-macs. If ever Tom needed to know what the weather would be like, he'd just check on what Scarlett was wearing and take it from there.

Overgrown conifers arched over the pathway up to the vicarage porch and the weeds that forced their way through the cracks in the concrete were up to their knees. Any sunshine that was visible only half an hour ago had completely disappeared. By the time they reached the porch they were soaked through.

'I can't believe you forgot to bring an umbrella,' Tom snapped.

Scarlett growled back

'Yes, all right, Mr Perfect,' she said, waving one of her crutches at him. 'I've got others things on his mind at the moment you know.'

Her running mascara made her look like Alice Cooper on a good day and her drenched hair reminded Tom of the dog he used to have when he was a kid. Tom was half expecting her to shake her head involuntarily to rid herself of the rainwater it was collecting, but she didn't.

It took three rings of the doorbell before the door was finally opened. The hallway was lit only by candlelight and the dim porch light made it difficult to see whom or what had opened the door. Tom helped Scarlett up the step and into the house before anyone spoke. Tom turned to close the door and was surprised to see the little old lady from the library. The look she gave him confirmed that she had no idea who Tom was – thank goodness!

'I'll take your coats and whatever else is wet, please,' she squeaked.

'Ooh er, missus!' Tom said in his best Frankie Howard voice. 'D'you mind if I keep my trousers on?'

Scarlett thumped him in the back – hard.

'Thank you,' she said, taking off her coat and plaster wrapping. 'Don't mind my husband. He's a bit of a joker, amongst other things.'

Tom resented that comment. The old lady came closer to him and gazed up at him though the musty darkness.

'Oh! It's you again.'

She remembered him. 'Enjoying the book?'

'Ah, well, I haven't started it yet. Thanks for asking.'

'Hmm,' she mumbled.

She took their things into a side room and they heard them thump to the ground.

'Perhaps if she turned a light on she would have found the coat stand,' Tom remarked.

'It is very dark in here, isn't it?'

'Daddy likes it that way.' It was the little old lady. She had joined them again and ushered them through to another room. It was lit, but only just. A dusty table lamp with a red bulb glowed on an old writing desk in a corner of the room. The lady beckoned them to sit down on the brown velour sofa.

'You said 'Daddy' just then. Did you mean the Vicar?' Tom asked.

'Yes. I'm Esmerelda, his daughter.'

'His daughter?' Tom asked. This little old lady didn't look a day under seventy. If Tom was right, then how old was the Vicar? From looking around the room, Tom noticed that everything seemed to be in a Victorian style. The curtains, carpet, chairs. The Vicar lived in a different time era.

'And do you still live here with Daddy, er, I mean the Vicar?'

'Of course, I do. When Mummy passed away in nineteen forty-two he asked if I would stay with him and care for him.'

Scarlett looked at Tom. 'So, you didn't marry at all?' she asked.

'Me? Oh dear, no. But...' She stopped and stared at Tom again in the same way she did in the library yesterday. Tom began to feel uncomfortable. He started to have a terrible thought. Perhaps she got them here under false pretences. Perhaps the Vicar was going to trade his daughter in for a younger helper, take Scarlett away from Tom, and lock her in the attic. Esmerelda obviously had the hots for Tom and Tom had a nasty vision of her dragging him by the follicles up to her bedroom where she would let go of all her years of abstinence, uncork the decades of lustful desires, and have her wicked way with him.

'Tom! Tom!'

It was Scarlett.

'Sorry! I was just daydreaming.' More like a nightmare.

'Esmerelda was asking if you wanted some tea.'

'Oh. Yes, two sugars, please.'

The little old lady left the room and apologised for the lateness of the Vicar.

'I'll just go and lock his cabinet,' she muttered as she closed the door.

Scarlett shivered. Although it was terribly muggy outside, it felt as though no form of heat had ever filled the room.

'I feel I'm in the home of Dr Jekyll,' whispered Scarlett.

'Well the Vicar's surname is Hyde,' Tom said quietly. 'Maybe he's related.'

They sat for a minute or two, just rubbing their hands together for heat, but then curiosity got the better of them. They started to filter through the bookshelves that encased all four walls. The books were all dusty except for theological texts. There were over twenty different books referring to Revelations and the end times. The Vicar was obviously a hell-fire and brimstone kind of preacher. One book was about Exorcism. Tom even found a DVD copy of the movie 'The

Exorcist' with '*for reference only*' written on the side of it.

'Tom, look at this.' Scarlett had found an old chest under a dustsheet. 'I wonder what's in it.'

'I don't think we should look,' Tom said. 'But who's going to know?'

She lifted the latch and then the top of the chest. Tom took out his pocket torch and switched it on.

'Oh, my!' Scarlett exclaimed.

'For the love of...' Tom breathed.

The box was full of leather bondage clothing, whips, and chains. There were handcuffs, face muzzles and other paraphernalia they didn't recognise.

'I think it's time we left,' Tom said. 'We're not hanging around to meet this sick, crazed...'

The door creaked open as Scarlett and Tom frantically tried to cover up the chest. They jumped back onto the sofa just as the main light was switched on. They both screamed and jumped back up again.

'Good evening, Mr and Mrs Farrow,' said a young male voice.

They both shut their mouths and let go of each other as the tall, bearded man walked towards them with a tray of tea and cakes.

'I'm so sorry to have kept you waiting.' He put down the tray on a coffee table in front of them and stretched out his hand with a warm, reassuring smile on his face. Tom shook his hand.

'I'm John Croft, the new Vicar.'

Scarlett shook his hand as she asked, 'You're the Vicar?'

'Yes, I am. I apologise if you were expecting Reverend Hyde. He finally decided to retire and I've recently taken over from him. I only moved in a couple of days ago. I'm afraid Esmerelda still thinks he's running things, so I'm sorry if you got the wrong end of the stick.'

He poured the tea into the cups and offered them to Tom and Scarlett.

'But, isn't Reverend Hyde still living here?' Tom asked quizzically.

'Yes. He and Esmerelda have lived here for sixty years and it would be too much for both of them if they had to move out straight away. I've let them stay here until they feel they're ready to leave.'

'Well, after what we've just seen it's about time there was a new Vicar.'

Tom could see John was confused. He got up, went over to the chest, and opened it.

'Not, what you would expect from a long-serving Vicar with the Church of England, would you say?'

The Vicar laughed. Tom personally couldn't see the funny side of a century year old preacher horsing around the vicarage, strapped in leather.

'What's so funny?' Tom asked.

'That doesn't belong to Reverend Hyde.'

'It doesn't?'

'No! It's mine!' He laughed louder.

Scarlett stood up, as fast as her crutches would allow. 'Vicar! How could you?'

'No, no, no. You're reading into it all wrong.' He asked them both to sit down again. 'When I say they're mine, I mean they're in my possession because I took them away from someone.'

'I'd rather not hear about your sexual exploits, Vicar, thank you very much,' snapped Scarlett.

'Oh, dear. Look. There's someone in our congregation who has an 'S and M' obsession. They want to overcome it and they asked if I would get rid of that lot for them. I only took them away this morning and haven't had a time to dispose of them yet. Now do you understand?'

They nodded and felt very stupid.

'Sorry, Vicar,' Tom replied, suddenly remembering about the darkness and the red bulb. He nodded toward the lamp.

'The Reverend Hyde has an eye condition and bright light aggravates it, so they try to keep the lights down for him. He finds the red light easier to cope with, and before you ask, the heating for the house is waiting to be mended. The boiler blew last month and they've been without heat ever since.'

That explained everything. Perhaps they were a tad over-judgmental. The rest of their time at the vicarage was great. The Vicar, or John, as he preferred to be called, was a lovely bloke and very encouraging about Scarlett and Tom swapping roles. They left at ten pm after retrieving their damp clothes from the study floor knowing that the Christening service was now left in capable hands. They would see John again then. The rain had stopped and there was a slight chill in the air as they drove home. They didn't really say much to each other. They were both feeling very foolish and guilty at how they had behaved during the evening. They had both jumped to the wrong conclusion and labelled two very nice people as sick and weird without finding out for themselves. 'Shouldn't judge a book by its cover, Mr Farrow,' Esmerelda had said as they left the vicarage.

'That's why she described the books to me when I met her at the library,' said Tom.

'Yeah, I guess so.' Scarlett folded her arms and huffed. 'I'm so ashamed of myself.'

'So am I,' Tom said.

Maud had heard the car pull into the driveway and prepared some hot chocolate for them as they came in.

'How was it?' she asked.

'Let's just say it was eventful.'

'Did you meet the new Vicar?'

'Yes,' Tom replied. 'He's a very *forgiving* young man.'

'Yes, he is. And non-judgmental too,' said Scarlett.

They said goodnight to Maud and then took their drinks up to bed.

'So what have you got planned for the weekend to keep the kids happy?' asked Scarlett.

'Nothing yet. I'll just see what happens, I think. Maybe we'll go swimming, and to the indoor playground. Geri said it's great fun for adults too.'

'Why don't you invite Jerry and Alex over for tea one evening? I'm sure Jerry would like some friendly adult company over a meal for a change. They probably get really fed up sitting in front of the telly every dinnertime. Must be difficult looking after a child on your own.'

For some reason Tom didn't know what to say. Tom was about to squash her idea and then realised Scarlett may get suspicious.

'Sure. If I see them again, I'll mention it.'

'Good.' She turned off her bedside lamp. 'Goodnight, darling.'

'Goodnight.'

Many thoughts ran through Tom's head as he lay in the dark, his eyes wide open. Why was he being cagey about Geri? Was he having feelings for her? He couldn't be. He'd only met her once. Perhaps it was just the 'Alex' connection that kept bringing her to his mind or just the thought of her being on her own with a little baby. Tom didn't like how he was feeling. He was mad about Scarlett and very much in love with her. He'd never do anything to jeopardise their marriage. Before nodding off Tom told himself that he'd speak to someone about it, probably George, or even John. Yes, probably John.

Maynard Tait

11

The weekend went by without much ado. The twins seemed to be settling into the Farrow way of life pretty well, considering. They spent most of their time at home that weekend so that Tom's hand and forehead could fully recover from the traumas they had experienced the previous week. All the bruising on his head had finally disappeared and Tom had an appointment with his hand specialist the following Tuesday. He'd told the twins they'd go swimming the following week and they were happy enough. They didn't make it to church after all either. It seemed like too much hard work. Two temporarily crippled adults with two toddlers and two babies – no thank you! They stayed at home and played Buckaroo with the twins while Alex and Jasper rolled around on the sitting room floor. At one point Tom was watching Jasper and feeling very sorry for Jackie, his mum. With all the crawling and pulling up he was doing it was certain that he would be walking in no time at all and she wouldn't be around to see it. Tom did mention to Scarlett that he could take Jasper to see his mum but she said that Jackie asked them not to. She wanted to get better as fast as possible and she believed that if the children were around her then her recovery would be prolonged. Poor kids! Then Tom got to thinking about their dad, Nick. Okay, so Tom didn't react as he would have liked when Alex was born but at least Tom didn't abandon him or Scarlett. Nick put his career before his family. How selfish could he be? Tom guessed there were more reasons for his behaviour than Tom could imagine. He was already in the Navy when Jackie became pregnant so it wasn't as if she didn't know he wouldn't be around much. Still, his wife needed him and he chose to carry on playing soldiers. What a prat!

On Sunday evening, Scarlett and Tom chose some hymns to sing at Alex's Christening. The service wouldn't be until September, but because they had so much going on, they thought it best to get things sorted as they came up. Scarlett wanted, okay, Tom wanted to have a little celebratory lunch at their house after the service, and Scarlett thought it necessary to call in caterers.

'Tom, we won't have time over the next few weeks to sort out stuff like that. They can do it all for us.'

'Yes, at ten times the cost,' Tom replied.

But, Tom gave in. She was right. After only one week with the twins, Tom knew that it wasn't going to be a lazy summer. They wrote lists of all the things they could do with the children over the summer. There was one for Tom when he was on his own with Polly and Ralph. Another for all of them at the weekends, taking into consideration Scarlett's delicate state, and one for when Scarlett was back on two feet. They had agreed that the weekend before the Christening they would all go to the south coast. A friend of theirs owned a cottage in the New Forest and had allowed Tom and Scarlett to use it whenever they wanted. They hadn't before because they felt it too big for only the two of them, but there were six of them now and the five bedroom retreat sounded very appealing.

On Monday morning, Scarlett found out all about Edward's Thursday night soiree from Sylvia, who had heard it all from Charlene, the typist who Sir Edward had an eye on.

'Well, apparently, none of the Board took their wives with them. It was an evening of ever-flowing malt whisky, fat cigars, and plenty of the other.' Sylvia tapped the side of her nose as if it was easier to do that than just say the words.

'What?' asked Scarlett. 'Sex? You mean all those married men were having...'

'No, no, no!' interrupted Sylvia. 'Gambling. Although, there were quite a lot of young ladies there to cater for the old rascals, pouring drinks, lighting their cigars, that sort of thing.'

'Sounds as though Edward had a very successful evening then, doesn't it? I just hope that little madam, Charlene, knows what she's up to.'

Sylvia smiled at Scarlett as she turned to return to her desk. 'Oh, I rather think she does.'

Scarlett was puzzled but didn't enquire what she meant.

Tom's appointment at the hospital was for midday and as he thought he'd be in and out, he had left the twins with Maud for an hour or so. Tom planned to have lunch at Maud's on his return but it wasn't to be. The waiting room clock just ticked past one pm and Tom was about to get up and complain about waiting for so long when Geri walked by. She was on her own, dressed in a figure hugging, black business suit.

'Hello, Tom,' she smiled.

'Geri! Hi! What are you doing here looking all beautiful and official-like?'

He didn't mean to say 'beautiful'. He was thinking it but didn't mean to say it.

'Thanks for the compliment, handsome. I'm here for an interview.'

'Oh?' Tom enquired.

'Yes, as much as I'd rather stay at home with Alex, needs must I'm afraid.'

'Yeah, well, at least you'll be able to meet new people this way. What job are you applying for?'

'Resident Orthopaedic Consultant.'

Tom's face froze. Beautiful and mega-intelligent. For a brief second Tom had that male jealousy thing going around his brain. You know, *how can she be cleverer than me – she's a woman*. But Tom rid himself of that stupid thought very quickly.

'Wow! That's...That's...That's great!'

Tom sounded like Woody Allen trying to find something more enthusiastic to say to a rather ordinary remark.

'Well, if I'm honest I really miss it and it would be such a shame to let all the years of training go to waste. I'll hear next week whether or not I've got the position, but I think I'm in with a good chance.'

There was an awkward silence.

'So, how about lunch to celebrate?' she asked excitedly.

'But you haven't got the job yet. Jumping the gun a bit aren't you?'

'Well, if I do get it then you can help me celebrate properly, next week. But seeing as we're both here now, we might as well have lunch together.'

Oh-no, what was Tom to do? Say no, of course.

'I'm actually still waiting for my appointment, so I'm afraid I'll have to pass on lunch.'

The overhead speaker boomed into action. 'TOM FARROW TO DR CARLTON'S ROOM! TOM FARROW TO DR CARLTON'S ROOM!'

Geri smiled at Tom as she sat down. 'I'll wait for you.'

Naturally, Tom wanted to tell her not to bother. Tom wanted to tell her he would probably be a very long time and that the twins were waiting to be picked up.

'Okay!' Tom said.

Lunch was at a very chic country restaurant, which Geri said she used to come to at least once a week before Alex was born. The building was mock Tudor but the interior was extremely modern. Diarmuid Gavin would have been very proud of the concrete and grass monuments that made up the garden. All the waiters wore jackets with a whiter than white cloth draped over their left arms. The tables were even far enough apart so that you didn't have to pull your chair in to let someone past – the place must be posh. Tom felt a tad out of place. Apart from the fact that he wasn't particularly well dressed for the occasion, he knew that he wasn't ready to pay over eighty pounds for a two-person lunch.

'Lunch is on me,' said Geri.

Here we go. Step forward, Mr Chivalry.

'No, please. Let me. You shouldn't have to pay for your own celebration.'

'Well, in that case, I'm paying for dinner next week.

'Next week?' Tom asked.

Where was this going? He has only met the woman twice and already he's buying her a ridiculously expensive lunch and she's offering to treat him to a romantic, candle-lit dinner followed by a passionate embrace, which would inevitably lead to something else. Okay, the last part Tom was making up, but momentarily hopeful for. Snap out of it, man. Where are your morals?

'Geri, I don't mean to be rude, but...'

'Oh, I'm sorry. I'm being pushy. I know, let's just meet up for coffee next week to celebrate. We can go to the indoor playground and let the kids go nuts.'

Well there wouldn't be anything immoral about that, now would there?

'That's just what I was thinking,' Tom answered.

Yeah, right! Their meals came and they ate in relative silence. Geri mentioned that it was just having the company that she enjoyed. All her family lived in Cornwall and she didn't really go home to see them too often. Her last hospital post was in Edinburgh where she had loads of friends, and she was still bitter about having to move to the south of England because of her estranged husband. Pudding and coffee lasted over a half-hour as they struck up conversation again. It was three pm by the time they parted, and Tom just knew he was going to have to think of a good excuse for Maud.

'I'm so, so sorry,' Tom said as he walked into the house. 'There were emergencies coming in to casualty left, right and centre and the doctors were being called away at a moment's notice. The average waiting time was two hours by the time I was seen to. So much for paying ridiculously high insurance premiums. I'll be on to my insurance company first thing tomorrow. It was appalling. What they should really do is...'

'Tom! You're waffling,' said Maud.

'Am I? Sorry, I didn't notice. I'm sorry I'm late.'

'You just said 'sorry'. What's wrong with you? Did the doctor give you something he shouldn't have?'

Tom was feeling guilty – that's what was wrong with him. He should never have gone to lunch with Geri. Beautiful women have a lot to answer for. Forget testosterone! A quote from William Scott Downey came to Tom's mind.

'Judge nothing by the appearance. The more beautiful the serpent, the more fatal its sting.'

'Pardon?' asked Maud.

'Oh, nothing. I'm just a bit hyper. Too much coffee while I was waiting for the doctor.'

Nice bluff!

'How's the hand?'

'Terrific! It's only slightly sore to the touch and it looks worse than it actually is.'

The skin on his fingers gave the impression Tom had them sitting in a bowl of water for twenty-four hours. They were all shrivelled up and felt clammy. Maud made a pot of tea and served it with freshly baked fruit scones. Clotted cream was part and parcel of afternoon tea with Maud and she always served it in a bone china bowl. It always made Tom think twice before shoving a big spoon into it to get a large amount of cream to spread over your scone for fear of breaking it. Polly and Ralph came rushing in from the garden where they had been playing hide and seek.

'I helped make these,' said Polly as she plopped down beside Tom on the sofa.

'They're delicious,' Tom said with his mouth full. 'I could sit and eat these all afternoon.'

Ralph sat on the floor in front of the telly. It wasn't switched on, but he sat and gazed into it none the less. Alex pulled himself up onto his feet and gurgled a very sweet smile before losing his grip on the playpen railing and falling back onto his bottom. Jasper laughed at him and then tried it himself. It wasn't a problem for him as he was a little bit older, but Alex was able to laugh too when Jasper tried to climb out of the pen. He managed to get one foot onto the top bar of the pen and just as he got his other foot of the floor, his top foot gave way and he bounced back down again. They were all in stitches, including Jasper. Tom just wished Scarlett was around to see all this.

The next morning, just after Scarlett had left for work, the doorbell rang. It was Sam, the postman.

'Morning, Tom. Long-time no see down the pub, me ol' mate,' he said.

'No. Haven't had time, mate. Fancy a coffee?'

'Love one, mate.'

Sam and Tom have been mates since they were five. They used to live next door to each other, went to primary school together, and even had their first swig of cider together at the tender age of thirteen.

Sam was one of the lads. He liked the ladies, but wouldn't let them get in the way of his social life. He was goalie for the local football team, captain of the pub's darts team and had a part-time evening job down at the snooker hall, but he always made time for a mate. He followed Tom into the kitchen and dropped his empty post sack on the floor. He kicked his boots off and shoved them under the table. Tom passed him some cereal and milk. It had become a habit for Sam to call in once a fortnight or so for breakfast before collecting his second delivery. Tom enjoyed it because it kept them in contact with each other and Sam was a good laugh.

'What have you been up to over the past couple of weeks then, mate? Little nipper keeping you busy is he or is the Scarlett woman pressing the thumb down on you?'

To say Sam was a bit of a chauvinistic, macho-pillock would be to underestimate him. He was very chauvinistic and the biggest wimp known to man. He had a skinny frame that would boost the ego of the thinnest coat and hat stand. His unbrushed auburn hair was slicked back into a greasy ponytail and had been for the last six years. The length of his hair had never receded but his fringe certainly had. Sam's strong point was his mouth. He could talk his way out of anything.

'Yes, Alex is keeping me busy and, no, Scarlett isn't putting the thumb on me. As a matter of fact there's more than just Alex now.'

Sam's mouth dropped, as did his buttered knife.

'Oh, sh..!' The knife landed in his lap.

'Quiet, mate,' Tom interrupted. 'They might hear you.'

'They?' he repeated. 'Tom, mate. I know we haven't seen each other in a while but even I know it takes a lot longer than a couple of weeks to make babies. What are you on about?'

'Well, in short, we've temporarily taken in two twins and a baby.'

Tom bit into a slice of toast and let the information sink in. Sam looked disturbed. Tom could tell he was trying to figure out in his own mind what Tom was talking about. Sam liked to figure things out for himself; it gave him a sense of wisdom.

'No, mate, you're going to have to tell me. I can't work this one out.'

Tom proceeded to tell him about Jackie, Nick, and the children.

'Are you out of your mind?' he shrieked. 'You mean there's four kids in there?' he was pointing over his shoulder towards the airing cupboard, but Tom knew where he meant.

'Yup!'

'She's really got to you, hasn't she?' he put down his toast and leaned over the table towards Tom. 'First she makes you get married and then she traps you with a kid and now she's gone and made you into a bloomin' housewife and nanny.'

Tom could see he was taking this rather well.

'What is it with today's women, mate? It's not good enough that they're taking over from us in business, but now they're trying to force their husbands to do the housework. They're always on about bloomin' equal rights, yet try and get one of them to pay for a meal out and they start on at you about not being a gentleman. Walk in front of a woman through a door and they spout on about a lack of chivalry. What a load of mutt's nuts that is. They just want their bloomin' cake and eat it.'

'I did have some say in it as well, you know.'

'Yeah, right. And if you knew women like I know women then you would have known that you were being taken for a ride. Tell me; what we're you doing exactly two weeks ago?'

'I was at the office taking a meeting.'

'Precisely. Two weeks later, you've given up your job that you've worked your butt off for and now you're wiping babies' bums and eating rusks for breakfast. You can't tell me she didn't have it all planned.'

'I'll get my job back in a few weeks when Scarlett's out of the plaster. You're out of your tiny mind sometimes, mate, you really are.'

'Yeah well, don't say I didn't warn you. Let things go on as they are and it'll be Scarlett getting that promotion, not you, you big mug. Ever since you got married it's been her that's made all the decisions and I reckon she's had you right from the start.'

As he threw his gums around a pain au chocolat Tom began to think about what Sam had said. Perhaps Scarlett had thought this all through. She'd planned it all along. Nevertheless, she couldn't have organised Tom burning his hand – or could she? She landed in hospital because of him. If Tom hadn't thrown that rolling pin over his head, she wouldn't have slipped on it. Perhaps she had already turned the cooker on and the hob was hotter than it should have been and that's why Tom burnt himself. Tom looked back at Sam. He was about to say something else but Tom beat him to it.

'Aw, shut-up and eat your breakfast. Stirrer!'

As Sam was leaving, he opened the sitting room door so he could view for himself what Tom actually had to cope with. Alex and Jasper sat in their playpen and Polly was running after Ralph playing 'Cowgirl and Native American'.

'Well, well. Look at this mess. I wouldn't do what you're doing for all the tea in China, mate, even if you threw in a million quid.'

'That's because no-one would trust you to do it, mate.'

'You're probably right, mate.'

Sam looked as though he had a mouthful of unsalted tripe in his mouth as he looked at the children, shaking his head.

'No. There's no way I'm having kids,' he said in disgust. 'If you want my opinion they're nothing but the result of a bad...'

Ralph landed his toy tomahawk right in Sam's crotch with enough power to land a heavyweight boxer. It was with no surprise that Sam dropped to the floor.

'Me Big Chief Ralphy. You naughty white man,' said Ralph as he hopped over Sam.

Sam got up and collected his breath. 'You little piece of sh...Oww!'

Polly fired her sucker gun and the arrow hit Sam in the eye.

Tom took hold of Sam's shoulders. 'I think you better leave now, mate, for the good of your health.'

'I'll get you, you little git! And you,' he shouted pointing a finger at Ralph and Polly.

Tom opened the front door and let Sam out.

'They're crazy, Tom. And so are you, you big sucker.'

Sam climbed on his bike and pedalled away, muttering under his breath. Ralph ran to the door and stood beside Tom.

'Git, git, git,' he shouted.

'Ralph! Don't say that. Get inside and wash your mouth out.'

'Git, git, git.'

'Ralph!'

Tom glared at Sam as he rode off. Some people have no sense of responsibility.

The rest of that week went smoothly with no major traumas or incidents. Throughout the week, however, Scarlett noticed Tom was checking everything she did at work, via her laptop computer. Tom wanted to make sure that she wasn't over-stepping her mark while she sat in for him. Not that Tom didn't trust her; it was just to confirm that all decisions being made were in the best interest of the department, and him, of course. Tom did receive a gentle, but playful slap in the face at one point when for some unknown reason he told Scarlett not to get too comfortable in his leather-bound chair as it was designed for hard-thinking men and not prissy little ladies. Ralph also got Tom into trouble on Wednesday evening when Scarlett arrived home from work. The two of them were sitting in the kitchen having a cup of tea when in walked Ralph muttering, 'git, git, git'.

Scarlett was shocked. She stared at Tom and he had to think quickly.

'It's just a pregnant camel. No harm in it.'

'What?' she replied in amazement.

'A git. It's what you call a pregnant camel. He was watching some nature programme this morning and they just happened to be talking about camels in the Saharan desert.'

Scarlett looked at Tom from under her lowered eyebrows. She could tell Tom was lying. It must have been the lack of eye contact.

'Tom. The next time Sam calls round,' she said as she stood to leave the room. 'Tell him to mind his language or there'll be trouble. Understand?'

'Yes, dear,' Tom replied.

Tom never was a good liar. It was stupid of him to try lying to Scarlett. She could usually sense when Tom was fibbing.

Without warning, Sunday came around. The way Maud came knocking on the Farrow's door that morning at quarter to ten would give anyone the impression that they had been trying to avoid going to church in the past. They had but for good reason. Tom was still nervous about bringing all the children along to church even after Maud's kind reminding that it was a child-friendly place. Scarlett and Tom put Alex and Jasper in their buggies while Maud put coats on the twins.

'Now, you two. We are going to a very special place today, called church and it would be lovely if you were nice and quiet for Uncle Tom and Auntie Scarlett.'

'What's church?' asked Ralph.

'It's a place were lots of people meet on a Sunday to sing praises and meet with God and meet with one another.'

Polly looked puzzled.

'Do you have to go to church to meet God?' she asked.

'Well, no. You can meet with God anywhere, anytime. He's wherever you are.'

This time Ralph looked confused.

'If God can meet us anywhere, then why can't we just stay here with him and watch telly?'

'Because God likes us to mix and meet other people so they can talk about him together and have fun, that's why we go to church. If we stayed here then we wouldn't be able to meet anyone else, would we?'

'S'pose not,' replied Ralph.

'So, let's go and have a good time. You two can go into Sunday school halfway through the service with the other children, if you like.'

'I didn't know there was school on Sundays,' said Polly. 'Mummy said when we start school after Christmas we will only go on a Monday, Tuesday, Wednesday, Thursday, and a Friday. She said Saturdays were for playing and Sundays were for shopping and lying in bed.'

Maud seemed a bit anxious. She didn't want to tell the twins that what their mum said wasn't entirely true. She hated the idea of becoming between people because of her faith, yet felt obliged to talk about her beliefs to anyone, children included.

'Well, why don't you try Sunday school and see if you like it. If you do then you can go again next week. If you don't then you can just sit in church with Scarlett and Tom. When you see your mummy again, you can tell her what you thought of it, right?'

The twins looked at each other. 'Okay!' they said. And they left.

The church was nearly full by the time they arrived. Tom was rather surprised at this, as the last time they had been to church the wardens had asked all the people who were sitting in the back nine rows to move forward to the empty ones at the front. Tom remembered feeling sorry for Reverend Hyde at the time as he looked down into what was basically a non-existent congregation, until Tom remembered that he probably couldn't see a thing as his head was permanently looking to the ground anyway.

Maud went and put on her robe as she was singing in the choir that day. Scarlett and Tom were offered a service sheet, which they took and then they walked into the main body of the church. It was a medieval church with a very high ceiling. The organ pipes looked majestic painted gold and red. An arched stained-glass window, depicting an empty cross, filled the building with brilliant colours as the morning sun burst through it. There were four columns of pews and there only seemed to be a few spare seats scattered around the room. As they were looking for enough seats to accommodate them all, the Vicar climbed into the pulpit and began to welcome the congregation. Scarlett pulled Tom by the arm to her ear.

'Where are we going to sit?'

'I don't know. I can't see any pews with six seats.'

'We only need four. The babies can sit on our laps.'

'I can't even see four seats. Who knew church was so popular?'

Suddenly, the Vicar stopped talking and the congregation all turned around to look at them. Scarlett and Tom froze.

'I didn't curse, did I?' Tom whispered to Scarlett.

'No. I think the Vicar was speaking to us.'

John, the Vicar, spoke again. 'I said would you like to come and sit up here, Tom and Scarlett? There's a choir stall at the front not being used today '

Tom hated it when that happens. You go to church once in a blue moon and somehow you manage to embarrass yourself in front of everyone.

'Ah...thank you, John...er...Vicar!'

They turned back to the buggies and tried frantically to get the babies out. The congregation didn't turn back and continued to watch them as they got themselves into a tizzy. Tom looked to John and motioned for him to carry on. Thankfully he did, as it took them a couple of minutes to get everything they needed for the next hour or so. They left the buggies and began to walk to the side of the inner pews to walk up the side aisle but it had been blocked with extra seats for guests. They tried the other side aisle but it too was filled with chairs.

'It must be a baptism Sunday,' whispered Scarlett. 'The water font is at the front of the church, that's why there are so many people here.'

'Yeah, well, if the heathens came out more often they would have known what to expect. Now there isn't even any room for the *real* Christians.'

'Tom! Don't be so facetious. Just walk up the middle aisle, quickly.'

Tom led his family up the aisle amid a mix of smiley, disapproving, and encouraging looks. He did notice that most of the disapproving stares were coming from the older folk. Tom knew exactly what they were thinking. They'd been through all this themselves and now that they were finally rid of their own kids, they looked forward to a nice, quiet service, but there was always a token family who disrupted things for them every week. Tom knew it couldn't be them as they hardly came at all, and as Tom thought of this, he began to wonder where the token family was that morning. Perhaps it was one of their kids who was being baptised because the daggers that pierced his eyes as Tom walked by the families in the front pews were sharp enough to kill. They finally made it to the choir stall where they unloaded the babies and shoulder bags which were stuffed full with milk bottles, nappies, nappy wipes, muslin's, rash creams, tissues, mats, rusks, nappy sacks and everything else that went with a short trip with a baby in tow. Tom smiled back apologetically at some who were still giving him the evil eye. This is why Tom hated coming to church. Although Tom had a strong faith in God himself, Tom hated the fact that people like himself were put off from coming to church because of the behaviour of other so-called Christians. Why can't they accept that we're not all the same, especially families? Some kids can sit still with their arms folded and listen to the most demanding of sermons, while others just switch off or turn their attention to the steps leading up to the pulpit, which is what Jasper did when Scarlett and Tom were sorting themselves out with the bags and Alex. Before they could react, he was at the top of the steps and yanking on the Vicar's trouser leg. John didn't seem to mind so much as he was singing 'Love divine, all love excelling', along with the congregation at the time. After the hymn had ended Tom crept over to the pulpit steps and tried to grab Jasper, but he crawled to the other side of the Vicar and just giggled. John began to read a passage from the bible. 'The reading is taken from James, chapter five.' He read on as Tom wriggled around behind him trying to reach for Jasper. Every time Tom thought he was about to grab him he would move. Then he sat on John's shoes. John had just read verse seven when he shuffled his feet from under Jasper's bottom. As he read out verse eight, he turned his wide-eyed gaze from the bible he was reading to Tom who lay prostrate across the floor of the pulpit. 'Be ye also patient; establish your hearts: for the coming of the Lord draweth nigh.' To an unsuspecting sinner it could have meant that the Vicar was about to send you to meet the Lord for judgement sooner than expected. Tom knew otherwise, but recognised the tone of a man who was beginning to lose his patience. John returned to the rest of the passage and Tom lay still until he had finished reading. As soon as he called for the congregation to stand and sing another hymn, Tom grabbed Jasper by the mid-riff and carried him back to his seat. Scarlett gave Tom one of those '*I don't believe you just did that*' looks.

'I had visions of a defrocked Vicar giving a sermon. What was I supposed to do?' Tom muttered.

'The children are behaving better than you are. Now just shut-up and sing: everyone's watching you.'

She was right. Tom glanced to his left and saw four hundred eyes looking at him as if the words of the hymn were imprinted on his forehead. Once again, Tom gave an apologetic smile, which seemed to appease most of them.

The children left half way through the service to go to Sunday school and then John gave his sermon. It was quite short but humorous, which made people sit up and listen, except Tom, of course. He fell asleep not long after the prayers and only woke up when Scarlett pinched the back of his hand.

'It's time for the peace,' she said standing up.

Tom jumped to his feet and kissed Scarlett on the cheek. He then turned to John who had crossed over to shake his hand.

'Peace be with you,' John said with a genuine smile.

'And also with you,' Tom replied.

'And don't be embarrassed about earlier, Tom. Happens almost every week in a church somewhere up and down the country.'

'Bit too late for that.'

Other members came up to Tom and Scarlett, shook their hands, and shared a sign of peace. Thankfully, none of them made a sly or rude comment about his behaviour. In fact, some even joked about it. One guy actually congratulated Tom on his discipline.

He began to feel much more at ease. At the end of the service, the twins came rushing over to Tom and Scarlett in the coffee lounge and showed them pictures of Jesus feeding the five thousand that they had drawn. Ralph obviously had problems with the number five thousand so he drew two people instead with 'Jeezis' scribbled above one and 'Kroud' above the other.

'Did you have fun?' asked Scarlett.

'Yeah, it was okay.'

During coffee and biscuits, several other members of the congregation came over to Tom to see how he was coping as a househusband. Maud had told just about everyone what had been happening in their lives and people actually seemed interested.

'Well, it wouldn't have happened in my day,' laughed an old man.

'It sure takes guts to do what you're doing, Tom,' one person said.

'You must be the most patient person I've ever met,' said one of the Sunday school teachers before trotting to the coffee table and taking a long drink from a coffee mug.

'Yes. I must,' said Tom as she walked away.

What a con. Tom was taking all this praise as if he was doing something extraordinary. He wasn't. Well, it depends what way you look at it. Most people see it as a backward step for a man to stay at home and run the household. Others see it as an opportunity to lift a man onto a pedestal for doing something brave and gallant. Why? Tom was simply looking after his family – it shouldn't matter who was earning the money or who was doing the housework. When Tom thought about it, Scarlett and Tom were both raising the family; they were both playing a part. Tom wasn't any better than she was. They were two equal partners trying to do the best in an abnormal situation. That Sunday showed Tom that it would be a long time before society saw men as being homemakers. But they can do it.

Tom certainly was.

'That went well, considering,' said Tom opening the front door.

'Considering you ripped a hole in the Vicar's cassock with your cufflink when you tried in vain to retrieve Jasper,' scolded Scarlett.

'It was an accident.'

Maud helped to take the coats off the children while Scarlett and Tom went into the kitchen to prepare lunch.

'Why don't you go and rest that leg of yours? I'll have a go at cooking lunch,' Tom offered.

'Why, thank you kind sir. Seeing as all you have to do is baste the chicken and put the carrots and parsnips on, I think I can trust you in here.'

Scarlett went to sit in the sitting room. A couple of minutes passed and as Tom was peeling away the plastic surround from a Black Forest gateau Polly shuffled into the kitchen and sat down at the table. She looked quite sad and upset. Tom licked the blobs of cream from his fingertips and sat beside her. Tom wasn't sure if she was just tired or if she had been crying.

'Polly, what's the matter?'

She sniffed and then started to cry. Tears gathered in the corner of her eyes before rolling down her cheeks and dropping onto the table.

Tom put his arm around her shoulders and lifted her head up with his other hand.

'You can tell me,' Tom said. 'Why all the waterworks, eh?'

She took a big sniff before saying, 'I miss my mummy.'

Tom gave her a gentle squeeze.

'I know you do, sweetheart. Your mummy misses you too.'

'Then why can't I see her?'

Tom didn't know what to say. He couldn't find the right words to make her understand. Simply telling her that her mum was mentally unstable and she was receiving the best psychiatric help there is just wouldn't do.

'You'll see her soon enough. Your mummy's a little bit ill right now, but she's getting better every day and she'll be here before you know it.'

'Will daddy come too?'

'I don't know, maybe.'

Right then Tom wanted to write a strong letter to Nick and tell him to come home immediately. His kids needed him. They missed him. He was their Dad for goodness sake.

'I know. Why don't you help me make the gravy?' Tom asked.

'Okay.' She raised a little smile.

Sometimes it's best to change the subject instead of guessing what the right words should be. Tom didn't want to make things worse for her.

That afternoon they all went to see Scarlett's mum. Tom hoped a change in scenery would be good for the twins. It was and Tom even managed to put a smile on Isidora's face when he handed back her precious videotape of '*Lady and the Tramp*'.

13

Edward called Tom the following Wednesday to rub in the fact that he had just won over a definite vote from Michael Pierce. Tom found this difficult to swallow, as he was usually a last minute voter on any issue.

'Oh don't beat yourself up over it, Tom, there are still seven out of twelve Board members who I haven't persuaded to vote for me, yet, perhaps they'll go for you.'

'If they've any sense, they will,' Tom said before hanging up.

Tom just couldn't understand it. Michael Pierce? How did Edward convince him to vote for him? Tom spent the rest of the day trying to think of a plan to get Edward out of the picture. His first thought was to hire a hit man to bump him off then Tom realised that just wasn't practical. He had too much to lose. His second thought was to start bribing the Board himself, but Tom realised he had nothing to offer them. His last thought was the best one and the one he decided to go with. Just to let things go on as they were and if Tom were the right man for the job then he'd get it. If he wasn't, then he wouldn't. It was as simple as that.

Scarlett had Craig and Howard running around the office like laboratory rats to try to coax their teams to work a little bit harder to increase productivity. Tom wanted to have the least amount of work outstanding come September, so that when Gilbert retired the department would be in a healthy position. The calculations Tom had made a couple of weeks before were proving themselves correct and he had to pray they would stay that way. Sir Wilfred had been to see Scarlett and had been bragging about his lunchtime rendezvous' with Charlene. Apparently, he had taken her to lunch every day for the past week, cancelling all his previous business appointments. Edward had also managed to take Charlene to dinner one evening to check that everything was going well between her and his uncle. The future looked fine and dandy for Edward. It was starting to look bleak for Tom.

The following day Tom decided to cheer himself up and take the twins to the indoor playground. Tom needed to get rid of some stress and anxiety and a roll around on a bouncy castle would do just the trick. Before Tom left he called Geri to see if she and Alex would like to join them. They would, so Tom said he'd see her there. He was very hesitant at phoning her, but his intentions were innocent. He'd already said that he'd call and he wouldn't want her to get the wrong impression of him. When Tom promises to do something, he always keeps his word or at least he tries.

As one would expect during the height of the summer the playground was bursting at the seams with children. Tom thought because it was such a lovely day that most kids would be outside playing in the parks or at the pleasure pool. He guessed all the other parents had the same thought, which is why they all ended up here. Nonetheless, they were here to enjoy ourselves and that's what they did. Geri hadn't arrived by the time they got there but they went in anyway. Polly and Ralph couldn't keep calm waiting in the foyer. They found an empty table and a couple of chairs. Tom relieved the twins of their shoes and warned them that if they took their socks off then they would leave, as it was a rule of the playground, fungal infections and all that. No sooner had Tom slipped their shoes under the table had they run off.

'Keep your socks on remember!' Tom shouted after them. 'I don't want you getting us thrown out!'

Geri and Alex walked through the entrance just as he'd sat down. Tom waved his arm at them to attract their attention.

'I'm sorry we're late,' she said with a wide smile. 'I've just had a phone call from the hospital and they've given me the job.' She bounced up and down a little in excitement.

'Wow! Well done, Dr...' Tom stopped. 'Blimey! I don't even know your last name?'

'Oh, it's Porter.'

'I'm very pleased to make your acquaintance, Dr Porter.'

Tom rose from his seat, took her right hand, and kissed it gently on the knuckles.

'So when do you begin this new job?'

'Not for another four weeks or so. I need to organise childcare for Alex and I know for a fact that I can't do that right away.'

'Don't they have a nursery at the hospital?' Tom enquired.

'They used to, but it closed down due to lack of use, so I'll have to try and find one close by.'

'I wish I could help.'

'You're sweet, Tom, but I think you've got your hands full already.'

173

'Yeah, that's true.'

Alex was too young to use the playground so Geri took him over to a closed in area for under one's. Tom watched her from his seat as she got down on her knees and played with her son. He thought of her life and how difficult it must be, juggling her career and her home life. What struck him was that not once over the two weeks that he'd known her had she complained or spoken about her situation with bitterness or in anger. She seemed content. At peace. We humans strive towards things that sometimes we cannot achieve and yet feel disheartened when we don't achieve them. Tom began to wonder how he'd actually feel if he wasn't offered the Director's job. How would he react if he knew he had to stay at home every day and look after the children? Or, as Sam pointed out, if Scarlett was offered the job, how would he react then? If it happened three weeks earlier Tom knew he would have hit the roof; his marriage would be going through a rough time, and Tom wouldn't see Alex because he'd be down the pub drowning his sorrows.

'Come and play, Uncle Tom. Come and play!'

It was Ralph, pulling his arm.

'Okay, okay, I'm coming.'

Tom flicked his trainers off and ran after him into the netted play area. He chased Ralph through the low-ceilinged rooms, almost crashing into other grown-ups, catching a whiff of sweaty t-shirts and socks as he went. He dove to the right and began to climb up the padded ramps to the first level. As Tom put his head out from under the overheard ramp, he got a wallop to the side of his head from an oncoming toddler. He shook it off and carried on chasing after Ralph. He ran across the floor and headed for the rope-bridge. Tom was having a terrific time. Whoever designed these places really had adults in mind. Most of the grown-ups seemed to be having more fun than the kids were. Tom followed Ralph to the bridge where two other grown-ups stood either side of the entrance. Thinking they were standing aside to let him through Tom ploughed on ahead. Ralph was stepping onto the platform at the other end of the rope as Tom put his second foot on the rope-bridge. It was then that Tom realised why the other two grown-ups didn't cross on the rope. Tom had just laid all his weight on the rope when he heard a snap. Before Tom had a chance to turn around and head back to safety, the rope snapped and Tom fell down onto the net below. The force of the fall made him bounce up once and then as he landed on his feet the second time, some of the net gave way and his legs fell through it, astride a supporting wire.

The attendant who helped Tom down gave him a right earful and then took him up to the first level again to show him the sign that hung outside the entrance of the rope-bridge. It read 'No Adults allowed – weight restricted to 9st only!'

'Guess I've put a little weight on,' was all Tom could say for himself.

Needless to say, Tom was banned from using the apparatus, but the attendant took pity on the twins and let them finish at their allotted time. Tom left the playground in shame and highly embarrassed. Geri said she had seen it all and Tom's face was a picture when he fell onto the wire. He bet it was. Tom bundled the twins into the car, strapping them into their raised seats with the seat belts. Geri stood behind him with Alex asleep in his carrier.

'Sorry we didn't get to talk much in there; these places aren't made with conversation in mind, are they?'

'No, they're not.'

Tom jangled his keys for something to do as the uncomfortable moment passed.

'Can I cook you dinner tonight?'

Geri wasn't smiling as she asked the question. She looked as though she'd regretted asking it in case she was rejected. Tom suddenly felt very vulnerable. Immediately, he thought of Scarlett and Alex. Things were bad enough. He already compromised any friendship Geri and Tom had by giving her the impression that he was a single parent. Tom knew that when he'd finally tell her that he was still married, he wouldn't see her again, yet he didn't want to hurt her.

'I'm afraid I can't, not tonight. Maybe some other time?'

'Tomorrow night? The next?'

She began to sound desperate, which in normal circumstances would have damaged his ego. This time though it made him feel a real idiot forever letting his feelings get involved.

'I'll let you know.'

'Okay. I'll wait to hear from you then?'

She sounded despondent.

'Sure. I'll call you.'

He knew he wouldn't.

'Bye, then.'

'Bye.'

She walked across the car park as Tom got into his car. He checked the rear view mirror and saw her turn around briefly in his direction. What was Tom doing? He was toying with someone's emotions and somehow he wasn't feeling as guilty as he should have done. A sense of guilt would at least show him he was doing wrong. He wanted to feel guilty. He switched on the engine.

'Are we going home now?' asked Polly.

'Yes! We're going home.'

Scarlett hobbled through the front door and dumped her crutches in the hallway. Sylvia stumbled in after her with a large box stuffed full of paper.

'What have you got there?' asked Tom.

'It's the quality control print-outs from the past three months. I'm going to see if there are any employees that aren't up to scratch and maybe move them to another department and take some old experienced staff back on temporarily for the next couple of months.'

'Very devious. I'm not sure the staff will thank you for it though.'

'It was your idea, remember?' said Sylvia from behind the box.

'Here, let me help you with that.'

'Scarlett's only doing what you would do yourself, Tom, so if anyone's devious around here, it's you.'

'Yeah, well, it is business,' said Scarlett. 'If we go ahead with this we may get a few abusive comments, but it'll be in the department's best interest in the long run.'

'Plus, no-one will get sacked will they?' Tom asked in desperation. 'I've already promised the Team Managers that I will not lower the current head count.'

'Well, you'll just have to help me decide what happens after we analyse all this stuff tonight.'

Tom remembered his conversation with George. 'Scarlett, please remember that any important decisions like whether we sack or hire people is entirely down to me. I'm still responsible for the staff in the department you know.'

She gave him a kiss on the lips and a smile. 'I know you are, darling.'

'Well, just as long as you do.'

Sylvia coughed before excusing herself to leave. Tom carried the box of reports into the kitchen.

'This is going to take all night,' said Tom. 'I hope you've enough stamina to keep you going till midnight, I'm not sure I have.'

'I don't mind finishing it off if you want to have an early night.'

There she was again. Trying to take control. George had sown a seed of doubt into his mind about Scarlett's intentions and Sam's remarks helped water it.

'Oh, don't you worry about me. Plenty of black coffee and I'll be fine.'

Tom turned his back on Scarlett and put his hand to his mouth to mask a huge yawn. He'd been up since five am and on the go all day. Truth be told, he was shattered.

'How'd it go at '*Tire'em'out*'?' Scarlett asked.

'Oh, just marvellous. Ralph practically dragged me onto the rope bridge and the attendants literally dragged me off it. I've got the friction marks on my inner thighs to prove it.'

'You didn't make an idiot of yourself again, did you?' Scarlett laughed.

'That's all I seem good for these days, making a fool of myself.'

She hobbled over to him and clung onto him. 'Aw, is my little man feeling sorry for himself?'

'No. Just a bit bruised.'

'Where? On your bum or your ego?'

Tom was confused.

'Why would my ego be bruised?' Tom asked.

'Well, the once big chief at work is now the housemaid and his squaw is running the office. I just thought you might have been feeling a little tender about it.'

Tom wanted to deny it, but there was no point. She knew Tom wasn't entirely happy over the past few days and she'd obviously worked out why.

'I'm not feeling tender about it. I just hope you realise that I will be going back to the office once you get your plaster off. I think you're getting too comfortable doing my job.'

'Tom, I'm doing this for you.'

'Are you?'

'Of course, I am. You know I'd rather be here with the children, but it's just not practical.'

'Are you sure there isn't another reason for all this?'

She knew Tom was fishing but she wasn't biting.

'I'm not trying to take your trousers from you, if that's what you mean.'

It was what Tom meant.

'Okay. I'm sorry. I'm just being stupid.' Tom squeezed her tight.

'I love you, Tom.'

'I love you too.'

They stood for a moment just hugging when Polly and Ralph came running into the kitchen. Scarlett laughed. They were playing doctors and nurses, but Ralph seemed reluctant to put on the nurse's pinafore as Polly chased him around the table screaming 'put it on – it's the rules'.

The twins sat with Tom and Scarlett in the kitchen for dinner. It was the first time they had done so since coming to stay. It was nice and cosy. Scarlett leant over to Tom just after they had said grace and whispered in his ear.

'Wouldn't it be nice to have a little sister for Alex to play with?'

'Scarlett, we have enough children to contend with at the moment. I don't even want to think about having another child until I've parted company with the present ones.'

Tom carried on with his dinner, but pondered over what Scarlett had said. Tom guessed it would be nice. Polly and Ralph seemed to enjoy each other's company so much. In the beginning, Tom would look at Ralph and often thought if Alex turned out like him by the age of four, he'd contemplate having a vasectomy. But when Tom saw him with his sister, he changed his view. A little daughter. Tom smiled to himself. Now that would be perfect.

Scarlett offered to put the kids to bed as Tom cleared up the mess in kitchen. Tom went into the sitting room to collect the twins' popcorn bowl when he heard a quiet voice. It was coming from the baby monitor, which he'd forgotten to switch off the previous evening. He turned up the volume button and sat down beside it as he listened to Scarlett read Alex a bedtime story. Tom could hear him gurgle and he was obviously putting up a fight going to sleep. She was reading 'Goldilocks and The Three Bears'. Her voice was soft and calm. He'd realised that he hadn't heard her read to him before, but it was because Tom was usually still at the office or at least on his way home. She read slowly and with a different voice for each character. Tom closed his eyes. When she had finished reading the story Tom heard her say sorry to Alex. She apologised that she couldn't be there for him every day, but that it wouldn't be for long.

'Daddy loves you too and he'll be around for you when mummy's not, and Auntie Maud cares so much about you as well.'

Tom could hear a faint sniffle. It was Scarlett. She was crying.

'I love you so much,' Tom heard her whisper.

Here he was complaining about her reasons for going out to work and thinking that she didn't want to be around the children, when in fact she was finding it painful to be apart from her son every day. She was sacrificing her time with Alex for him. Tom began to well up. Not because he was feeling sentimental, but because he was such an idiot. A few minutes later Scarlett joined him in the sitting room.

'Have you cleared up in the kitchen, yet?'

Tom got up, took Scarlett in his arms, and gave her a tender kiss on the lips.

'What's brought all this on?'

'Nothing. I just want you to know that I do love you and appreciate you.'

She looked into his eyes and smiled. 'I know you do, Tom.' And she returned the kiss.

'Now, we've got work to do.'

'Work can wait,' Tom said. 'Let's go upstairs.'

Scarlett dropped her crutches and Tom lifted her up and carried her to the bedroom. They didn't get any work done that night.

Maynard Tait

14

Sam brought the morning post at eight thirty am on the dot just as Tom was getting Alex and Jasper into the buggy.

'Is it safe to come in?' he asked.

'I'm just on my way out, mate. Scarlett's still here in you want to go in and have some toast.'

He thought better of it.

'Nah, perhaps next week, mate.' He handed Tom his post and Tom shuffled through it. 'Looking for something in particular?'

'I'm waiting for a reply from the insurance company about a claim I made. It's been two weeks now and we haven't heard a thing.'

'What do you expect, mate? The only thing an insurance company insures is that their customers never get a satisfactory reply within a satisfactory time. What you need to do, mate, is call them and ask for the Customer Service Director and give off stink. It always works for me.'

'Really?'

'Yup. If I were you, I'd think twice about this promotion of yours, mate. It'll be nothing but complaint after complaint.'

'We'll see about that. Anyway, was there anything else you wanted only I need to get going?'

'Just to tell you that the boys are meeting down the pub tonight to send off young Jimmy. He's off to Australia tomorrow for a couple of years. Fancy joining us, mate?'

Tom was about to say he needed to speak to Scarlett, but he made his own decision.

'Yeah, I'll be there.'

His reply took Sam by surprise. 'Gordon Bennett! Sure you don't want to check with the old trouble and strife, mate?'

'I said I'll be there, didn't I?'

Sam laughed and picked up his bike from the pavement. 'See you about eight then.'

'See you later, mate. You owe me a pint by the way.'

Tom strapped Alex into the buggy and pulled down the rain cover, as the skies looked threatening. Sylvia pulled up and beeped her horn to let Scarlett know she'd arrived. She hobbled outside and closed the front door.

'I'll see you later, handsome. Try not to get into any trouble today please.'

'I'll try, but I can't promise anything.'

They kissed and Tom helped her into the car. Sylvia sounded her horn again as she drove off. The twins held hands as Tom pushed the buggy out onto the pavement. They had only walked twenty yards or so when Sylvia's car pulled up alongside them and Scarlett wound down her window.

'What's the matter?' Tom asked.

'It's Jasper's birthday,' Scarlett uttered.

'When?'

'Today. It's his birthday today.'

'Oh! Well I'll buy him a little cake this afternoon and stick a candle in it.'

'No. I promised Jackie he'd have a party. She's already invited the children and she told the parents where the party would be.'

'A party? Where?' Tom couldn't believe it. He knew exactly what Scarlett was about to say and he dreaded the thought of it.

'I said they could have it at ours.'

'Oh, that's just great, Scarlett.'

'I wasn't expecting to be in crutches at the time, was I? Anyway, it's at two o'clock so you have all morning to prepare. There's an envelope in the bureau with ideas for what to bake or buy. I'll try and get home as soon as I can to help.'

'Scarlett!'

'Sorry, darling. I'll see you later.' She rolled up her window as Sylvia drove off.

'Scarlett!' Tom shouted in vain.

Tom looked heavenward for sympathy but none came.

After leaving the babies with Maud Tom headed straight into town to start buying what he thought he'd need for a children's party. Tom went to the supermarket first to buy some jelly and ice cream, which was always the pièce de résistance at any party – at least it was when he was a kid. Tom scanned the dessert freezers for some other treats. Profiteroles seemed an obvious choice, so Tom threw a couple of boxes of those in his trolley along with a multipack of frozen ice-lollies. From the confectionery aisle, he took several packets of marshmallows, assorted nuts, and toffees. Spicy chilli crisps always went down well at a party so he grabbed a couple of bags of those too. Tom was almost finished buying the food when he remembered about a cake for Jasper. He saw a row of readymade and iced cakes but the price of them put him off.

'I can bake a cake. How hard could it be?' he said.

Polly and Ralph stared at him in wonder. Tom lifted some eggs and flour and then headed to the checkout. The girl on the till gave him a weird look as she scanned his purchases.

'Got a sweet tooth, have you love?' she said.

'It's not for me.'

'Oh, yeah. Whose it all for then?'

'It's for a baby's first birthday party, if you must know.'

She raised her eyebrows. 'The parents will love you after their kids have eaten all this. Seventeen pounds and twenty, please love.'

Tom wasn't going to argue. He paid and left. The first thing he did when they got back home was to check the list that Scarlett had left in the bureau. To call it a list was slightly conservative, it was more of a manual. There were six pages of instructions and ideas of what to do for the party. Jackie had thought of everything. After all, she had done it a few times for the twins, so Tom figured she knew what she was talking about. There was also a list of names of the people she had invited to the party. Hoping it would only be about half a dozen, Tom nearly had a coronary when he counted nineteen children's names.

'Oh boy! This is going to be a nightmare.'

Tom checked off the food he had just bought against another of Jackie's lists. The only two things that he had managed to buy that matched her list were jelly and ice cream, even Tom knew he couldn't get that wrong. There were recipes for top hats and chocolate crispies, trifle and banoffee pie. Tom ruffled through the bags of shopping and thought that he'd done rather well, so he wouldn't have to bake or cook anything apart from the cake. The party was due to start at two o'clock, which gave him three hours to prepare. No problem. Tom sent Polly and Ralph out to the back garden. The threatening skies of the early morning had dispersed and it was turning out to be another beautiful, warm day, so he turned on the lawn sprinklers in the hope that it would keep them happy for the next couple of hours. Polly also had her Wendy house up, so they could cool off in there if need be.

'And keep away from my flowers!' Tom shouted through the window.

It took him over half an hour to find a suitable cake recipe from Scarlett's selection of seven cookbooks. Delia Smith was his first choice, but there just didn't seem to be any sense of fun in the way she presented her cooking. Tom plumbed for Gary Rhodes. At least he did for the first crack of an egg and then realised that not even Raymond Blanc could end up with a cake that would resemble the masterpiece that was presented in the photograph, so Auntie Bessie's Victoria sponge it was to be. Any fool could follow Aunt Bessie's recipes and that gave him comfort as he ploughed on with the task in hand. The phone rang as Tom was beating the sloppy mixture into a less sloppy mixture. It was Isidora, Scarlett's mum.

'Hi, Isidora. What can I do for you this fine day?'

'Scarlett tells me you have a birthday party this afternoon and I thought I'd grace you with my presence.'

Oh, no! The last thing Tom needed was a fire-breathing dragon bouncing toddlers on its knee. What would the parents say when they collected their hair-singed children at the end of the party?

'Isidora, I appreciate the offer, but Scarlett will be back in time, so there's really no need to come over, thanks all the same.'

'But Scarlett has just called me to say she can't make it, something about an urgent Board meeting. Hasn't she called you yet?'

Typical. This was exactly what George and Sam were on about. Scarlett decided to tell her mother first, so that Tom couldn't do anything about it. She knew there was no way Tom would have the guts to turn away Isidora. What a cow!

'Ah, no, she hasn't called me yet, but honestly, Isidora, there's no need to come, I'll cope.' Tom wobbled on a few words, which gave Isidora the impression he couldn't cope.

'Nonsense. I'll be there at one thirty sharp. Bye!'

Before Tom could argue, she was gone. He was about to curse when the twins heads popped up from beneath the window.

'Go and play,' he shouted.

Tom returned to his sloppy mixture and began to pummel it until no lump was safe from the wooden spoon.

'That's all I need. A chaperone.'

He poured the mixture into a round tin, chucked it in the oven, and then called the office. It took a while before Sylvia finally answered it.

'Sylvia. It's Tom. What's going on?'

'Tom, Sir Wilfred has called an urgent Board meeting and asked for Edward and Scarlett to join them. She hopes to be out by one, so she'll be home in time for the party.'

'She better be or there'll be trouble,' Tom warned. 'And you tell her that I want a satisfactory explanation as to why she didn't call me before calling her mother.' Then Tom remembered what Isidora had said. 'Hang on. Scarlett told her mother she wouldn't be back this afternoon.'

'Well, she did take her mobile phone in with her perhaps she called her from there. I'm afraid I'm not allowed to disturb the meeting, Tom.'

'Why not? What's it all about? And why wasn't I invited?'

'Tom, I think you have to remember that Scarlett is doing your job at the moment and Sir Wilfred is very happy to have her back, so just trust her will you.'

Trust? That was the point. Tom was beginning not to.

'I do trust her,' Tom replied. 'Completely.'

'Well then. Have a nice time this afternoon. Oh, one thing Scarlett did say...'

'What?'

'Party bags. Each child will need a party bag to take home.'

'What do you mean?' Tom really was beginning to think he couldn't cope.

'You will need to give the children a bag each filled with some things to take home, like a balloon, stickers – things like that.'

This was getting too much. The idea of not answering the door this afternoon suddenly went through his head. He could hide in the back garden in the Wendy house and bribe the twins to keep quiet. Then he thought about what Scarlett would do to him if he did that. It wasn't worth it. Tom would have to go through with the party. He said goodbye to Sylvia and began to make another list of what to put into the party bags. Balloons, stickers, sweets, and bubble-gum cards. They were always a favourite when Tom was a kid. He remembered chewing a whole pack of bubble-gum in ten minutes just so he could see what football players he had on his cards. One hour later Tom was rushed to hospital with a bloated stomach and gum stuck in his windpipe. He was banned from eating gum for the next two years, but he still had an impressive collection of football cards to swap with. Those were the days.

Tom was going to have to go into town again to buy some more stuff. It would be easier without the twins so, once again, he asked if Maud could have them for an hour. She could.

The sweet shop he stood in front of hadn't changed in over twenty years. His last visit here was on his twenty-first birthday when Tom was given twenty-one pence by the 'worms'. A practice his mum got into when she wanted to give him some little presents was to say they were from the animals that lived in the garden. Tom thought she was loopy but he never complained. He decided to spend it on a twenty-one pence mix-up. He always made up half of his mix-ups with white chocolate mice and the other with different sweets.

As Tom opened the shop door, the little bell above it announced his arrival. It was a pokey little shop, but every spare inch was covered in shelves full of every kind of confectionery imaginable. It was like Aladdin's cave. He smiled as he took in the names of all the sweets he used to buy as a kid every Saturday afternoon with his pocket money. His favourite was candy tobacco, which came in realistic tobacco pouches. It was flavoured coconut and it tasted fantastic. Tom spotted a box of it and just had to have some, so he took half a dozen packets. There were jars full of midget gems and candy mushrooms, toffee teacakes and peanut brittle. They brought back so many memories. Tom was just drooling over some other jars when he felt cold air on the back of his neck. He turned around to find an obese-looking character, at least six foot five in height, with greasy black hair that rested on the dirty collar of his pale blue polo shirt.

'Morning!' he grunted. 'Anything I can get you? Anything... special?'

Every Saturday, when Tom was a kid, a fragile old man who smiled gently at you as you made your purchase, served him. He would never speak, just smile. Where was he now?

'Do you work here?' Tom asked the guy.

'Yes. I run the place.'

'Oh. There used to be an elderly man who ran the shop. What happened to him?'

He frowned and turned his gaze to the floor. 'Daddy died a couple of years ago. He left me the business. I was his only child, you see.'

'I see. I'm sorry to hear that.'

The man walked along the aisle and back behind the same old wooden counter.

'I haven't changed anything in here. I still order all the same stock as Daddy did over the forty-eight years he ran it.' He slowly looked up at Tom and gave a yellow-toothed grin. 'But I have begun to sell... extras.'

Tom had no idea what he meant and had no intention of finding out.

'Well, there is something I would like.'

The doorbell tinkled again as a scrawny looking teenager came in with both hands shoved deep into his pockets. His eyes were blood shot and sunk deep in their sockets. The shop owner excused himself from Tom and walked to the other end of the counter. The teenager spoke loud enough for only the shop owner to hear. The overweight shopkeeper turned around and lifted down a jar covered in brown paper from the top shelf. He unscrewed the top and turned his back to Tom as he pulled out its contents and passed it to the boy. He in turn handed over some money and then left with his gaze fixed to the ground. The shop owner walked back over to Tom and rested his bulk on the counter.

'Now, what was it you wanted?'

The curiosity was killing him.

'What did he just buy? The boy that just left.' Tom asked.

'Oh, he's just got a thing for...liquorice.'

'Liquorice, huh?'

'Liquorice,' he repeated.

Tom tried to concentrate on his own business.

'Well, I was wondering if you still sold the packets of gum with cards in.'

The man smiled that same creepy smile again and lifted himself up.

'For you?' he asked.

'Well, yes. I know I'm a bit old for them, but they give me a little pleasure, if you know what I mean.'

He continued to grin. 'Oh, I wouldn't say you were too old for that. It takes all ages.' He walked off towards a side door. 'Just give me a minute. I'll get something special for you, seeing as you're an old customer of my old man.'

'Oh, wow! Thanks.'

Tom was feeling giddy with excitement. He felt like a little boy again about to experience something good for the first time. Goosebumps covered his arms. As he waited, he gathered some more candy for the party bags. He took some strawberry laces, sherbet dips, and candy necklaces for the girls.

'I'm Barry, by the way,' said the owner as he returned. He had a plastic bag in his hand and he let Tom look inside. There were about thirty small, unmarked white boxes, all wrapped separately in cellophane.

'It is gum, isn't it?' Tom asked rather naively.

'Of course its gum, with special collectors cards, hence the unmarked packaging.'

He passed Tom the bag. 'Here,' he grinned. 'Get your gums round them.'

'Thanks, Barry. I'm Tom, Tom Farrow.'

He shook Tom's hand and then counted up the bill. Tom was rather surprised at the final tally, but assumed it was because of the collector's cards.

'Enjoy!' said Barry, as Tom opened the door to leave.

'Oh, I will, don't you worry. I'll see you again, I hope.'

'Oh, you'll be back. I can guarantee it.'

Tom drove home first before collecting the twins from Maud's and it was a good thing he did too. He couldn't believe his eyes as he drove toward his house and saw a fire engine parked in front of his driveway and three fire fighters running through the front door. Tom stopped the car and as he got out, he saw smoke coming from the back of the house. It must have been the kitchen. Running to the front door, another fireman grabbed Tom by the arm.

'Stop!' he shouted. 'You can't go in there.'

'But it's my house,' Tom cried.

'I wouldn't care if it was the Queens palace. I'm not letting you in. The fire won't take long to sort out, it looks worse than it is.' He walked Tom back to the fire engine, his hand cupping his elbow.

'What happened?' Tom asked.

'You tell me. It's a small fire coming from the kitchen. They don't think anywhere else has been affected. I assume there's no one upstairs?'

'No.'

'Have you been gone long?' he asked.

'About an hour or so.'

'What were you doing before your left?'

That's when it struck him. This was going to be embarrassing. Tom sighed and then swore.

'I was baking a cake for a birthday party. I must have left the oven on or something.'

'Or something?'

Of course, it was the oven. What an idiot. And Tom thought he could cope. The fireman didn't laugh as Tom expected him to. Instead, he reassured him that oven fires were very common, caused only by forgetfulness. Not much in the way of consolation. A couple of minutes passed before the hose was turned off and the fire fighters came out of the house.

'Not much damage, sir,' shouted one of them to the man beside Tom. 'More smoke damage to the ceiling and walls than anything else.'

'Thank heavens for that,' Tom said.

Just then, the nightmare got worse.

'What in heavens name, happened here?'

It was Isidora and she was in a right old panic.

'Tom, are you all right? Where are the children? Have you burnt them?' She practically sprinted across the road in her high heels, carrying a bakery box.

'No, I haven't burnt them you stu...' Tom thought better than to continue. He took a deep breath. 'They're all at Maud's house. I just had a little accident baking the cake, that's all.'

'That's all! You almost burnt your house to the ground. It's a good thing I bought this on the way.' She lifted the lid to show off a triple-layered chocolate and vanilla cream cake, topped with fresh strawberries and kiwi fruit.

A few choice words came to Tom's mind.

'You didn't have to. I could have made another one,' he said.

'No you couldn't, mate,' laughed one of the fire fighters. 'Not unless you wanted to bake it on a gas stove.' He pointed to the front door where a couple of firemen were carrying out the remains of the black cooker. 'That's had it, mate. Better call your insurance company.'

Tom turned to the fire engine and began to bang his head against it, chanting incessantly. 'Scarlett's going to kill me! I know she's going to kill me! She's definitely going to kill me!'

Maynard Tait

15

Isidora threw the rubber gloves at Tom as if to remind him that all this was his fault. He didn't need reminding, the black walls did a terrific job of that. They started scrubbing the walls as hard as they could to remove the chargrilled pattern that covered them. Their feet splashed in the puddles of dirty water that surrounded them. The flooring would have to be replaced; as would a few of the wall units but other than that, he'd been lucky. Before he'd left the house, Tom had opened the two kitchen windows as wide as they could go. It was a hot day as it was and the heat from the oven made it almost unbearable to be inside. If Tom hadn't left the windows open the damage would have been much worse, apparently. As he scrubbed, he began to mutter to himself how all this wouldn't have happened if Scarlett hadn't said 'yes' to Jackie.

'I'd still be at work, dealing with my own promotion prospects. My wife would be at home with Alex, where she belongs. We wouldn't be forking out for a nanny. I wouldn't have crashed into a policeman and I wouldn't be standing here in a burnt out kitchen!' His annoyance was evident.

'Tom! None of this is Scarlett's fault. You left the oven unattended, not her. And another thing, Scarlett isn't just a mother, she needs to feel valued and you know how much she loves working at the office.'

'I value her as a wife and Alex values her as a mother. How much value does she need?'

'Enough to feel happy. Don't deny her happiness, Tom. She's doing all this for you, remember? I'm sure she'd rather be at home with Alex. I should know, I can remember what it was like to be a new mother.'

'Way back in the Middle Ages,' Tom muttered.

'Don't be impertinent, Tom, it doesn't suit you.'

She was right, it didn't.

'Sorry! It's just that things are always going wrong. I can't seem to make this father business work. If I can't cope with Polly and Ralph, who I can actually communicate with, how am I going to cope with Alex?'

Isidora stopped scrubbing and took off her gloves. 'Tom, I think you're trying too hard. You're trying to build a model blindfolded without instructions. If I'm honest, and I haven't shared this with Scarlett mind, I did have my fears when she told me about the twins and Jasper. The two of you are still getting used to sharing your lives with your own baby and all of a sudden instead of learning how a new life progresses, you've been thrown in at the deep end and made to adapt quickly and learn the hard way. The problem is, this is how it is and you need to take things as they come and not charge ahead to make the path clear because something will always get in the way.'

'I guess you're right. I don't want to let anyone down, least of all the children.'

'Then just take it easy. Relax and go with the flow.'

She gave Tom a hug, and for once he didn't squirm away from it.

'And another thing, don't be too proud to accept help when you need it.'

Tom laughed. 'Sure thing, Isidora. Thanks.'

'It's okay. Now, we haven't got long before people start to arrive so we better get cracking.'

'Tell you what, if you don't mind clearing up in here, I'll decorate the sitting room and get the food out on the table.'

She raised an eyebrow. 'Don't push your luck. You made the mess, you clear it up. Now get mopping. I'll do the rest.'

She had a point.

The first party guests arrived bang on two. Tom was slightly surprised that the two children who had been invited were actually the same age as the twins, which also reminded him that he hadn't collected them from Maud's. Tom opened the front door to run down the road and get them, but he didn't have to. Maud and the twins were climbing the steps already.

'I knew you'd have your hands full,' smiled Maud.

'You are an angel in disguise. I'm sure of it.' Tom clasped her face and gave her a kiss on the cheek before she turned and left.

'I'll take that as a compliment.'

Within fifteen minutes, all the guests, bar one, had arrived and Tom felt like a stripper at a hen party. He was the only man in the house and the fact that he was the host seemed to amuse the ladies. He was just about to start proceedings with a game of pass the parcel when the doorbell rang.

'That must be Linda and little Mark.'

Tom opened the door, but Linda and Mark weren't the only people standing under the porch.

'Hi, I'm Linda. This is Mark. I hope you wouldn't mind, but I brought a friend with me. She's somewhat new to the area and I thought this might help her get to know people. You must be Tom.'

'Yes, I'm Tom.'

'Then, Tom, this is Geri and Alex. Geri and Alex, this is Tom.'

Linda trailed Mark passed Tom as she made her way to the sitting room. Tom just stared at Geri and she stared back. It was an awkward moment. His first thought was of how they parted company the previous day. Then he remembered Isidora as he heard her high heels click on the hallway behind him.

'Okay, Tom, that's the kitchen taken care of. The cake is sitting on the table with a candle on it. Are you sure I can trust you with a match to light it?'

Tom looked at her and laughed. 'Ha-ha, very witty, Isidora. So, you're leaving now, are you? That's great.' Tom grabbed her coat from the stand and put it on her as he wished her a pleasant drive home. 'Thanks for all your help. Couldn't have done it without you. I'll speak to you later. Bye- bye!' Tom walked her past Geri and Alex out onto the steps.

'Are you going to be all right on your own, Tom?'

'Me? I'll be fine. Take care, now.'

She kissed Tom on the cheek and walked to her car. He looked back at Geri.

'The nanny?' she asked.

'Nanny?' Tom looked back at Isidora. 'Yes, of course. Who else would it be?'

'You're obviously very close.'

'Closer than you think,' Tom whispered as he closed the front door behind him.

Tom asked one of the mothers if she didn't mind running the party games while he went to the kitchen and have a quick whisky. He didn't tell her that of course. He told her he was going to get dressed up like a clown for the kids. It was the only thing he could think of as he felt under considerable pressure and duress, but at least it let him escape to the kitchen to think what to do. In the sitting room was the woman Tom was mentally having an affair with and his wife could arrive home at any minute. What was he to do? He sat at the kitchen table and poured himself a drink while the joyful screams of over twenty children echoed around him. He was about to pour another drink when Geri came in.

'Tom. Now I know why you seemed a bit distracted yesterday. You were just worried about the party, weren't you?'

Was he?

'Yes! Yes, that was it. I was distracted. So much to organise; so little time. You know how it is.' Tom tried to be calm. He took another swig. 'Would you like a drink?' he offered.

'Not yet. Maybe in a minute or two.'

'Well don't mind me. Just a little tense at the moment.'

Geri walked towards him. 'Really! How about I ease some of that tension?'

She put her arms around his neck and brought her face toward his. Tom eased out of his seat, trying to remain in control.

'Ah, sorry, Geri. Look, I need to go and dress up as a clown. Don't want to keep the kids waiting.' He bumped his way passed the table to the door. Geri just stood and smiled at him.

'Need a hand with your make-up?' she asked.

'No!' Tom shouted. 'I mean, no, thanks, I can manage, I hope!'

Tom left the kitchen, closed the door behind him, and leant against it. One of the ladies came out of the sitting room.

'Is the clown ready to come in or should I get them to play something else?'

'Give me...er, him, ten minutes.'

'Right!'

Tom began to feel faint and sweaty at the same time. 'This can't be happening. What have I done to deserve this, Lord? Whatever it was, please forgive me!'

He ran up the stairs and rooted through his closet to find something that would pass as circus wear. Tom knew he wouldn't find anything. If there was one thing he had pride in it was his appearance and he had a habit of changing his wardrobe every year. He never kept any old clothes. They always went to the charity shops. Tom remembered one time he left an old leather jacket at one particular shop and the price tag read more expensive than when he first bought it. Inflation, he guessed. He pulled down the stepladder to climb up to the attic. Scarlett kept a box of old clothes up there from her days in amateur theatre. He was bound to find something up there. Luckily, he did. There was a pair of huge, red pantaloons, which she wore in a production of '*Pirates of Penzance*' and a black and white striped T-shirt she donned for the part of a French onion seller would have to do as his top. He managed to locate a blond, curly wig with blue bows tied into it. All he had to do now was put on some make-up. Tom emptied the contents of Scarlett's make-up case onto the bed and then plastered his face with all different colours of lipstick. Looking in the mirror, he painted a sad pair of lips on his face in bright red. It mirrored how Tom was actually feeling. He outlined them with some black mascara. He smothered his eyelids and cheeks in pink and purples and put on a couple of Scarlett's over-pretentious earrings for good measure. Before running downstairs, Tom checked himself up and down in the mirror. He didn't look like any Bobo the clown he'd ever met, but at the last minute it was the best he could do. His toes were all curled up and squashed into an old pair of builder's boots that he once wore while doing an apprenticeship on a work site. He never thought his feet could grow any bigger than they did at the age of seventeen, but these proved him wrong.

After stumbling down the stairs Tom burst into the sitting room and the crowd went wild. Children screamed and the parents all laughed as Dipstick the clown tried to entertain. At first, Tom didn't really know what to do but he took his cue from a rather pathetic looking lemon meringue pie that someone had left in the centre of the food table. Tom lifted the pie and pretended it was heavy and he wobbled around the room giving the children the impression he was going to trip and splat the pie in someone's face. At least that was the idea. Just before Tom had planned to trip himself, he actually did trip over Ralph's foot. If he didn't know any better he'd swear Ralph did it deliberately. He lost his balance and fell forwards losing his entire grip on the pie. As Tom crashed to the ground, the pie flew over a few heads before landing in the lap of one of the ladies. The children roared with laughter. The lady didn't. Tom picked himself up and made his way to the lady and without thinking, helped to wipe the mess off her skirt. She landed the back of her hand right on his left ear and the sting went around his head for the next five minutes. Tom apologised and attempted to carry on his act. The children loved it, so what was he to do? He did the '*split my thumb in two*' trick, which wowed even some of the parents. For his next and final trick, he pretended to have nothing in his hands before pulling a five-pound note from his right ear, which he had squashed up and placed under the wig before coming down the stairs. On that note, Tom left the room and urged everyone to start eating and the birthday cake would follow soon after. All the kids got up off the floor and pushed their way to the tables. The parents didn't get a look-in but from the expressions on their faces, that was just part of the course. They'd all clearly had past experience of children's parties. Tom wished he had too.

He retreated to the kitchen to find Geri had beaten him to it. If it weren't for the fact that Tom was dressed as a clown and she had seen him come in, he would've tried to sneak back out. It was clear that Geri was beginning to have serious intentions about them and Tom was getting nervous about being in her company. He was very glad that Scarlett couldn't make it to the party after all. This would have been one predicament even he couldn't have escaped from.

'That was a very nice show you put on in there, Mr Clown.'

She sat behind the kitchen table and had obviously had a glass or three of his whisky. The bottle was in her right hand and her left hand was beckoning Tom towards her. He moved to the table, gingerly. No sudden movements. In a matter of thirty minutes, their relationship had changed course. She was the cat and Tom was the mouse. He had to be careful. He sat opposite her and he could tell that she was under the influence of the whisky. Her head lolled, ever so slightly, back and forth and her eyelids were almost closed. Suddenly she swept her left arm across the table clearing it of plastic plates and napkins. She dropped the bottle and threw herself across the table. The momentum pushed her face into Tom's and he was forced back into his chair. Her lips squashed tight up against his. Her eyes were shut tight. Tom could tell because his were wide open in sheer panic and surprise. She moved her lips around on his as he tried to wriggle out of the situation. His resistance only encouraged her and she pressed her lips harder, her tongue trying to find entry into Tom's mouth. He finally managed to free his arms that had been trapped between his body and hers with his hands in a compromising position. Just as Tom took hold of her head to push her away, the kitchen door flew open.

It was Linda.

'Oh, my goodness! Tom, I'm so sorry!' she said as she tried frantically to pull Geri off him and into a chair.

She was sorry? What had she to be sorry about?

'It's okay! Nothing happened,' Tom lied.

Geri flopped into the chair and let her head fall onto the table. She moaned a little.

'I should have known this might happen,' said Linda. 'You being the only man here and her desperate for...well, you know, and an open bottle of whisky. It was a calamity waiting to happen. I shouldn't have let her out of my sight.'

Tom was confused.

'What are you on about? Nothing happened. She just fell across the table. It was all very innocent.'

'Tom, you don't need to cover for her. She's been like this ever since her husband left her. She's been trying to get off with any man she could get her claws into.' She checked over her shoulder that no one was coming in. 'She's got a problem, you see.'

'Yeah, she can't control her drink!' Tom said.

'No! It's a sex thing.'

Tom looked at her, still confused. 'What do you mean?'

'She's a nymphomaniac, Tom. She feels she needs to have sex as often as possible.'

Tom couldn't believe his ears. For the past two weeks, he had been leading on a nymphomaniac.

'She's been coming to my therapy sessions for the past couple of months and I thought we were beginning to make progress, but evidently not!'

Tom tried to cover his tracks.

'But nothing happened, Linda. She just kissed me. We haven't had...y'know. Just lunch and coffee. There was no sex. Definitely no sex. I would have remembered had there been sex. She never mentioned anything about to me about sex.'

'What are you talking about, Tom? Lunch? Coffee?'

She obviously hadn't cottoned on that Geri and Tom had met before, and he had nearly put his foot in it. Tom backtracked.

'It's dribble. I'm talking dribble. I'm just a bit shook up, that's all.'

'Well, don't worry. We'll sort her out soon enough. She got offered a new job today so maybe that'll help.' She began to lift up the plates and napkins. 'Tell you what, you take in the birthday cake and I'll sort her out. When you've done that perhaps you could come back and help carry her out to my car and I'll take her home.'

'Sure. Probably best. Take her home I mean.' Tom shuffled around for a moment before composing himself and then lit the candle on the cake. Linda boiled the kettle to make Geri a cup of coffee while Tom escaped to the comfort of the sitting room.

He opened the door of the sitting room and began to sing 'Happy Birthday'. Everyone joined in and one of the ladies lifted Jasper from the playpen and set him in the middle of the room. He gurgled happily, as Tom carefully lowered the cake in front of him. When they had all finished singing and cheering, Polly and Ralph both leaned over Jasper and blew out the candle for him. He clapped his hands and gurgled again. Tom left it for someone else to cut the cake and put slices into the party bags before trotting back to the kitchen where Geri was still in a different world but able to drink the coffee Linda had made.

'I'll go and put Alex and Mark in my car. Keep an eye on her for a minute, will you, Tom?'

'Er, yeah,' he said reluctantly.

She left and Tom heard her call for the boys. Geri opened her eyes and laughed aloud. She waved her finger at Tom to come over to her. Tom did, but kept a safe distance of about four yards away from her. She blew him a kiss and then giggled like a schoolgirl. She snorted so much that some snot flew out of her nose onto the table.

'Oh, Tom. Darling Tom. Can I ask you something?' she managed to say.

'Yes? What?'

'Does this mean our dinner engagement for next week is off?'

'I'm afraid so,' Tom replied.

'Oh well. I'm sorry.'

Tom finally took some responsibility. It was easier when she was drunk.

'No, Geri. I'm sorry!'

Tom could tell she didn't know what he meant, but he didn't think it necessary to explain. Linda came rushing back in. 'Right, madam. Let's get you home. Alex can stay with us tonight.'

The two of them tried to carry Geri to the front door, but Tom found it easier on his own. He lifted her into his arms and Linda went on out ahead of them. Tom stepped out onto the top step and stopped. Scarlett was getting out of Sylvia's car and her facial expression was one of bewilderment. Geri's face was dropped backward over Tom's arm, so he tipped his left arm up a bit to make her head roll into his chest. Her hair was just long enough to cover her face. Tom had on enough make-up to hide his shame. He didn't know why he wanted to hide her face. It wasn't as if Scarlett would ever see her again. He hoped. He began walking again as Scarlett hobbled toward him.

'Tom, what on earth is going on? What's happened to her?' She was nodding at Geri.

He kept on walking towards Linda's car. 'Too much party spirit. Linda's taking her home.'

'At a kid's party? Daft woman!'

Tom set Geri into the back seat and did up her seat belt. He thanked Linda for her help and she promised she wouldn't say anything to Scarlett. 'Patient confidentiality and all that. I didn't really have much choice in telling you, but please keep it to yourself if you don't mind, Tom.'

'No fear of that, Linda. Oh, the party bags. Let me get two for Alex and Mark.'

'Don't worry, Tom. They're both a bit young for party bags anyway. To be honest I think they've had enough rich food for a while. Those chilli crisps went down Mark's throat like there was no tomorrow. Bye!'

'Bye, Linda! Bye, Geri!'

Geri groaned again as Tom closed the door and waved.

'I don't recognise her,' said Scarlett.

'Oh, no-one special. A client of Linda's.'

'Of Linda's? Blimey! So that's what a nymph looks like. She must have been here to try and see if she could control herself around a sexy, strong man, like you.' She grabbed hold of Tom's right bicep and squeezed.

'Oh, please,' Tom laughed. 'She couldn't have been more polite!'

Scarlett let her coat drop on the floor as she walked through the door and headed towards the kitchen. The last thing Tom wanted was a full-scale argument about a kitchen fire, so he coaxed her into the sitting room to say hello to some of her friends. People were getting ready to leave and Tom quickly finished off preparing the party bags, filling them to the brim with the goodies he had purchased earlier in the day. Each party bag had lots of sweets, a pad of stickers, a badge, and a piece of cake and, of course, a packet of gum with collectible cards. Tom had bought twice the amount of gum packets that he needed so he could treat himself later. That evening he had planned to eat all of them to see what his collector's cards consisted of. As the children left, he handed them a bag each and reminded them that if they wanted to swap anything, they could get their parents to call him. It was as Tom closed the front door behind the last guest that Scarlett screamed.

'What have you done? My kitchen's ruined.'

'Oh, don't exaggerate!'

'Exaggerate! Tom, you have ruined my kitchen.'

'It's my kitchen too. In fact I spend more time in here these days, so if anyone should be annoyed, it should be me!'

'I just can't trust you with anything, can I? A simple party is all that I ask and I come home to find a drunken nymphomaniac in your arms, you dressed up like a transsexual clown and my house in tatters. Would you please give me the space to be angry and upset?'

'Well, I'm sorry if things didn't go the way you were planning. Perhaps if you were here in the first place then none of this would have happened.'

'Oh, so it's my fault, is it? I wondered how long it would take before you shifted the blame to me. For your information I was at a very important meeting trying to convince the Board that some changes you had proposed would be for the benefit of the department.'

'Oh yeah? And did you?'

'Yes, of course I did, but only because I'm a woman. They wouldn't have understood it from a man's point of view so it had to be me.'

'So you think you're doing a better job than me, eh?'

'Couldn't be difficult, the proposed budget cuts you made were skewed. If I hadn't rearranged them a little, the Board wouldn't have gone along with them.'

'Fine. If you're happy doing my job, then just leave me to do yours.'

'But that's just it; it's not a job, Tom, its life. I'm not a Board of Directors you have to prove anything to and the children aren't the staff who you have to keep satisfied when you make a difficult decision. This is more important than any job, Tom!' Scarlett's voice dropped. 'I just worry I've left you to cope with too much.'

'I can cope.'

'Can you?'

Tom had to think about it. 'Yes, I can. But I still wish you were here with me.'

'I wish I was too, Tom.'

'Do you? Really?'

She reached out her arms for a hug, so Tom obliged.

'Of course I do, it's just not practical, is it?'

'No, I guess not.' Tom gave her a big hug. 'The quicker you get that plaster off, the better.'

'I know.'

Polly and Ralph arrived at the door.

'Do you think they heard us?' Tom asked.

'Probably.'

Scarlett called them over and told them to stand up on the chairs.

'How about a hug?' she asked.

They both smiled and threw their arms around Scarlett. Ralph told Tom to join them. It was lovely. It was like a big family huggle and then Ralph spoke.

'Uncle Tom?'

'Yes Ralph?'

'Can I have a party bag too?'

'Of course. I should have given you one earlier.'

Tom lifted Polly and Ralph down and gave them a bag each and they ran off into the sitting room to open them.

'Looks like they all went down a treat. What did you put in them?'

'Oh, the usual stuff,' Tom said taking a seat. 'Cake, stickers, sweets, gum.'

'Gum?' Scarlett asked in disbelief.

'Yeah. Why? I used to get gum with collectors cards when I was a kid.'

'Not when you were only four or five, for goodness sake. What kind of message are you trying to give the youth of today?' She laughed at him as Tom pulled out a few packets of the gum to open for himself.

'But it's fun. You get free cards in the packets and you swap with your friends.'

'What kind of cards?'

'Oh, all sorts. Football players, sports cars, cartoon characters. Stuff like that.'

'So what have you got in these packs.'

'Don't know. The guy in the shop said these were special collectible ones which is why they're unmarked.'

'Well open one and find out. I'm going to the loo.'

Scarlett left the kitchen as Tom opened the first packet. He did think it strange that the packets had no pictures on them, as how were you supposed to know what was in them? He ripped off the cellophane, pulled out a piece of gum, shoved it in his mouth, and began to chew. Nice flavour. Tom pulled the card out slowly between his thumb and forefinger and closed his eyes. He always did that as a kid to lengthen the anticipation. He pulled the card right out and turned the picture side towards him. Tom opened his eyes and the huge grin that was on his face suddenly dropped. He couldn't believe his eyes. He grabbed another packet of gum from the bag and ripped it open, quickly. He removed the card and saw the same picture, well almost the same, as the one on the first card. He grabbed the bag of gum packets and furiously ripped open the third and the fourth and fifth and carried on until he'd opened them all and was totally shocked to find the same kind of card in every pack. Tom pushed his chair back and covered his mouth with his hands. He couldn't believe what he was looking at. Now he knew why the packets were unmarked and what Barry meant when he said that Tom wasn't too old for them.

Scarlett came back in. 'So what kind of cards are they?'

Her eyes fell on the kitchen table and she gasped as she took in the sight of the cards.

'Don't tell me you put *them* in the party...' She choked on the last word.

'I didn't know. How could I have known?' Tom was reaching paranoia.

Scarlett looked back at the cards. 'They're naked. They're all naked, Tom.'

'I know. I know.' Tom began to chew his nails.

'All those children have got them.'

'I know. What am I going to do?'

'We'll just have to get them back.'

Suddenly, there was a heavy thumping on the front door, followed by a persistent ringing of the bell. The letterbox flap banged open. 'Open, this door, Farrow, you little pervert!' It was Karen Jackson's husband. 'We know you're in there, so you better open up!'

'He said 'we'. He said 'we'. There's more than one of them.'

Tom was frantic. He didn't know whether to run and hide or face them like a man and explain what had happened. Yes, he did. He ran to the kitchen cupboard as Scarlett made her way to the front door.

'What are you doing, woman? They'll kill me!'

'Look, calm down. I'll open the door and you can tell them it wasn't your fault – they'll understand.' She reached the front door. She was as cool as a cucumber.

'They won't understand, they won't! They'll kill me, I'm telling you! Scarlett! Scarlett!'

They didn't understand and they did kill Tom. Well, not quite. Scarlett managed to get through to some of the parents just as Brad Jackson finished flattening the bumps out of a chopping board with Tom's head. Prior to that Tom spent a full minute with his head in a sink of water, with only two pull-ups for fresh air. When he finally got enough breath to tell him it wasn't his fault he then moved to the chopping board to get the name and address of the shop where he'd bought the gum. All twelve parents left appeased, but with the promise that they'd be back if his story didn't fit. Scarlett slammed the door behind them and put across the deadbolt.

'They won't be bothering us again. Now would you like a drink?'

'No thanks. I'll just wait until I go out later.'

'Later?'

'Yes, I'm meeting up with Sam and the boys down the pub, and after today I could do with a pint.'

Scarlett scowled at him. 'Oh you are, are you?'

Tom wasn't in the mood to be frowned upon, so Tom scowled back.

'Yes, I am. And no-one is going to stop me, not even you.'

Scarlett was a bit shaken by the anger in his voice.

'Whoah, easy tiger! I won't wait up for you then.'

'Don't then!'

'I won't!'

'Good!'

'Good!'

Maynard Tait

16

Scarlett didn't wait up that night. Tom fell onto the porch at about one twenty in the morning so he wasn't too surprised. The climb up the stairs and the thought of undressing himself quietly in the dark was too much for him. Instead, he crawled into the sitting room and into the playpen for the rest of the night. If it was good enough for babies then it was good enough for a drunk who didn't know any better.

The next morning Tom was disturbed from his slumber by the piercing sun, as Scarlett opened the curtains at lightning speed. The torture had begun. It was inevitable really. Tom hadn't had a night out with the boys for months and as expected, it proved too much for his stomach and his brain cells. Scarlett knew as much and was going to punish him further for not thinking about the consequences well in advance. Tom watched her walk to the Grandfather clock, which stood in the corner of the room, and flick the switch inside it that turned on the mechanism to allow the bell to strike as the clock passed the hour. As his brain was working a little slower than normal, it took him a few seconds too late to realise why. The hammer struck the bell with an almighty force that would not only wake the dead but send them packing as well. The noise whooshed through his eardrums and around his head before piercing into his temples. The pain was unbearable and for some insane reason, it pleased Scarlett. Tom clutched his ears with both hands to try to stop the banging but it continued until all seven strikes had completed. He could see Scarlett standing over him; arms folded like a schoolmistress trying to think of how to punish him next.

'Why don't you just shoot me in the head and get it over with?' Tom groaned.

'Because that would be too quick a death,' she shouted.

It sounded like shouting to him. She later told him it was just a whisper. Like Tom was going to believe that.

'It's time to get up. Alex and Jasper are awake and I don't want to bring them down here and see you like this.'

'They'll just think I'm tired.'

'Maybe, but I know otherwise, so shift!'

Tom swung his legs under him so he could pull himself up on the bar of the playpen.

'Just look at you, it's pitiful. One of these days you'll learn that when you go on a binge after a long period from abstaining you're going to wake up worse for wear.'

'Yeah, you're right, but when everyone's buying you drinks you don't say no, do you?'

'You would if you were sober in the first place.'

She helped Tom out of the playpen and pushed him upstairs to the bathroom. She took off his clothes and shoved him into the shower. 'And don't come out until you've lost that smell of stale smoke and kebabs!'

It's funny how hearing just one word can spin the world around you and make you lose all control of your gut. Tom wasn't going to make it to the toilet in time, so Scarlett shut the door of the shower just in the nick of time to stop her from being covered in regurgitated lamb and salad.

'And make sure you clean in there properly as well!'

What a morning. The rest of the day wasn't much fun either. It was extremely hot and the heat aggravated Tom's sensitive condition. Scarlett had some work to do on her laptop, so Tom was to keep watch of the children while they played in the garden. Sunday of that weekend wasn't up to much either. Scarlett went to church again with the babies, but left the twins with Tom. She had a good time and a nice chat with the Vicar. Tom was bounced on, trampled, punched, and stabbed and that was just from playing soldiers. He was glad they weren't doing it for real. When he asked if they could do something else less violent Ralph snapped back at him. 'Why can't you be like my Daddy?'

Tom would never forgive himself for the reply he gave him. 'If I was more like your Daddy, I'd be miles away from you two brats having a good time. If he's any sense he'll stay where he is and never come back!'

Ralph walked off in a sulk and Tom couldn't believe how callous he had just been.

It was the following Monday when the lives of the twins would change forever. They'd all had a good night's sleep and Alex didn't wake up until seven twenty, which gave Scarlett and Tom an extra three quarters of an hour to sleep. They felt better for it and they even managed to have breakfast eaten before the twins began to stir. It was eight forty-five when the telephone rang and Tom was just about to take the babies to Maud's and then the twins to the swimming pool.

Scarlett was waiting in the hallway for Sylvia to arrive. Scarlett picked up the receiver and said hello. But that was all she said. She just listened to the person who was talking at the other end of the line. She had her back to Tom so he couldn't see her reaction to the news she had just heard but he sensed it was bad. She replaced the receiver and turned around. Tears rolled down her cheeks and she took a deep breath to hold back her emotions.

'Honey, what is it? What's wrong?'

She looked at the twins and put her hand to her mouth as she began to cry. She turned her back and Tom told Polly and Ralph to go into the sitting room for a minute. Tom made sure the door was closed so they couldn't hear Scarlett crying. She turned and wept further upon looking at Jasper.

'Scarlett, tell me what's wrong. Please.'

She wiped her eyes with a tissue before speaking.

'It's Nick – Jackie's husband.'

'What? What about him?'

Tom felt he knew, but he had to ask.

'He's dead.'

'Dead? But...how? When?'

Tom knew the questions weren't important, but it helped to understand.

'He was killed during a live ammunition training exercise yesterday. One of the ships gun turrets exploded and Nick was caught in the blast along with another officer. They died instantly.'

'Oh dear Lord.'

Tom felt physically sick. His immediate thought was of Jasper. As Scarlett and Tom held each other, he sat in his buggy blissfully unaware of the immense change his father's death would cause to his life. Tom thought of Polly and Ralph, sitting in the other room, waiting for him to call them to come outside. His stomach churned as he recalled the cruel words he said to Ralph the day before. How evil his thoughts had been. They stood for a moment unsure of what they should do next. It was Jackie's consultant who phoned them, so she was obviously aware of the situation. How must Jackie be feeling? Did she want them to tell her children about their father?

'The doctor said we should wait for a call from Jackie's mother. He called her immediately after telling Jackie about Nick and he said she took the news very badly. He had to sedate her, she became hysterical and overwrought.'

'So what do we say to the twins? They'll want to know why we're not going swimming. What do I tell them?'

The phone rang again. Scarlett answered and indicated that it was Jackie's mother calling from Ireland. As she talked, Tom undid the straps on Jasper's buggy and lifted him out. He cuddled him and thought how sad it was that neither of his parents could be at his first birthday party and that his daddy wouldn't be at the next one or the next. A tear ran down his cheek and it fell onto Jasper's. He giggled and wiped his cheek with his hand. Scarlett said goodbye and put down the phone.

'She has asked that we tell Polly and Ralph about Nick. She'll fly over tomorrow morning and stay at Jackie's house while she sorts everything out. Nick's family has asked for a civil burial as opposed to a regimental. Apparently they were against him joining the Navy and are blaming them for his death, so the funeral will be held here in Frankfield on Wednesday at noon.'

Tom handed Jasper over to Scarlett.

'I'd better go in and tell them then.'

Deep down, he wished that Scarlett had offered to tell them, but somehow Tom felt obligated. The following few minutes were the hardest Tom had ever had to endure and never wanted to repeat. He had often watched news reports about the deaths and murders of people and always felt sorry for the ones who had to break the news to the relatives, especially the children. Now he knew how it felt. Choosing the words that would make them understand was not the hardest thing, it was seeing their sad faces as the news sunk in was. Tom felt as though he was the one who had taken their father away. He was only bringing them the terrible news, but yet, he felt guilty. After a few minutes, Scarlett came into the room to help comfort them. Neither Polly nor Ralph cried heavily. It was as if they still hadn't fully registered what Tom had said. After all, they were only four years old. They were too young to understand. Tom had just prayed that he had said the right words.

Maud came later that morning to take Alex and Jasper for the rest of the day.

It made no sense for Jasper to stay with them. He had no idea who his father was, let alone understand that he had died. He could be with Maud and Alex and be himself. Scarlett called Craig, told him of the situation, and asked that he look after things for a few days while they waited to find out about Jackie and if she could leave the hospital. The morning dragged on and on as they waited for Jackie's call. The twins sat in front of the television watching videos Tom had borrowed from the library. It may have been the hottest day of the year, but neither Scarlett nor Tom felt it right to force them to play outside if they didn't want to. It was lunchtime before they heard from Jackie. Scarlett took the call and was on the phone for over an hour. Tom made the twins pizza for lunch and only Ralph managed to touch his. They were both miserable and not surprisingly, pining for their mum. Scarlett came into the kitchen as the twins left to go and watch more telly. She closed the door after them to keep them from hearing the conversation.

'So? How's Jackie?'

'Not good. Apparently, she was doing very well with her treatment but this has just knocked her right back. There was the possibility she could've been allowed home this weekend to see how she would cope. Not anymore.'

'What about the funeral? Is she going to be able to go?'

'Yes, she'll be there. Her doctor will come with her. At first he wasn't sure about letting her out, but he believes she'll cope pretty well and he feels it necessary for the children to see her even for a short while.'

Tom thought of the twins. 'I just hope the kids can cope.'

The next forty-eight hours was a waiting period. Nothing got done. Nothing happened. They just waited. The morning of the funeral was a very tense time for everyone concerned. Scarlett and Tom were particularly worried about Polly and Ralph, and how they would react when they saw Jackie. Would they be able to let her go at the end of the day? Would Jackie let them? They arrived at Jackie's house at about eleven am. It seemed fair to let the children see there mum in their usual surroundings than at a morbid church full of unfamiliar faces. Jackie's mum answered the door and immediately fell on her knees and hugged Polly and Ralph. She began to sob loudly, but still held onto the children.

'Now listen. Your mummy's in the living room waiting for you. I want you to put on big smiles and run in there and give her a huge hug, okay?'

The twins easily understood her heavy Irish brogue and they both squeezed past their grandmother and ran inside. Tom helped her up onto her feet and introduced Scarlett and himself.

'Oh, you are the best two friends anyone could ever have. Please come in. Please.' She stood back and outstretched her arm to guide them into the hallway. She closed the door, turned towards Scarlett, and gave her shoulders a squeeze as she kissed her gently on the cheek.

'And you, Tom. What a lovely man you must be to give up so much for a friend in need.'

'It's okay. I'm glad we can help.'

So much guilt, sorrow, and anger ran through him. Tom couldn't get out of his head the words he'd said to Ralph last Sunday and hearing praise and thanks from others made him feel worse. He'd wanted to say something to someone, to apologise. Scarlett had told him it would do nothing to talk about it. The family was grieving and his feelings were not important or even valid to them right now. She was right. Tom knew it but who could forgive him. Tom felt he needed forgiveness.

'I'm Siobhan,' said the lady. 'I think we should leave Jackie and the children alone for a few minutes. Come into the kitchen and I'll make some tea.'

'I'll make it for you, Siobhan, please,' said Scarlett.

'Oh, don't be daft. Look at you with your crutches. Now behave and sit yourself down. I've a feeling you haven't been able to rest up for quite a while, what with your own family to contend with.'

'Well, that's true, but it hasn't been as hard as I'd thought it would be.'

Tom gave her an incredulous look. It was only because she hadn't been around. Tom was the one taking the flack.

'And as Tom said, we're only too glad to help. Jackie needed friends and well, we couldn't say no, could we, Tom?'

For a moment, Tom thought about giving his first reply, but then thought about the circumstances and gave his honest one instead. 'Course not. It's been a...a very emotional time for everyone.'

Siobhan poured the tea and sat down. They drank in silence. A few minutes later Scarlett and Tom went in to see Jackie. They opened the sitting room door and saw the twins sitting either side of their mother as she flicked through a photo album.

'And that's me and your dad on our Wedding day.'

'You look very pretty, mummy,' said Polly.

'Thank you, darling. When you grow up you're going to be even prettier.'

She reached down, kissed Polly on the head, and asked the two of them to stand up.

'Why don't you two go and ask Granny to butter some scones for later and see if you can help her?'

'Okay!'

They left the room and Jackie got up and gave Scarlett a long hug as she burst into tears. Tom felt he should leave them alone and he made a move to the door.

'No, Tom,' said Jackie. 'Please stay.' She was still embracing Scarlett as she smiled through her tears at him. 'You have no idea how much you two mean to me. I don't know what I would do without you.'

'It's okay,' said Scarlett. 'We're here for you, both of us.'

They all sat down and Jackie began to tell them of how she had felt when she heard about Nick. How she had gone from feeling more positive than she had for over a year back down to the depths of despair and all within a few seconds.

'I was doing so well,' she cried. 'I was getting used to the idea of being on my own with the kids for long periods of time and knowing that the few times I would see Nick were to be treasured and exciting times for all the family. Now I'll never see him again and I'll be on my own forever.'

Her crying got heavier and Tom felt he was invading her grief. Scarlett wrapped her arms around her again.

'Jackie, you will never be on your own. We will be here for you whenever you need us and for as long as you need us. Nick's family and yours will support you, you'll see.'

As Tom watched Jackie weep, he couldn't help but feel totally responsible for her children's welfare. It suddenly dawned on him that Scarlett and he were their foster parents, even if it was only temporary. Tom not only had responsibilities to Alex, his own son, but to them as well.

The funeral car arrived at eleven forty-five. Jackie had asked that Scarlett and Tom go with her, the children, and her mum. In the back seat of the car, Tom sat with Ralph on his knee while Jackie had Polly on hers. At first, Tom didn't think they should come to the funeral, but it was evident that Jackie needed them with her. They were the only things that seemed to keep her going that day. They were her comforters.

The service was short and concise. The small church was packed to its capacity. Over half of the congregation were Nick's colleagues. They were not dressed in uniform as a mark of respect to his family. They had made their feelings clear about no uniforms, but welcomed anyone and everyone who wanted to commemorate Nick's life. Tom watched Polly and Ralph throughout the service and they sat still and quiet the whole time.

Afterwards Jackie had arranged for anyone who wanted to, to come back to her house for some food. She wanted to thank everyone personally for coming and she would feel more comfortable if it were at her home. Scarlett and Tom helped pass round food and drinks while Jackie accepted condolences from family and friends. When everyone had been served, Tom managed to slip out to the back garden for a minute on his own. He was feeling claustrophobic and needed some air. He had just sat down by a flowerbed when his mobile phone began to vibrate. He thought he'd turned it off completely in fear of it chirping during the service and when Tom answered it, he wished he had.

'Tom! It's Geri!'

'Geri?' She surprised him. Tom looked around to check that no one had followed him out. 'Hi! How did you get this number? I thought I only gave you my home number.'

'You did, but I really needed to speak to you about my behaviour last week, so I drove over to your house this morning to see you, but you weren't in.'

'You went to my house?'

'Yes. Luckily, you're postman was delivering your second post. I was walking back to my car and he asked if he could help.'

'My postman?'

'Yes! Sam isn't it?'

'Yes! Sam!'

'Well, he told me he was a mate of yours and he gave me your mobile number. Didn't hesitate. He was very helpful.'

'I bet he was,' Tom whispered.

'Pardon?'

'Nothing. Look, Geri, this isn't a good time. I really think we should talk later – if we have to.'

'Okay, how about I come over later and...'

'No! No. I'll call you later and we can talk then. Okay?'

'Fine. I'll be waiting for your call.'

'Whatever, Geri. Bye.'

'Jerry? What did he want?'

It was Scarlett. She scared the life out of Tom and he dropped his phone as he jumped around to face her.

'Scarlett! It's you!'

'Yes, it's me. What did Jerry want?'

'Oh, just to talk about a personal problem. Nothing important.'

'Oh, a man thing, eh?'

'Sort of.'

She sat down on the wall and dropped her crutches. 'Oh, I'll be so happy when I lose these things, they're such a nuisance. So, have you invited Jerry to dinner yet?'

Oh-oh! He'd really hoped she'd forgotten about that. Fat chance! Scarlett has the memory of an elephant.

'Well, I did, but it was for tonight, so I had to cancel, what with the funeral and everything. I thought it would be a bit much to have guests afterwards.'

'You're right. Some other time perhaps.'

'Perhaps.'

Tom called Geri that evening just after Scarlett had gone to bed. He was in the sitting room pretending to watch a documentary about extinct animals that may have resurfaced in the hidden jungles of the Congo.

'Hi, it's Tom.'

'At last, I was beginning to think you weren't going to call. I've just got into bed. Want to come over and join me?'

'Geri, you know I can't.'

'I know. All those children. A lovely man like you weighed down by kids. It must feel like you've a millstone around your neck.'

'Well, not really actually. Some parents accept their responsibilities, unlike others.'

'Yeah, well, that's why I needed to talk. Tom, I'm so sorry about last week. I don't know what came over me? Must have been the whisky.'

'Geri, you don't have to lie. Look, Linda told me about your problem.' There was a silence from Geri's end. 'Geri? Geri?'

'She had no right to tell you. How dare she?'

'She had no choice. You were practically lying on top of me chewing the lips of my face.'

'And what beautiful lips they are too.'

'Geri, pack it in.'

'Sorry! Look, I'm sorry I lied. I didn't know what to do. If I'd told you about my problem when we met would you have met me again? No, you wouldn't. Men dream of having a woman like me with a high sexual drive. They think it's like owning a high performance sports car. Only, when they get behind the wheel for the first time they realise it's beyond their control, so they resort back to their basic model and only look at the car of their dreams and don't touch.'

'That's why Stephen left, isn't it?'

'Yes. He felt he wasn't in control of the relationship, I was. He couldn't keep up so he left.'

'I'm sorry, but there's something I need to tell you.'

'Look, whatever it is, forget it. I'm sorry I lead you on or upset you. Perhaps when I finally get over all this we can try again.'

'I really can't see that happening, Geri.'

Tom really was sorry. He knew he was at fault as much as she was, if not more!

'Well, let's just see what happens, eh? Goodbye, Tom.'

'Bye!'

17

The day after Nick's funeral Jackie returned to the hospital accompanied by her doctor and her mother. It was a difficult farewell as the children wanted to stay with her and explaining that they wouldn't see her again for another few weeks made things worse. To try to cheer them up Tom took them to the shopping mall and promised he would buy them any toy they wanted. It seemed to do the trick. Polly returned home with a rag doll and Ralph with the biggest box of Scalextric that he could find. Tom realised too late that he should have put a monetary limit on the cost of their chosen toy but he had to admit he wanted to play with the electric-powered cars himself, so he didn't make a scene. That afternoon Tom went up to the attic and cleared away all the old boxes of rubbish that Scarlett had collected for years. She didn't mind in the end, as they were full of junk that didn't have any sentimental or monetary value – except for a porcelain doll that was given to her by her Grandmother before she died. Monetary value – two thousand and three hundred pounds. Sentimental value – priceless! Tom would spend the next few years of his life searching for a replica.

Tom dusted down the attic and laid a few new floorboards. He fitted a couple of extra lights to help brighten up the dark space. By teatime, he had turned the attic into the Grand Prix circuit of Monaco complete with slopes and hills made from foam sheets he had bought from a DIY store. The water feature was an old blow-up paddling pool that Scarlett used as a child. Posters of famous drivers covered the walls and Tom even rooted out his tape cassette of the 'Top One Hundred Racing Noises' and put it into a previously unused cassette player. He always knew it would come in useful one day. He waited until Alex and Jasper had been put to bed before showing the twins what he had been doing all afternoon. When Ralph came up the ladder, he couldn't believe his eyes. He clambered into the attic and started jumping up and down on the relatively loose floorboards. Tom was almost as excited as he was. Ralph dropped to the ground and picked up the controls.

'Let's race! Let's race!' he shouted happily.

Scarlett helped Polly up the ladder and she gasped when she saw what Tom had done.

'You are a genius, Mr Farrow.'

'I do try, Mrs Farrow.'

She blew him a kiss and Tom reciprocated.

'Can I play?' asked Polly.

'Of course you can. Here, take this control.'

Tom counted them down from three and as soon as he said 'Go', they were off. The twins laughed and laughed as their cars flew around the track and they didn't stop until almost nine pm. It was terrific to see them so happy after such a horrible few days.

During that weekend, Scarlett and Tom had agreed that they should get out of the house as much as possible to let the children enjoy the beautiful weather. On the Saturday, they took them all to an adventure park. Alex and Jasper were obviously too little to go on any rides, but Tom did take Alex onto a miniature carousel. Jasper had eaten too much ice cream at lunchtime and Scarlett didn't want to risk him throwing up on anyone, so he just watched from the comfort of his buggy. The twins went on everything that wasn't height restricted. They had a whale of a time. Afterwards, they took them swimming at a huge indoor water park. They were very grateful that there was a separate paddling pool that had extra supervision so they could let the twins go there, while Scarlett and Tom took Alex and Jasper into a larger pool. Tom found it hard to relax completely though. He kept an eye on the twins throughout, regardless of the superb supervision they were under. Alex giggled and laughed as he splashed in the water. They took it in turns to lay him on their front as they swam across the pool. Jasper was a bit nervous of the water at first, but when Scarlett put a floating ring around him, he seemed happy enough.

On that Sunday, they made a family trip to church. They made sure they were early this time and sat in a pew that was right at the back of the church. Tom was not going to have a repeat of the last time they came. People were very friendly and several people did come over to say hello and welcome them. Reverend Croft sat with them for a few minutes just before the service to talk over some minor details about Alex's Christening. He obviously wasn't nervous about his sermon. Tom was, especially after the bible reading which was from Matthew chapter five. Tom winced as the reader read 'But I say to you that everyone who looks at a woman with lustful intent has already committed adultery with her in his heart.' Tom didn't hear any other words after that and he could have sworn that the lady doing the reading was looking at him the whole way through that verse.

'Okay, okay!' he prayed. 'I'll sort it out, I promise.'

They had lunch at Maud's after the service. She had prepared a magnificent feast that would have fed the four thousand. Luckily, Tom was there to empty all the dishes of their contents and he spent most of the afternoon fast asleep on the couch.

The following couple of weeks passed quite by quickly, but thankfully, without any fires, car crashes, or beatings. Scarlett tried to spend as little time as she could manage at the office that fortnight to try to help Tom out a little more at home. She did bring a lot of work home with her though which Tom carried on with in the evenings. Time was moving on and he felt as though he wasn't doing enough to secure the promotion. Scarlett did reassure him that there was nothing to worry about; that Craig and Howard had been 'working their butts off' for the last month in the hope that Tom would get the job. He knew they both had their own interests at heart, which was why they had been working so hard, but Tom did fully appreciate what they were doing for him, and for Scarlett. Everyone needs friends in times of trouble and they were two of the best. Tom wasn't looking forward to the decision he would have to make if he did become Director.

One afternoon George popped by with an order of meat Tom had made. He knocked on the door just as Tom switched on the kettle.

'Hi, Tom. Thought I'd pop round personally with your order and to see how the househusband is getting on. I've thrown in some more of that venison, seeing as you liked it so much.'

'Aw, thanks, George. Come on through. It's only the twins and me again today. They're in the sitting room doing jigsaw puzzles. Maud's still happy to look after the babies.'

'She's a real diamond, that Maud,' said George.

'Yes, she is. We'd be lost without her.'

George followed Tom and sat down at the kitchen table as Tom prepared a pot of fresh coffee. They sat and chatted for quite some time about the past couple of weeks and then suddenly, without warning, George burst into tears. At first, Tom didn't know where to look or what to say. His head fell onto the table and he wept and wept. This was very out of character for George. He prided himself on being a very jolly yet stoic man. He had always said it was bad for business to show emotions in front of customers. Tom was a customer, what was George playing at? Tom was also a friend, so he tried to find out what was wrong.

'George, come on. What's the matter? Is it work?' Tom was stabbing in the dark. He had to; George wasn't helping him out here. 'Is it money problems? Are you short of cash?'

He shook his head sideways. Perhaps it was his eldest sons. Two of them had already spent time in prison for theft and arson; they were the bane of his life!

'What about your boys, is it family trouble again?'

'No.'

What was left? Tom tried to think of what was important to him. The only things Tom could think of that George craved and loved more than anything were food and women. He was quite a hefty man and Tom thought that maybe he'd been told he had to go on a diet due to an illness he'd just found out about. That would certainly upset him.

'Your health, is it your health?'

No.

'Your liver? Kidneys? Your eyes? What?'

No, again.

'Is it your heart? Too much cholesterol or something?'

Tom was very frustrated and getting bored at playing guessing games.

'Oh, will you stop blubbing and tell me what it is, for crying out loud.'

He stopped blubbing briefly to lift his head high enough for Tom to see his eyes and mumbled something that Tom couldn't quite hear.

'Sorry George, I didn't hear you.'

'I said…I'm in…love,' he said before the blubbing began again.

His reply knocked Tom for six. George? In love? This was Frankfield's answer to Russell Brand sitting here. How could he be in love?

'What do you mean 'in love'?' Tom asked. 'With whom? And why are you crying about it? Surely this is a good thing.'

'I've never felt this way before, Tom,' he cried. 'I feel like every relationship before now has been a sham. I'm in an emotional turmoil.'

Tom had no idea how to deal with this.

'Well, it's never too late to turn things around, so look on the bright side. You're proof that there's always a chance of change and for good things to happen, no matter what stage of life we're at.'

George lifted his head and slowly the sobbing stopped.

'You're so right Tom. Forget the past, look to the future, eh?'

'Er…yes, I guess so.'

George stood up and rested his large hands on his hips.

'Thank you Tom. You're so wise. Now I need to go and tell my new love how I really feel.'

He turned and headed toward the front door.

'So,' said Tom. 'Aren't you going to tell me who this amazing lady is then?'

'All in good time Tom. All in good time.'

And as fast as he had answered he was out the door and gone.

'Strange,' uttered Tom. 'Very strange.'

Maynard Tait

18

'It's August eighteenth. Don't you have an appointment with the leg doctor today?' Tom was shaving when he noticed the date circled on the calendar. They have two calendars in the house, one belonged to Scarlett, and the other was Tom's. Like any normal person, Tom would write on his to tell him what he was to do on a specific day. Scarlett just puts a circle around the day and uses different coloured pens to indicate different things. She had circled the eighteenth in red, which Tom knew to be a health colour. Tom put two and two together and assumed it was to do with her leg.

'Ah...Yes! I do. It's this afternoon at four o'clock. Could you drive me there?'

'Sure. Maud hasn't had the twins for a while. She won't mind having them for a couple of hours.'

'Great.'

She joined Tom in the bathroom and sat on the edge of the bath. He carried on shaving and he could see her smiling at him through the mirror. She never did this. She knew Tom hated distractions while he was shaving.

'You've really enjoyed having the twins and Jasper here, haven't you?'

'Well, it's been an experience, I can tell you. I suppose I have laughed more than I've cried over the past few weeks. Why do you ask?'

'Oh, no reason. I just want to know if you'd do it again.'

Tom dropped his razor and it took a slice of his chin with it. 'Ow!'

She knew Tom didn't like distractions!

'Scarlett, you haven't agreed to take on more kids, have you?'

'No! Don't be silly. But you have enjoyed having more children around?'

'Yeah, I guess I have. The twins have kept me on my toes and I think it's been good for Alex to have other kids around him.'

'Hmm!' she said with a smile.

She stood up, pinched his bum, and gave him a kiss on his wet face. 'You really are a sexy man, Tom Farrow.'

'Only because you make me sexy, Mrs Farrow.'

She left the bathroom and left him to wonder what she had just been on about while stemming the thin trickle of blood rolling from his chin.

Tom parked in Sylvia's parking space knowing that it would be empty. She had a half-day as she was going to Paris for the weekend with her sister and she had a mid-afternoon flight. Terry opened the door for him and made another joke at his expense – something about suspenders and a duster. Tom didn't quite hear all of it as the lift doors shut just before Tom heard him and the receptionist burst into fits of laughter.

Craig greeted him with a worn look on his face. Tom asked if he could bring Howard to his office to have a quick chat.

'So! What has Edward been up to the past few weeks?'

'I'm afraid things aren't looking too good.' said Howard. 'From the information we've been able to get out of Charlene, Edward has got practically all the Board in his pocket including Sir Wilfred.'

'What! But it can't be! Scarlett has said I've nothing to worry about. Why hasn't she told me any of this?'

'She didn't want you to worry. She believes she has it all under control. The Board have gone with the proposals she made; the staff seem happy even though they're working a little harder for no extra money and she trusts the Boards' better judgement.'

Howard seemed more stable than Craig did. Tom did need to correct one comment though. 'They were my proposals, excuse me. Scarlett just rearranged them.'

'Whatever,' he replied. 'They still worked.'

'Yeah, well. Just keep everything going as directed and keep your fingers crossed. How's Gilbert doing these days?'

Craig chirped up. 'Oh, he's good. Not doing much work though. He's been more than happy to let Scarlett make the day to day decisions.'

'Really!' Tom snapped. 'Sounds as though she's been doing a lot of decision making around here.'

'Only what she would expect you to do, Tom.'

'Maybe!'

Tom was growing more and more suspicious of Scarlett every day. Tom just wondered what she was playing at. It seemed to him she was planning for him to stay at home permanently, while she played at being Director. Tom thought if they had never met and got married, she'd be the one being offered the promotion anyway. She was bitter, that was it, she was bitter at his success. The thing was there wasn't anything Tom could do at this stage, except wait. That's why she was asking those questions this morning. She was going to blackmail him, emotionally, to stay at home with the children. Well, he would see about that, even if it meant a showdown at the eleventh hour.

The drive to the hospital was a quick one. All the roadwork that had been happening over the past couple of months had been completed and the traffic was back to normal. It meant Scarlett was over half an hour early for her appointment, so after helping her to the waiting room, Tom decided to pay a visit to Barry, the dodgy sweetie man. As Tom pulled up alongside the shop, he was surprised to see it boarded up. He got out of his car and walked up to the front door. There was no board on the door window so Tom peered through it into the darkness. He could see that all the shelves had been cleared, and the old wooden counter had been ripped apart and lay in pieces on the floor. The floor was covered with sweets that had obviously spilled from jars as they were removed from the shelves. The place was a mess. Tom felt quite sad. Not for Barry, not at all, but Barry's dad. The old man had been a symbol of this shop and it held happy memories for Tom. When he first entered the shop a couple of weeks ago, he became a child again. He had hoped that he would feel as he had felt years before and that he'd be able to bring Alex here in a few years' time to experience the same joy. It was a simple joy but worth having nonetheless. As he sighed, an elderly gentleman came and stood next to him. He looked very familiar but Tom couldn't place him.

'Sad, isn't it?' he said.

'Yes, it is. Very.'

'He only had it for two years and during that short time he made a mockery of his own father's lifetime work.'

'You knew the old man?' Tom asked.

'Yes, I knew him,' he replied with a smile. 'He was my brother. Jim bought this shop in nineteen forty-nine, for nearly fifty years he served every child who lived within a two-mile radius of the place, and they were only the ones who walked here. People came from miles around knowing that whichever piece of candy they were looking for, they would find it here. He made this shop a little paradise for everyone with a sweet tooth.'

Tom sniggered. 'Yeah, me included. I used to come every Saturday to spend my pocket money. He would sit on a stool by the counter and read his paper while I shuffled up and down every aisle trying to decide what to buy. Those were the days.'

'Yup. And now they're gone.'

The two of them stood side by side and smiled at the vacant shop as they both relived their past.

'How I wish it could be what it once was,' Tom said.

Scarlett was standing at the entrance to the hospital as Tom pulled up to collect her.

'Where have you been? I've been waiting here for over an hour. My appointment only lasted fifteen minutes.'

'I'm so sorry. I went to see someone.'

'Who?'

'Oh, no-one you know. So, how's the leg?'

Scarlett giggled. 'It's great! The doctor reckons I can have the plaster off next Friday.'

'Terrific! That means I could go back to work the following Monday.'

'Well, he did say I would have to take it easy for a week or so, so it's probably best if I carry on at the office, until we go away for the weekend at least.'

Tom couldn't disagree with the consultant. 'Okay, if it's for the best.'

'It is.' She giggled again. 'It's great to know I won't have to hobble around on crutches while we're away in the New Forest.'

Tom was looking forward to that too. It would mean she could run after the kids for a few days while he put his feet up in the sun and drink a few beers. Lovely!

The following Monday Tom made a call to the insurance company. It had been six weeks since he put in his claim for the sofa and he was getting impatient. Every time he walked into the sitting room, he would wince as his eyes caught sight of the ink-splattered sofa. Tom really wanted rid of it, but he needed confirmation that his insurers were going to fork out for a new one. He still got a headache whenever he thought of the painting. He spent twelve minutes going through the details with a Customer Service Advisor, who just happened to be a trainee. Tom's patience wore thin after he was asked to 'just hold' for the umpteenth time.

'Listen, junior, I want to speak to your manager because this is becoming farcical.'

'I'm only doing my job, Mr Farrow. There's no need for the attitude.'

The cheeky little gimp.

'Attitude! I'll give you attitude if you don't hurry up and put me through to your manager.'

'If you continue with that tone, Mr Farrow, I will have to hang up. I'm not here to take abuse.'

'Hang up? Abuse? I'll hang you up, you arrogant little fart. I'll...'

The line went dead.

'Son of a...' Tom dialled the number again. This time Tom was taking no prisoners.

'Hello! I wish to speak to your Customer Service Director... er...what's their name again?' Tom fished. 'Miss Dartnell, yes, that's right. Please tell her Mr Tom Farrow is on the line, Customer Service Director at Thornes Printing Ltd. I wish to speak to her about certain office practices that she has adopted.'

Okay, so Tom was lying through his teeth, but it worked. He managed to explain his predicament to Miss Dartnell and she had promised to have a settlement cheque in the post that evening. Tom apologised for his uncouth manner, but he felt it was the only way to get a result. And it did. The next morning Sam brought the post and as hoped, there was an envelope from the insurance company. Tom opened it quickly and was gobsmacked, but pleasantly surprised, to find a cheque for five thousand and three hundred and fifty pounds.

The accompanying letter from Miss Dartnell apologised for the incompetent way his claim had been administered and also for not processing the inclusion of the painting onto the policy correctly. The money not only covered the cost of replacing the sofa and the painting, it included seventy-five pounds for his inconvenience. What a result!

That afternoon Tom took the twins into town to purchase a new sofa. They had great fun trying out all the chairs. The shop assistant seemed a bit reluctant to let them bounce on the sofas but a twenty-pound note popped into his blazer pocket soon brought him round. Choosing the new sofa was a more difficult task than it had been the first time round. Tom was now considering how the new one would stand up to spillages, chocolate stains and ink pens. Eventually Tom settled on a large three-seater sofa with loose back cushions. Ralph said they could make a great little hut for Alex to hide in. It was a light blue colour with stain resistance fabric, guaranteed for three years. It was perfect. Scarlett loved it and said Tom had good taste. When she asked why Tom couldn't wait until the weekend so that she could choose it with him, Tom replied that it proved he was capable of making some good decisions. She agreed, thank goodness.

'All we need now is a new picture to go on the wall above it,' she said.

'I think a simple print in a cheap frame will do, don't you?'

She laughed. 'You're probably right.'

A week later Scarlett asked if Tom could take her to the hospital again to have her plaster removed. She had asked Sylvia to type up some important reports and didn't want to take her away from it. Once again, Tom left the twins at Maud's and made the journey to the hospital. They arrived at four pm, Scarlett's appointment time, and were directed into the doctor's room where he would remove the plaster. Tom felt a bit nervous coming into the hospital for fear of meeting Geri. Tom was aware she had started her new job and the thought of explaining that he was still married while standing next to Scarlett gave him the shivers. Tom envisaged himself lying on the trolley in a body cast with both legs in plaster with Scarlett stood at the end of it clutching a mallet in both hands.

'The doctor will be back in a minute. She's just finishing scrubbing down from a surgery,' said a nurse as she left the room.

'She?' Tom said to Scarlett. 'She said 'she'.'

'Yes. Doctor Singh is on holiday this week so I have to see someone else. A Doctor Porter.'

The mint imperial Tom had been sucking on flew out of his mouth as he coughed unexpectedly. He coughed and coughed trying to catch a breath.

'Tom, are you all right,' Scarlett asked.

'Fine. Almost swallowed my sweet, that's all.' Tom coughed a little more and regained composure. 'So, Doctor Porter. Did you know you would be seeing her...I mean him...I mean it could be a her, you just never know do you? You can't tell just from a name.'

'Yes. Doctor Singh told me last week. He said she's very good.'

'I'm sure she is.'

Tom's forehead began to sweat as he took in the grave implications of his current situation. Tom thought hard for an excuse to leave the room before Geri came in. The blood drained from his face and he felt ill. This was one predicament he didn't want to be in.

'Tom, you look pale. Are you sure you're okay.'

'Ah, perhaps I'll go and find some water or something.'

'Okay, but come back quick.'

Tom stood up to leave but the door began to open.

The person entering began to speak. 'Sorry to keep you waiting, Mrs...er... Farrow.'

It was Geri. Tom immediately began to cough again and bent himself over to try to hide his face as she came into the room. He turned his back to her and began to shuffle towards the door.

'I'm sorry about my husband, Doctor. He's having a coughing fit. He's just going to get a glass of water.'

'It's okay, Mr Farrow. There's a jug of water here on the desk. I'll pour a glass for you,' said Geri.

Tom kept moving towards the door waving a hand frantically dismissing her offer.

'Tom! Wait!' urged Scarlett.

Geri put a hand on his shoulder. 'Here you are...Tom.'

He had no choice. Tom stood up and turned around to face both Geri and Scarlett. Scarlett looked at Tom and then at Geri.

'Oh, have you two met?'

'Yes,' replied Geri. 'I met your husband a few weeks ago. Didn't I, Tom?'

'Yes,' Tom muttered.

Geri stared into his eyes. Tom couldn't sense what she was feeling or planning.

'When?' asked Scarlett.

He was scared stiff. He gulped heavily and tried to swap his gaze from Geri to Scarlett as he tried to reply.

'When he came in to have the bandages removed from his hand,' lied Geri.

'Oh! Right.'

The look Tom gave Geri was of immense relief and gratitude.

'Perhaps you could wait outside, Mr Farrow.'

Oh no! She was going to tell her. 'Outside?'

'Yes, please.' She opened the door and took a step towards Tom. She looked disappointed. 'Don't worry. Everything will be fine.'

Tom hoped it would be. She took a step closer as he backed out of the room, the door blocking their sight of Scarlett. 'I may be a nymphomaniac and have feelings for you, Tom, but I'm not a homewrecker. I won't say a word.'

She closed the door as Tom whispered, 'Thank you!'

He waited for half an hour before Scarlett limped out of the room, cast removed, followed by Geri. 'Your x-ray shows the bone has healed magnificently. You'll feel some discomfort for a while but you should be back to normal in a week or two.'

'Thanks so much, Doctor Porter. I hope you settle in here okay.'

'I'm sure I will.'

Tom stood up to escort Scarlett to the car.

'I need to go to the bathroom, Tom. Bring the car round to the entrance and I'll see you there.'

'Okay.'

She walked slowly to the bathroom and Tom turned to Geri. 'Geri, I wanted to tell you. I didn't mean to deceive you all this time. I'm so sorry!'

'I know you didn't. You did well not to lie though.'

'I did?' Tom asked innocently.

'Uh-huh! You never said you weren't still married and you never said you were, either. I think I'd known all the time, but that wasn't going to stop me. I wanted you, while you wanted the idea of an affair. You didn't lie because you had it in your mind that if you did then you would have crossed a boundary. You didn't tell the whole truth because you enjoyed the cheap thrill of it all.'

'I guess you're right.'

'How did you keep it secret from Scarlett? Most wives notice straight away.'

'It was your name. The day we first met, I implied that you were male. She never questioned it and I never told her.'

'Clever!'

Tom felt uncomfortable. It was only now that he really felt guilty and he actually wanted to tell Scarlett, to get it all out in the open.'

'You're not going to tell Scarlett, are you?' she asked.

'I feel I should. She's my wife for crying out loud. I've cheated on her. It's only fair.'

'Fair to whom, Tom? And you didn't cheat on her. Well, in thought maybe, but not really. The idea may have gone through your head, but that doesn't mean you committed adultery. It was me who kissed you remember?'

'I know, but I still feel terrible. I've hurt you too.'

'Oh, don't worry about me. I'm getting help for my problem. Who knows, I may become a nun. Choose celibacy for life.'

They laughed.

'Tom, you are so very clearly in love with Scarlett. Don't ruin it by opening your big mouth. It would only ruin the trust she has in you. What you did was what most married men think about all the time, and some women! We all love to dream. Perhaps we just need to keep are dreams more realistic.' She kissed Tom lightly on the cheek. 'Goodbye, Tom. Go love your wife and don't let me see your sweet face again.'

She turned around and went back into her office.

'Goodbye, Geri. And good luck!'

'You too. Now go!'

The door closed.

Tom was still on his way down the corridor when Scarlett came out of the bathroom.

'Tom! What's keeping you?'

'Oh, nothing. I just wanted to thank the doctor for looking after you.'

'That's sweet, darling. Come on. Let's get home. I'll cook your favourite – lasagne, baked potato, and green salad.'

'You're too good to me, you know.'

'Don't you ever forget it.'

Maynard Tait

19

Tom was in the garden mowing the lawn when Scarlett came out of the kitchen. She waved at him to get his attention over the roar of the mower's engine.

'What is it?'

'Come over here and I'll tell you.'

She made a gesture with her arms towards the Wendy house, which Polly and Ralph were sitting in until he'd finished mowing.

'Can we come out now?' shouted Ralph.

'In a minute.'

Tom walked over to Scarlett. She had a huge beam on her face. Not the wooden kind, but the kind that stretches from ear to ear.

'What are you so happy about? Have we won the lottery?'

'Don't be daft, we don't do the lottery.'

Sarcasm's lost on Scarlett.

'That was Jackie on the phone. Her consultant has allowed her to go home for the weekend and he feels it would be good for her if the kids were with her. She'll be over in an hour to collect them.'

'That's marvellous. It seems quite soon though, doesn't it? It's only been three and a half weeks since Nick's death. Do you think she'll be all right?'

'I hardly think her consultant would let her home if he didn't think so.'

'Hmm!'

'Tom! Don't be so negative. It's great news. She'll be fine and so will the kids. Let's go tell them.'

When told about their mum Polly and Ralph reacted as though they'd won a month's holiday to Disneyworld. They jumped up and down in the Wendy house until it toppled over on top off them. They were ecstatic. Scarlett had to remind them several times that it was only for the weekend, but they just kept on jumping. When Jackie arrived later, the twins ran to the door, flung their arms around her, and held on tight. Jackie reciprocated. Scarlett told the twins to go and grab their rucksacks from the bedroom while she had a quick chat to their mum. Tom had to comment on how good Jackie was looking.

'You look fantastic, Jackie. How are you feeling?'

'Pretty good, thanks, Tom. I've had to do a lot of very hard thinking over the past few weeks. I just kept focusing on the kids more than anything and I realised that they need me and I need them. A lot of my thoughts used to be selfish ones, but I can't afford to be selfish anymore, not now Nick's gone.'

'We're just glad you're all right,' said Scarlett. 'So, what's going to happen from now on then?'

'Well, I start day treatment as of Monday for two weeks which means I'll be able to have the kids at home every night. I'm sure you'll be relieved.' She looked in Tom's direction. 'No more reading bedtime stories till all hours, eh Tom?'

If Tom were honest, he would miss that. He had gotten used to tucking them in at night and choosing which story to read them. 'Er... no. I suppose not.'

'Well, if you don't mind, I think we should be off.'

Tom looked at Scarlett and she looked at him.

'Right! Yes, of course.' Tom shouted up the stairs. 'Come on kids. Your mum's waiting.'

They came charging down the stairs, raring to go. Jackie set Jasper in his buggy and strapped him in.

'We'll see you on Monday morning then. Have a nice time and don't give your mum any trouble.'

'We won't,' shouted Polly and Ralph.

Scarlett showed them out as Tom waved goodbye. When she joined him in the sitting room Tom lifted Alex up off the floor and cuddled him.

'Just the three of us again for a while,' Tom said.

'Yes, for a while,' said Scarlett with a smile.

Later that day they went for a walk. Well, Tom walked, Scarlett limped and Alex was pushed, but they enjoyed being their own family again. It was quiet too.

Sunday was even better. By the time they arrived at church, Alex was fast asleep in his pram, so they had a lovely, peaceful service.

Tom, once again however, thought the bible reader had it in for him as she read from the book of Genesis chapter six and he felt her eyes pierce his soul as she read 'The Lord saw that the wickedness of man was great in the earth, and that every intention of the thoughts of his heart was only evil continually.' With every word, he heard his body slumped further and further down in his seat, his eyes closing tightly in a vain attempt to stop the lady reader from reading his thoughts.

'I'm trying, God, I'm trying!' he prayed. 'I'll tell her, I promise I will.'

Scarlett nudged him with her elbow thinking he was falling asleep.

'Sit up, Tom!' she whispered. 'You're embarrassing me.'

He shuffled himself upwards. 'Sorry,' he said.

When the service had ended, they decided stay for a cup of coffee afterwards and Scarlett even got invited to the mother and toddler group. Tom noticed she didn't say she couldn't make it because she would be working, as it was held on a Thursday morning, which made him feel that she wasn't planning to take his job after all. Things seemed to be going his way that week, job-wise anyway!

On Monday, Tom collected the twins and Jasper from Jackie's before she headed back to the hospital to begin her day patient treatment. She looked a bit worn, out but after having her children stay for seven weeks Tom could understand why. It turned out to be a good week. Tom even managed to relieve Maud of the babies on Wednesday so that she could visit her sick brother in Royal Tunbridge Wells. To keep them occupied Tom returned to the indoor playground. The attendant made it clear that under no circumstances was he to go on any of the apparatus.

'Just keep an eye on them because I'll be keeping my eye on you,' he warned.

Tom let the twins run around to their hearts content and he had to admit, he was very pleased about how well they behaved. He sat in the baby section and made holes in the sandpit with Alex. Jasper fell asleep in his buggy. It was almost relaxing.

That Friday afternoon Jackie collected the children at three pm as arranged. She looked even happier that day than she had the previous weekend. It was obvious she was getting better. Scarlett had taken the day off to pack and sort all the twins and Jasper's things out. She was looking forward to getting away for the weekend and wanted to leave at a half decent time in the day so that they didn't arrive at their destination too late. They waved to Polly and Ralph as Jackie drove away. Now it was their turn. They got into their car and Tom pulled away from the house. Just Scarlett, Alex, and him. The sun was shining, Alex was asleep, and Scarlett looked radiant. What more could a man ask for?

Tom had only driven to the end of the street and indicated to turn left when Scarlett burst his bubble.

'Why are you turning left? You know Maud's house is up there,' she said nodding to the right.

'What's Maud got to do with anything?'

Scarlett turned away from Tom mouth agape.

'You invited Maud, didn't you?' Tom asked.

'I thought I'd told you.'

Tom sighed and then caught sight of Alex, through the rear-view mirror, fast asleep in his seat. If Tom blew his stack, he'd wake Alex up.

'I just thought she could do with a break too,' said Scarlett. 'I mean, she has been looking after two babies practically non-stop for the past two months.'

'You're right. I just wish you'd told me earlier.'

'So you don't mind?'

'Mind? No, of course not. It was a good decision.'

A decision that Tom wish he had made. Scarlett was incredible. It was as if she was always one-step ahead of him, but Tom was beginning to not mind. Soon enough Tom would be making all his own decisions, with her help of course!

They collected Maud and headed west. By the time they finally found the cottage, which was hidden down an overgrown lane, it was pouring with rain. Alex was testing his lung capacity with screams that would put a banshee to shame and Scarlett was trying to resist being sick again. She had been sick a couple of times on the way. She never travelled well on long journeys, but this was something else. Maud snored unceasingly for the whole journey. Tom pulled up in front of the cottage, jumped out, and ran to the porch. He opened the front door before unloading his wife, his child, and the luggage from the car. Maud would have to wait until she was awake. Tom was soaked through to the skin, his teeth were chattering and he needed a drink. Scarlett toured the building searching for the necessities.

'The drink's cabinet's locked,' she shouted from the drawing room.

Tom caught his reflection in the hall mirror. 'Good job I brought my own!'

They spent the evening in front of a roaring log fire and the telly. Alex got over his tantrum and managed to crawl up the flight of stairs on his own for the first time, to his bedroom, just before '*The Bill*' started. They were all feeling relaxed and bloated from a heavy Chinese take-away and were glad they could watch something without having to think about an in-depth plot. After all this was to be a break. Scarlett had been feeling exhausted so went to bed early. Maud and Tom stayed up to watch an old Hammer horror movie.

'They don't make them like that anymore,' she said at the end of the film.

'No, they don't. It's all blood and guts nowadays. Everything is done to shock instead of making us hide behind cushions like they used to.'

'Hmm! Bring back Vincent Price, that's what I say.'

Tom switched the telly off and blew out the candles before stoking the fire.

'Fancy a night-cap, Tom?' asked Maud.

'Oh, go on then. Scotch, please, no water.'

'I'll have a little port.

She clinked the glasses together several times before pouring in the stupefying liquids. As Tom watched her pour the drinks, it occurred to him for the first time how resilient Maud was. Most women her age were in either a nursing home or being cared for by family. Yet, here she was, old enough to be Methuselah's mother and still caring for little children. What a testament she was to the older generations. Watching Maud gave him comfort. She was strong physically, mentally and most importantly to her, spiritually. It may seem strange, but being with Maud gave him a feeling of closeness to God. Her faith shone out of her and just being in her company five minutes you could count almost all the fruits of the Holy Spirit in her.

She made all his insecurities seem like nothing, but she always had a knack of reminding him that they were something. 'Something to deal with and something to be conquered,' she would say. This evening was not going to be an exception. She handed Tom his drink and sat down opposite him in an old scuffed leather armchair.

'So, how are you, Tom?' she asked.

Her gaze was intense and Tom knew she was waiting for a little white lie to jump from his mouth, but this time, Tom would surprise her. He looked back at her with a warm, genuine smile and said 'Great! Absolutely great!'

She smiled back and took a sip of her port.

'You know I actually believe you mean it this time,' she said.

'I do. Things are turning out very well.'

'Oh! In what way?'

Tom pushed himself deeper into his armchair and let out a deep sigh.

'Let's just say I've made a decision.'

Maud looked curious. 'What kind of decision?'

Tom smiled again. 'A life-changing one.'

Maud sat up straight and set her glass down on the coffee table in front of her.

'Do you mean you've decided to come back to your faith?'

He laughed and reassured her. 'Maud! I have never lost my faith in God. Yes, I feel it's become deeper over the past while, but I was never away from it. No, what I mean is...' Tom stopped himself after having a thought about Scarlett. He wanted her to be the first to know, so he refrained from saying anything to Maud. 'Well, let's just say, the future looks sweet, very sweet.'

Maud didn't know what to make of what Tom had said, but she didn't push him any further. She picked up her glass and raised it.

'Then here's to the future whatever it may bring. And may God bless you!'

Tom raised his glass. 'He already has, Maud. He already has! Cheers!'

'Cheers!'

The next day, Scarlett and Tom took Alex for a pony trek across the New Forest. He sat in front of his mummy on a small brown and white horse named Rocky. He was strapped on to Scarlett, just in case, but he didn't seem to mind. For the whole hour-long ride, he giggled continuously and it was infectious. Tom laughed with him and at him the whole time. It felt perfect. Seeing Scarlett and him together made him feel so proud. Tom was thankful he had them. They met Maud in Beaulieu village afterwards for lunch and sat beside a pond, which overlooked an old manor house. It was a busy day. Large air-conditioned buses thundered along the village roads taking tourists to the nearby car museum. Somehow, it didn't detract from their idyllic picnic.

'This world is always so busy,' said Scarlett. 'No matter where you go people are always rushing around. Time never sits still for some of them, does it?'

It was a rhetorical question but Tom thought he'd reply anyway.

'No, it doesn't. They live in a fast, advancing world never looking back to the good things it has; just pushing the boundaries to make life ever more convenient and richer for us all. Just depends on what makes your life rich.'

Scarlett looked at him. Tom knew it wasn't what she was expecting, but hey, spontaneity and the element of surprise make life more fun. That's what Tom felt anyway.

'Sure, Tom. Are you trying to tell me something because I didn't really understand what you just said?'

'All in good time, darling.' Tom picked up a large bag of crisps. 'Cheese'n'onion, anyone?'

That evening, Maud offered to baby-sit while Scarlett and Tom went out for dinner. The last time the two of them had a meal out was on her birthday, two weeks before Alex was born. They found a beautiful old pub that was renowned locally for its home-cooked food. The owner guided them to a secluded table, out of sight of the bar.

'Can I get you anything to drink while you make your mind up about the food?'

'Sure, I'll have a pint of bitter please, and a Dubonnet and bitter lemon for my wife.'

'Actually, I'll just have an orange juice and lemonade, please,' interrupted Scarlett.

'Are you sure? You're on holiday, go on have a drink.'

'It's fine, Tom. We can stay out longer if one of us has a few drinks and I volunteer you. I'll drive back.'

'No, you can drink, I'll drive. It's been a while since you let your hair down.'

She leant forward over the table. 'No, I'll drive, I don't mind.'

'But darling, it's not a problem.'

She scowled at me, fiercely and kicked me in the shins from under the table. 'Tom! I'll drive. You drink. Understand?'

Boy, was she tetchy!

'Okay, okay! No need to waste all your hormones on me, not in that way, anyway!'

Tom bent down and rubbed his legs. She managed to get both of them in one foul swoop.

'That hurt!'

'And it'll hurt more if I have to do it again.' She picked up her menu and as fast as she turned on me, she turned back to the gentle lady she had been moments earlier. 'Now, are we having a starter or are we going straight to the main course?'

'Whatever makes you happy, sweetheart. You have whatever you want.'

She did have whatever she wanted. One starter of melon wasn't enough so she had two. She seemed frustrated that she couldn't order the duck pâté. When Tom asked why not she said it contained too much garlic and she wasn't in the mood for garlic. This confused him because for the main course she ordered Chicken Kiev with a side order of garlic bread, a side order of Lyonnaise potatoes and French fries not forgetting the jacket potato with cheddar cheese and chives. After the kick to the shins, Tom didn't question anything. As long as she was happy, Tom was happy. Dessert came not a moment too soon for her and when she complained that her hot apple pie was only warm apple pie she took the opportunity to order a second helping. Tom ate his dinner in relative silence as she pigged out on hers. Conversation had to wait until the coffee and shortbread arrived.

'Are you looking forward to getting back to the office on Monday?' she interjected between a mouthful of coffee and a mint chocolate crisp.

She took Tom by surprise with this question and then he recollected the conversation they had on the day they visited casualty with their injuries.

'To be honest, darling, I think it would be best if you just stayed on for this last week. You seem to be enjoying it so much. It would be selfish of me to not let you work this one last week.'

His reply seemed to take her by surprise too.

'But we talked about this, Tom. Don't you want to be ready for next weekend when the Board announces who the new Director will be? There's still some final work to be done on the work plans and staffing levels.'

'Don't worry. I'm as ready as I need to be. You've worked hard over the past few weeks, I'd just get muddled up with what you've started. I'll take care of the children. I'm actually enjoying it now. In fact, I'm going to miss the twins and Jasper when they leave for good next Saturday.'

She put her head to one side and gazed at Tom with half-open eyes.

'You really have grown used to being a Dad, haven't you? Only two months ago you'd run a mile when any parenting was required of you, now you don't even want to go back to work, and for you that's quite a dramatic change.'

'I didn't say I wouldn't go back to work, it's just that I'd want to go back to work on my own terms. Decide my own hours; which people I have working for...I mean...with me. This time with the children has made me see things differently. Understand what's important. Rearrange my priorities.'

Tom sipped his coffee and bit into a piece of shortbread.

'I really am proud of you, Tom. I knew you'd get so much out of this. I'm also overjoyed that you've loved having more than just Alex around. It's very reassuring.'

'Well, they're a real handful at times, but it's been great. At least I'll be prepared when Alex turns four.'

'You're a terrific father, Tom, and the children love you.'

It was the first time she had said that. It only took eight months, but she finally said it. It was only as she said it that Tom realised he had been waiting to hear it, to confirm that he was good enough for Alex. It was the confirmation Tom needed to go ahead with his plans. She got up from her seat and came round the table, bent over and kissed him. Tom was a little embarrassed as there were people nearby, but he soon got over it.

'Let's pay the bill and go for a walk. I could do with the exercise after that meal and we haven't walked hand in hand for a long time,' said Scarlett.

'Good idea. I'll get your jacket on the way back from the bar.'

Tom paid and they left. They took a long walk into the forest. It was quite chilly, but not cold enough to stop them from walking for the next hour and twenty minutes. They crossed five cattle grids during the walk and saw wild ponies galloping across the almost flat shrub land. They stopped to watch them as the bright moon shone down to light the ground all around.

'Do you think Alex will miss Jasper and the twins?' Tom asked.

'Certainly he will. He's got used to having a little friend around him.'

Tom looked up at the stars as he sifted through the thoughts he was having.

'Do you think he'd like having a little brother or sister?'

Scarlett lifted her head off his chest and tried to search for the star his eyes were fixed upon. 'I think he would.'

A small cloud cloaked the moon leaving them in darkness. Tom pulled Scarlett closer as the cold air nipped at them.

'Perhaps we should consider getting him one then.'

She laid her head back on his chest and looked up at him.

'It's too late for considering,' she said.

For a second Tom kept his eyes on the cloud that was covering the moon and then it dawned on him. Not the moon, but what Scarlett had just said.

'Scarlett? Are you saying...are you actually...are you...?'

It was almost the most sense Tom had made in a long time.

'If you're trying to ask if I'm pregnant, then the answer is yes.'

Tom's mouth dropped as he tried to think of a sensible, adult way of responding to the best news he had heard in weeks. Instead, he let go of Scarlett, jumped up and down a few times and then ran into the middle of the empty road and threw his arms out wide, shouting from the bottom of his larynx 'Yippee! I'm going to have a baby! I'm going to have another baby!'

Suddenly, a window opened from the top floor of a nearby cottage and an old man appeared. 'If you're going to have a baby, have it somewhere else. I'm trying to get some sleep!'

'Sorry!' Tom shouted back.

He ran back to Scarlett and gave her a long kiss.

'How long have you known?'

'A couple of weeks.'

'A couple of weeks?' Tom gasped.

'I'm sorry, darling. I didn't want to tell you until next week, after your promotion. I didn't want anything to get in the way. I wanted you to concentrate on that. But this just seemed like the perfect moment. After hearing you talk earlier about things it made me want to tell you.'

'Scarlett, we agreed never to keep secrets from each other. Especially a secret like this.'

'I know, but you've got a secret too. Haven't you, Tom?'

The moon returned in all its splendour pouring light onto Scarlett's face. Tom kept his eyes on hers as he tried to work out what she meant. Tom was so ecstatic from hearing that she was pregnant that he couldn't focus his brain properly.

'Secret? Me? What secret?' Tom asked in absolute innocence.

She looked into his eyes. What did she know? She reached into her jacket pocket and pulled out a small piece of paper. She held it up in front of Tom.

'What's this?' he asked.

'Have a look,' she replied passing it to him.

He held it up in the moonlight and gulped deeply as he read Geri's mobile phone number. Time stood still. It didn't really, but Tom wished it had. What was he going to say? How could he get out of this? If he'd only been honest in the beginning, he wouldn't be standing here almost soiling his best pair of trousers.

'Where did you get this?' As soon as Tom asked the question, he knew it sounded accusing. What right did he have to accuse Scarlett? 'I mean, did I drop it in the house or something? What?'

'No. I actually took it out of your wallet.'

'Ah!' It wasn't unusual for Scarlett to look in his wallet. They had an agreement that she could look in his wallet for money or stamps and Tom could look in her purse for the same.

'I needed some cash to buy some snacks at work last week. After all, I am pregnant and I needed something to keep me going until lunch. As well as relieving you of ten pounds, I took that piece of paper. You hadn't invited 'Jerry', she emphasised the name, 'to dinner, so I thought I'd do it for you. When Dr Porter answered the phone you can imagine how I felt.'

Tom had a fairly good idea as to how she felt but he wasn't going to ask her to tell him.

'Scarlett, I can explain.'

'I think it best that you don't, Tom.' Tom shut his mouth and let her talk. 'As soon as Dr Porter mentioned her name I began to put two and two together. The day you met, you obviously disguised who she was by giving me the impression that she was a he. You didn't actually lie, so I kept calm and thought about the rest. The expensive lunch that I noticed on last month's bank statement. Yes, I know you do the accounts, but I did have my suspicions, so I checked. Then there's the day that I had my plaster removed. You must have thought I was a real idiot not to notice that you had met her before. Her excuse that she had met you the day you had your bandages removed was so clearly a lie, but again, it wasn't you who had said it, it was her.'

She took a step away from Tom and rested against a signpost. 'You weren't ever going to tell me, were you, Tom?'

The guilt rushed back. His legs went weak and Tom began to shiver. The last thing he ever wanted to do was to hurt Scarlett. Tom thought Geri was right when she advised him not to say anything but now he wished he had.

'I wanted to tell you, honest I did. Nothing actually happened, well, we did kiss, but that was at the party when you weren't there and we'd been drinking! I mean she kissed me. It was her fault. She was drunk. You saw what state she was in when you arrived home that day, didn't you?'

Tom's voice began to crack. Tom stepped towards Scarlett, timidly, in fear of being punched on the nose or worse, being kicked in the shins again. 'She told me not to say anything, I mean, not that there was anything to talk about. Well, okay, there was. I liked her, slightly attracted to her, but only slightly.'

Tom realised how puny and pathetic he was being, so he just gave up. He couldn't stand it anymore and he wanted to get it all out in the open. Tom began to sob like a little baby and he dropped down onto his knees on the damp grass. 'Oh, Scarlett, I'm sorry. I'm so sorry. It was entirely my fault. It was a moment of weakness and God will punish me in the lake of fire when I die, but please don't punish me now. I don't want to lose you, Alex, or the new baby. Please forgive me, please, please, please!'

Tom stopped spouting on and came to rest against Scarlett's knees. Tom sobbed and sobbed, and then realised that she hadn't said anything or even moved. Where was the screaming and the spitting? Why hadn't she walloped him across the ear-hole with her handbag or clouted him over the head with one of her shoes? He raised his head, cautiously. When Tom caught her eyes, she was staring down at him with a look of bewilderment.

'Look at the state of you,' she said. 'Pitiful. Really pitiful.'

She almost smiled as she shook her head at him.

'You're not angry,' Tom asked. 'Why aren't you angry? I cheated on you. You should be angry?'

'You didn't cheat on me, Tom.' Her voice was calm and quiet. 'You had a few lustful thoughts about another woman. You had what most men have every day when watching '*Baywatch*' or '*Hollyoaks*'. Some women actually have them too, including me, Tom. Remember when we went to see '*Gladiator*'? I must admit, and I'm sure I wasn't the only woman in the cinema, that I wouldn't have minded if Russell Crowe had taken his body armour off a little more than he did.' She helped Tom up to his feet. 'If it's forgiveness you need, then pray about it, Tom, don't ask me for it. I've nothing to forgive you for. Besides, I know exactly what happened between you and Geri.'

'You do? How come?'

'She told me. I persisted and she eventually told me about her problem and she told me all about how she felt about you.'

'She did?'

'Yep! And you know what, Tom?'

'What?'

'You are the most wonderful husband a woman could ever hope for.'

Tom must admit he was quite shocked by that remark.

'I am?'

'Uh-huh!'

She grabbed his cheeks and planted a long kiss on his lips.

'I would never cheat on you, Scarlett. I love you and Alex, and the little one in there.' Tom rested his hand on her tummy.

'I know you wouldn't Tom, and I know you do. That's why I love you so much and that's why I said earlier that you're a terrific father. Alex has the best Daddy in the world.'

Tom hugged Scarlett for ages after that and he thanked God for her as he did so.

'I think it's time we went back. Maud will be getting worried.'

'Oh, somehow I don't think so.'

She wasn't. By the time they got back, she was fast asleep in the nursery. Tom covered her with a heavy blanket and lifted her legs gently up onto a beanbag. She looked too comfortable to disturb. He gave her a kiss on the forehead.

'Goodnight, Maud. Thanks for everything,' Tom whispered.

He crept to the door and closed it quietly.

'Goodnight, Tom. You're welcome!'

After lunch on Sunday, Tom packed the car and checked the oil level before leaving the cottage. It had been a pleasant weekend and Tom drove home feeling revived, relieved, and ready for the week ahead. It was to be a tense week but he would get through it with help. The twins were great and were looking forward to moving back home for good. Jackie seemed in fantastic health every day she dropped off the kids and it was evident she was ready to take on the world, in small doses at least. Scarlett had a couple of sick days that week as she was beginning to feel the effects of pregnancy all over again. Nothing serious, but breakfast always made it to the toilet bowl before hitting the floor of her stomach. She was feeling much better on the Thursday so they decided to take all the children out for a pizza. They walked to the restaurant via Maud's house and the park as she was coming with them too. She had never eaten pizza before and not being one to miss out asked if she could join them. They had just been seated in the restaurant when the front door opened and in walked Geri with Alex in his pushchair. Tom swallowed nervously as Geri began to walk over towards them. Scarlett noticed her and turned to greet her. 'Geri! Hi! Glad you could make it.'

'Hi, Scarlett. Thanks for inviting us.'

'You're welcome. I've wanted to have you over for dinner for the past two months, but I thought this would be okay.'

'It certainly is. Hi, Tom!'

Tom pretended to only just notice her and jumped to his feet. 'Oh, Geri. Hi! How are you?'

'I'm fine.'

'Down, tiger!' Scarlett whispered with a smile.

Tom took Scarlett by the elbow. 'Why did you invite her? Haven't I suffered enough? You're making me look stupid!'

'Tom, I never have to help you with that. I invited her because she needs friends and that's what we're going to be, okay?'

As if he had a choice. He shrugged his shoulders and sat down. 'Well, if it's okay with you then it's fine by me.'

'Oh, thank you for your approval, sir!'

'That's all right.'

Scarlett sat beside him on his right while Geri took the empty chair to his left. Tom thought he'd better try to converse.

'So, how's the job?'

'It's great. Great.'

'Great!' Tom replied. 'I was beginning to wonder why there were so many places set at the table.'

'I'm sorry if this makes you uncomfortable, Tom.'

'What? Don't be silly. I'm fine, I'm fine.' Tom was feeling very weird but fine all the same. 'Oh, look, there's still an extra space. I'll get a waiter to clear it away.'

'No, it's okay,' said Scarlett. 'Geri's boyfriend is joining us too, isn't he Geri?'

'Yes, he's just parking the car. He'll be here in a minute.'

Boyfriend! She said boyfriend. Tom was so relieved. When Tom saw Geri come in he had visions of her and Scarlett both squeezing his knee under the table and having a catfight in the middle of the restaurant to the amusement of the other customers.

'Oh, here he is.'

The door closed behind a stocky man, wearing a denim jacket and a pair of leather trousers. His jet-black hair was pulled back in a ponytail and his pearl white teeth shone through his bronze skin. He had that chiselled look that made the more insecure man weep. Tom managed not to!

He walked over and Geri introduced him. 'Everyone, this is Paulo. He's from Italy.'

As if they needed telling! He seemed a very nice, wealthy, strong, handsome man, and Tom was able to breathe normally again. Tom was off the hook. He just hoped Paulo knew what he was letting himself in for. It was nice to know that Geri was getting on with her life, and finally Tom had closure. For the first time in weeks, he could look across a table at his wife and not feel guilty. It was a marvellous feeling and one he would recommend to any married man!

Maynard Tait

20

Jackie dropped by the next morning at eight am. It was to be her last day of treatment at the hospital and she was very excited at starting the rest of her life with her children. Once the twins' cardigans were off Polly ran out to the back garden and Ralph ran up the stairs, shouting at Tom to help him up the ladder to the attic. Every morning for the past month had been the same and Tom enjoyed it immensely. The Scalextric track had been a great hit and Tom was sad to know that this would be the last morning that Ralph and he would drive the Monaco circuit together. Before chasing him up the stairs Jackie had something to say.

'Ah, Tom, I need to tell you that, if it's all right with you, I'll be collecting the kids at lunchtime today.'

'Oh! Right! I'd just assumed it would be the normal time.'

'It should have been, but my counsellor called me last night to say she needed a half-day today as she was going to a conference this weekend and that she really didn't see why they couldn't finish everything this morning, so if it's all right with you guys?'

Scarlett and Tom looked at each other and then back at Jackie. Tom had hoped to take the kids to the indoor playground that afternoon but he would just have to change his plans.

'Of course, Jackie. We'll have them all packed and ready to leave by twelve,' said Scarlett. 'Won't we, Tom?'

'Er, yeah! 'Course!'

'Thanks you two. Look, I've got to go. I'll see you around midday then.'

She turned and opened the door and waved with a wide smile.

'Bye! Have a good morning!'

'I will.'

Tom closed the door behind her and considered the afternoon. It was going to be strange not having them around. It would just be Alex and him.

'Tom! Are you okay?'

He hadn't realised he was in a daze. 'I'm fine. Just feeling a bit funny.'

Scarlett put her arms around him. 'I know. I am too. But it's great to know that we've helped a friend, isn't it?'

'Certainly is. That's what friends are for after all.'

Scarlett ruined the moment with a burp. Then another one.

'Are you alright?'

She moved away from Tom and then turned and stood still for a moment.

'No! I'm feeling funny too. Sick kind of funny!'

'Oh dear!'

She ran to the downstairs toilet and hurled. And hurled. And hurled once again.

'I don't know why you bother eating breakfast these days, I really don't!' Tom muttered quietly.

Tom called Gilbert to tell him that Scarlett wouldn't be in for work that day but to say that they would both be at his farewell party in the evening, all being well. Gilbert had been a good, helpful boss and Tom wanted to be around to wish him good luck for his retirement. On returning from Maud's, after leaving the babies with her, Tom tucked Scarlett back into bed and checked on Polly in the garden before joining Ralph in the attic. He opened the Velux window so he could look down on Polly every so often.

'Right, Ralph. Who are you going to be today?'

'Umm! Michael Shoe Maker.'

Tom tried once to correct his pronunciation, but it was like flogging a dead horse, so he gave up.

'But you're always him. Why not be someone else for a change?'

'Because he's the best,' he said arrogantly.

'So what? Why don't you be Eddie Irvine?'

'Don't like him!' he replied in disgust.

'Well, no-one actually likes Eddie Irvine, Ralph, but he's a good driver. Go on, be Eddie.'

'No!'

'What about Mika Hakkinen?'

'Too ugly!'

'Johnny Herbert?'

'No!'

'David Beckham?'

'Too pretty!'

'I notice you didn't say he was a footballer.'

'Just play, Uncle Tom.'

'Okay, how about Ralf Shoe Maker. He's Michael's brother.'

'Yeah! It's the same name as mine. Yeah, I'll be him. Let's start.'

Hurrah! Tom was going to be David Coulthard, so that meant he'd definitely win!

Tom placed the two cars on the starting grid. His was the slightly slower red one and Ralph had the slightly faster blue one. Tom switched on the 'noises' CD and the tape of a commentary by Murray Walker that he had recorded from the telly during a Canadian Grand Prix. He turned on the water pump that he'd inserted in the water pool. It blew bubbles and was Ralph's favourite bit. Tom lay down beside him on the floor and picked up his control.

'Okay, we're ready to go.'

Tom switched on the timed lights that would start the race. They watched them intently. Red light. Red light. Red light. Red light. Red light. Green! They were off! As always, Ralph giggled continuously as the cars raced round the track. Over the past two months, they had both learnt where to take the power off and when to strangle the throttle. Halfway around the track they were neck and neck. Murray Walker was becoming more and more demented and the roars of the engines from the stereo added to the excitement. At a hairpin bend, both cars spun and Ralph's flew off the track. He scrambled to his feet and tiptoed across the mass of road to replace it. Tom had a lead now, but that wouldn't stop Ralf Shoe Maker from making a fantastic comeback. He flew down the box-covered curved stretch and braked hard at the right-angled chicane. He was on his tail now and the tension grew every single second. His car was climbing the uphill straight and suddenly Ralph was beside Tom. He laughed unremittingly as his car began to overtake Tom's at the crest of the hill and turned to the right as both cars began their descent. It was to be a race of two laps and Ralph was winning. The engines roared louder and louder from the stereo and Murray Walker was interrupted by a commercial break, but the cars kept going on relentless. As both cars entered the tunnelled curve once more, they were side by side. It was going to be a close call. As they came out of the shoeboxes, they let off the throttles as the cars approached the sharp left-hand bend. Tom's car turned first, but it was still going too fast. It skidded around on the track. Ralph's car did too and it thumped into Tom's knocking it off the track and into the water feature. Ralph's car straightened up and he pulled the throttle back and headed towards the finish line. When it crossed the line he dropped his control and jumped up and down and all around the attic floor, yelling, 'I won. I won. Ralph Shoe Maker is the winner. I won. I won.'

A small puff of smoke rose up from Tom's car as it lay on its roof in the pool. He raised his eyebrows and lifted it out. Ralph just kept jumping and jumping. Tom left Ralph to enjoy his victory and to play on his own for a while. Polly had been on her own for some time, so Tom thought he'd go out to the garden and play with her. The garden was empty and the Wendy house had been moved to behind the shed at the bottom of the lawn, hidden behind an overgrown willow tree, but the bright yellow tent was easy to spot. Tom crept up to the house, quietly, to surprise her. As he approached, he could hear her talking. He knelt down at the door and peered in through a gap in the closed window. Polly was sitting with her back to the door, opposite her favourite dolly. When Tom realised what she was saying he stayed where he was and kept quiet.

'And Daddy is in Heaven now, Auntie Maud says, and he's looking down on us every day so we shouldn't be sad, Jemima. You know, Jemima, I'm glad I can tell you anything. Mummy hasn't been well for a while, so she hasn't been here to talk to me, but you have. Thank you, Jemima.' She picked up the doll and kissed its face before putting it back in its place. 'Yes, I know Daddy isn't here either, but it's been fun staying with Auntie Scarlet and Uncle Tom. Uncle Tom is very funny and silly too. He's very good at reading bedtime stories too and Auntie Scarlett makes lovely gingerbread people. I love them very much. I hope they love me too.'

A solitary tear rolled down Tom's cheek and stopped as it reached his mouth. He slowly opened the door of the Wendy house, went inside, and sat beside Polly. She turned and looked at him and asked, 'Do you love me, Uncle Tom?'

What else could he say?

'Yes, Polly. Scarlett and I love you very much, and Ralph and Jasper. But you know what?'

'What?'

'Your mummy loves you a hundred times more and she can't wait to have you home this afternoon. And your Daddy loved you too, every day he was away.'

'But he's not here anymore. Will I ever have a daddy again?'

'I don't know, sweetheart. Maybe.' Tom closed his eyes and squeezed her gently. 'But if you ever want someone to play Cowboys and Native Americans with you, you know where to find me. Right?'

'Right!'

A moment later, Tom was drinking a cup of imaginary tea with Jemima from an imaginary cup but the joy he felt inside was very real.

Jackie arrived at midday and the excitement of having her children home with her for good was clear to see. Her face glowed as she lifted the kids' backpacks into her car. Tom arranged their suitcases into the boot leaving enough room for the abundance of toys that would give them back a few square feet of space in the sitting room. Maud gave Jasper a long, tearful hug before setting him into his car seat. Scarlett kissed the twins a dozen times in the time it took them to walk from the front door to the car. Tom helped them into their seats and then buckled them up.

'Now you two, your mummy's going to need your help for a while, so try not to be naughty or anything, will you?' They both nodded. 'Your Granny's going to be around too and that'll be good, won't it?' They nodded again, both staring back at Tom.

Tom didn't know how to say goodbye. He didn't really want too.

'I'll miss you!' said Polly.

Tom gave her a sincere look. 'And I'll miss you too, Polly.' Tom then tickled Ralph on his tummy. 'I'll even miss you, Mr Grand Prix champion!' He giggled.

'Me too!' he shouted. 'Thanks for the races, Uncle Tom. I really loved them.'

'Well, how would you like to play it whenever you wanted to?'

'But I can't. It lives here and I start school soon anyway.'

'Well, you're mum has agreed to let me decorate her attic and guess what I'm going to put up there?'

He looked at Tom as if he had two heads.

'What?' he asked.

'Monaco,' Tom replied.

'You mean the race track?' asked Ralph.

'Yes, duh! The racetrack. It's all yours. When I get a chance to take it apart next week I'll bring it round, so you can practice on a smaller circuit in your bedroom.'

He began to bounce up and down in his seat and then Polly joined in.

'Yippee! Yippee!' he screamed.

Tom kissed them goodbye before closing the car doors.

'That's everything, Jackie. You're all set.'

'Yes, Tom. I am. And it's all thanks to you guys. I don't know how to repay you.'

Tom put his arm around his wife and smiled at Jackie. 'Oh, believe me, Jackie, there is nothing to repay. I think we've, at least I've, gained so much from having them. Two months ago I never thought I'd say this but it's been a privilege and I mean this so sincerely, a joy.'

Jackie came closer and squeezed them as they stood. 'Well, thank you anyway. I couldn't have got through all this without you, and you too Maud,' she said over their shoulders.

'You're more than welcome, my dear. Take care.'

'I will.'

She hugged them once more and then climbed into her car. As she reversed out of the driveway, Tom noticed Alex waving at them from his pushchair. It was his first wave. Tom picked him up and they waved together.

'I'll be in touch about the decorating,' Tom called to Jackie and she sounded her horn in recognition before driving off.

Scarlett, Maud, Alex, and Tom stood and waved even when the car was out of sight. They all cleared their throats to try to dismiss the choking sensation they were all feeling.

Maud broke the silence. 'Anyone for a spot of lunch?'

Lunch was a quiet affair. Maud helped Scarlett wash up afterwards and the conversation was still only about the weather. Tom took Alex into the sitting room and rolled around on the floor with him for a while. His leg strength was getting better and better and he could stand on his feet extremely well with the aid of his hands.

'You're going to have a baby brother or sister soon, young man. We weren't planning on it so soon, but I reckon the big man upstairs had other ideas. His timing's always perfect apparently, so I'm certainly not going to argue.'

Alex blew bubbles and the dribble collected at the corner of his mouth and ran down his chin dropping off into his lap. Tom smiled at him. 'That's my boy!'

It had taken Tom almost eight months to get used to having a baby of his own, and within a further eight, he would have another one. In the short space of two months, his outlook on fatherhood had changed dramatically. Gone were the fears of failing Alex, and his doubts of making a good father had disappeared. Tom had realised that his role wasn't mainly to provide for his family, but to be there for them, to love them and to cherish them. No longer would Tom only see his son five minutes in the day and for a few hours at the weekend. Tom was going to be the father he wanted to be, helpful, caring, and available. It would not only benefit him and Alex, but Scarlett and the new baby too. Tom had missed too much of Alex's early months and he wasn't going to miss anymore. His mind was made up. The decision had been made. All Tom had to do now was wait.

Later that afternoon Tom went for a walk on his own to collect his thoughts and to see a few people. The last one was George. He skipped up the step into his shop, whistling merrily. George was wrapping up some sliced ham for a lady customer who wouldn't have looked shabby even if she were standing next to Jane Russell. She had long brunette hair that drew Tom's eye down to the beginning of many curves that were modestly covered up by a cream coloured suit. Tom quickly averted his gaze as she turned to leave after receiving her change from George. As she left, Tom noticed that George wasn't drooling or mentally undressing her with his lecherous eyes. He struggled to resist the temptation himself, so how could George?

'Morning, Tom. Glorious day, isn't it?

He just had the world's most beautiful woman in his shop and he mentions the weather. What's happened to him? Surely he couldn't change from a lifetime of womanising in just a few weeks, could he?'

'It's marvellous, George,' Tom replied. He leant against the counter and peered over it, watching as George refilled an empty tray with minced beef.

'George?'

'Yes, Tom?'

'You did see that woman that was just in here a moment ago, didn't you?'

He glanced up at Tom with a curious look. 'Of course. I may have lost some of my faculties in my old age, but I can assure you that my sight isn't one of them. Why do you ask?'

'Well, it's just that she was magnificently beautiful and you didn't seem to notice. Now, forgive me if I'm talking out of turn here, but that's just not like you, George.'

George smiled as he packed the meat onto the tray.

'I did notice, Tom. But I didn't feel the need to ogle her. That would have been rude.'

'Rude? It's never stopped you before. I've seen you slap the rear end of many a pretty customer and if that's not rude then I don't know what is.'

'Yeah, well, not anymore. I don't need to.'

He shoved the full meat tray into the counter display and then walked into the back to wash his hands. Tom was a bit confused.

'Why not? What's changed? I know you're 'in love' as you put it. But how could you change the habit of a lifetime.'

'Tom, Tom, Tom. It's just that I've finally found the right woman, and when you've found the right woman you'll do anything to keep her.'

'You have? You would?'

'Uh-huh! And she's more beautiful than any woman I've ever had in this shop. What's more, she's been a real comfort over the past few weeks. She's made me forget my problems and concentrate on other enjoyable things in life.'

'Such as?'

'Oh, Tom. You really must get out more. Like sport. We play

tennis twice a week and we've joined a bowling club. She's given me a new lease of life.'

'That's great, George. It really is. I'm so happy that you've found your true love. Looks like we've both found a new lease of life.'

'Oh! I hope you haven't been playing about, Tom. Tut-tut!'

'No, I mean...'

Tom was interrupted as George stood up straight and a wide grin came across his face. He was looking over his shoulder at someone who had walked in.

'Tom, here she is! I want you to meet the new woman in my life.' He grabbed Tom's shoulders and spun him around. 'Tom, this is Isidora.'

The sight of his mother-in-law gave Tom another one of his visions. He had pictures of her wearing a skimpy tennis outfit writhing around on a bed with George dressed in bowling whites and a peaked cap.

Then he fainted.

When Tom came round Scarlett was kneeling over him and Tom could hear Alex cooing beside him. 'Tom, can you hear me? Please wake up.'

'What happened?' Tom groaned. Tom tried to lift his head up, but changed his mind once he felt a searing hot pain come from the back of it.

'Careful. You banged her head when you fell,' replied George.

Tom saw Isidora and George standing behind Scarlett.

'It was you. You did this,' Tom said deliriously.

'Sorry Tom!' George apologised. 'We were going to tell you sooner ,but Isi thought you had your hands full with the kids, so we thought it best to leave it until after the Christening when everything had settled down.'

'I think they'll be good for each other,' said Scarlett as she helped Tom up to his feet.

'You do?'

'As do I,' said Isidora. 'I love Disney movies and George loves cuddly toys. It's a perfect combination.'

'Ahh,' said Tom. '*The lady and the tramp*' video. It makes sense now.' Tom looked at George after hearing his revelation, but George wouldn't meet his eyes. Cuddly toys indeed! 'Well I'm thankful for you telling me before the Christening. It makes sense now for you to be Alex's godfather. You can't be his actual grandfather, so it's the next best thing, I guess. You don't mind do you, Scarlett?'

'Of course not. It's perfect.'

George didn't know what to say. For once, he was speechless. He just nodded and then picked up Alex and kissed him on his head. He actually did look happy even if it was thanks to Tom's mother-in-law.

Maynard Tait

21

Scarlett and Tom arrived at Thornes just after eight thirty pm and the party seemed to be in full swing. It was a formal do and Tom was glad his fast-expanding stomach could still fit into his tuxedo. Scarlett looked a million dollars in a full-length sequinned dress that gave no indication of her fragile condition. The boardroom was smartly decorated and full with Board members, department Directors, and staff, dancing to the Brian Setzer Orchestra as it pumped from the PA system. Swing was obviously the theme for the evening and it certainly looked as though the senior members of staff were making the most of it on the dance floor. Scarlett and Tom made their way to the drinks table, but were intercepted by Edward Thorne.

'Well, Hello, Mrs Farrow. How absolutely stunning you look tonight with that dress just cut low enough to give us mortal men something to dream about when we go home to bed.'

'Shut up, Edward or you'll be singing along to the music, only you'll be doing it two octaves higher.'

'Ooh! Scarlett please put away the claws. You've got Tom to stand up for you this evening. Not babysitting then, Tom?' He leant towards

Tom and sniffed. 'Not sure about your aftershave, old boy. Smells like baby wipes to me.'

'Give it a rest, Edward. Anyway, shouldn't you be over there making sure the Board are all being taken care of.'

'Oh, don't need to, old fruit. You see I already have them where I want them. I'm so sorry to have to tell you, Tom, but a little birdie told me that they've already decided who's going to be the next Customer Service Director and I know for a fact that it's not you, so it looks like I'll be the one celebrating. Hope you're not too disappointed.'

He laughed aloud and Tom had to grab Scarlett's right hand before she slapped him.

'Ignore him, darling. He's drunk and not worth it.'

'You see Scarlett. He's always there for you. In fact he'll always be there for you after tonight because as soon as I become Director my first job will be to get rid of him.' He pointed at Tom and began to jab his finger into his chest. 'You see, Tom, Raymond has never forgiven you for getting him fired and he's been helping me with my plan all along and once you're gone he'll be back in his rightful place as Head of Department.' He laughed again scornfully before turning and tripping his way across the dance floor.

'Tom didn't get him fired. I did!' shouted Scarlett, but he couldn't hear her.

'Don't worry Scarlett. It wasn't you or me. He did it to himself.'

'What are we going to do, Tom? It's too late. He's won.'

'Let's just wait and see, shall we?'

They both had a drink and Scarlett was annoyed that she couldn't have any alcohol to help her feel at ease. She became more and more nervous as the evening wore on wondering what was going to happen.

Craig and Howard found them sitting at a table in the corner of the room.

'What are you doing over here? You should be up there dancing,' shouted Craig.

'We're not in the mood,' Tom shouted back.

'Why not? You're going to be a Director in five minutes time. You should be celebrating.'

Tom nearly choked on his drink. 'Five minutes? What do you mean five minutes?'

Howard sat down next to him. 'Sir Wilfred told the Team Managers today that he's going to announce the new Director at ten o'clock tonight. Sorry, I meant to call you and let you know.'

'Yeah, you'll be a big cheese on Monday, Tom,' said Craig.

'No I won't.'

'Yes you will and you'll have to decide who gets your job.'

'No I won't, Craig, and anyway it's not even nine o'clock yet. What's happening in five minutes?'

'The Board want to tell you, Scarlett and Edward first, so you'd better get over to the meeting room. They'll be waiting for you.'

Tom stood up and saw Sir Wilfred lead the Board members out of the door towards the meeting room. This was it. This is what Scarlett had been working so hard for. It was crunch time.

'Come on, Scarlett. We'd better get in there.'

Tom helped her up and they shoved their way across the dance floor towards the door. Edward got there first. How he managed it Tom had no idea as his legs seemed to be going in opposite directions to one another. He was as drunk as he could be, but confident with it.

He fell through the door and out into the corridor and across to the boardroom. As they followed him, he carefully composed himself and straightened his bow tie before making himself comfortable in one of the three chairs that sat next to each other at the end of a long table behind which sat all the Board members with Sir Wilfred at the top. Tom offered Scarlett the middle chair but she didn't want to sit next to Edward so Tom sat in it himself. As they all settled themselves, the Board members coughed and spluttered as they sucked on oversized cigars, which Edward had supplied.

'They're from Havana,' he whispered in Tom's ear. His breath reeked.

Sir Wilfred stood up, as the room became silent.

'Good to see you again, Farrow...er...Tom, I mean.' His voice echoed around the room as he spoke. 'Getting to grips with domesticity?'

'Sort off, Sir Wilf...'

'Lovely, lovely! Well, you know why you are all here so there's no point beating around the bush, but I'm going to anyway. I love suspense, don't you?' he chuckled.

His mood was jovial, as though he was about to honour a scout with his fire-starting badge – if there is such a badge! He began to walk slowly down the length of the table puffing at his cigar as he went. Suddenly he stopped and took a deep breath.

'The Board and I have had two months to decide who would be Gilbert's successor and I can confirm that we have not found it easy. Due to certain circumstances our decision has changed once or twice, but we have finally come to the natural one.'

Scarlett glanced at Tom sideways and smiled. She rested her left hand on his right and squeezed it tenderly. Edward's head swivelled towards Tom to reveal a smug grin that seemed to have been there for a very long time. Tom was hoping and praying that what Sir Wilfred would have to say would remove it.

Sir Wilfred continued. 'The person who has been selected has been loyal ever since they joined Thornes and they have pleased the Board no end. They enjoy a challenge and go out of their way to get what they want.'

Edward shuffled in his seat, his smile broadening.

'This person is capable of anything and can be ruthless and yet charming at the same time.' He walked to the top of the table again and stared at all three of them before fixing his eyes on Edward. 'This person has dedicated themselves to this promotion over the past two months and has pulled out all the stops to make sure the Board choose the right man for the job.'

Scarlett squeezed Tom's hand again, but this time, it was due to shock.

Edward jumped to his feet and screamed in delight. 'Yes! Yes! Yes! Thank you, Uncle Wilf. Thank you!'

Sir Wilfred continued. 'However Edward, that person is not you.' He paused and grinned as he spoke these words. 'Edward! You're fired!'

Sir Wilfred kept his grin and all the Board members joined him. Edward's mouth fell open as he tried to find the words to retaliate.

'But...but...but...you...you...can't. You can't!' he shouted. 'I've done everything for you.' He began to trip his way around the table and all the Board members. 'I've catered for your every whim. I've given you what you wanted. I've bought you cigars, cars, women..., and static caravans! Including you, Uncle.'

'Actually, you didn't. What you did do Edward was manipulate, deceive and lie to all of us over the past couple of months, believing that we wouldn't see through your smelly little plan and give you the promotion. But I'm glad to tell you that we're not that naïve or stupid. You tricked us and cheated us and used everyone around you to get what you wanted, but it hasn't worked.' Sir Wilfred walked towards Edward making him stumble over his feet as he shuffled backwards towards the door. 'You're sacked, Edward. Fired. Dismissed. Let go. Kicked out. So turn around, open the door, and get out!' He bellowed the last two words loud enough to raise the hairs on the back of Tom's hands.

'But Uncle!' cried Edward.

'Get out!' yelled Sir Wilfred as he opened the door for him.

'But!'

'Out! And don't ever come back!'

Edward tripped over his feet and fell out into the corridor as Sir Wilfred slammed the door behind him. Simultaneously, all the other Board members stood to their feet and politely clapped Sir Wilfred. Some congratulated him vocally. 'Jolly good show, old boy!' 'Here, here!' 'Spiffing execution, Wilfie old chap.' 'Couldn't have done better myself!'

He returned to his seat and pressed a button on a console. 'Howard, please ask Miss Fleck to join us in here, will you?'

Tom leaned over to Scarlett and whispered, 'Looks like she's for the high jump too!'

'I don't know how she ever thought she'd get away with it,' she replied.

Howard opened the door and Charlene Fleck walked in, not in fear, as Tom had expected, but confidently and with a smile. She stopped at the chair beside Tom and Sir Wilfred asked her to sit down.

'My dear, Charlene. Thank you so much for your help over the past few weeks and as promised I would like to officially offer you the position as my Personal Assistant with two months back pay, of course. What do you say?'

'I accept, Sir Wilfred. Thank you.'

Bemused and bewildered Scarlett and Tom looked at each other, at Charlene, and then at Sir Wilfred who just smiled back at them.

'Okay, I see you're confused. I'll let you in on a little secret,' he laughed.

'I wish you would. We seem to be the only ones in the dark here,' Tom said.

'Well, it's quite simple, my dear boy. As you know, we've been trying to get rid of Edward for a long time and this promotion scam seemed like the perfect opportunity.'

'I still don't follow, Sir Wilf...'

'Well, stop interrupting me and let me explain.'

'Sorry!'

'The Board and I agreed to give Edward the impression that he may get promoted when Gilbert retired and knowing what Edward would do I set him up by asking Miss Fleck here if she would be willing to play along.'

'On the basis that she would get the job as your PA?' asked Scarlett.

'No, no. I'd already offered her the job beforehand. I needed someone new who would not know Edward and wouldn't arouse suspicion.'

'But the two of you have been seen out together in public as a couple. I don't understand.'

'Well, the fact that Charlene and I have been a couple for a while needed to come out at some point, so we played it into our little game, but Edward was the only one who didn't know. He just thought I'd been smitten with her and she was stringing me along. Not the case, is it my dear Charlene?'

Their heads turned towards her.

'No Wilfie. I've been smitten with him since the first day I met him at Ascot. He's such a cuddly big bear.'

Sir Wilfred tried to hide his embarrassment by coughing and chewing his cigar butt.

'Ah, so...er...there you have it. Edward's gone; I have a new PA, and all that's left for me to do is to publicly name the new Director of Customer Services.'

Tom tightened his grip on Scarlett's hand knowing what was coming. He had been waiting for this moment for weeks and here it was. He just hoped Scarlett would understand.

'I would like to offer the position of Customer Service Director,' said Sir Wilfred. 'To you Scarlett.'

The smile on her face slowly fell as she replayed in her head what she had just heard. She looked at Sir Wilfred and then at Tom and then back at the Board.

'Me? But I...I mean...Tom...ahm...' She faltered on every word as she spoke.

She looked at Tom again and almost cried. 'Tom! I didn't know. They've got it wrong. This is for you, not me!'

'Obviously not, Scarlett,' said Tom flatly. 'But if you don't want it then you'd better tell them.'

She stood up and leaned on the table to give her some support.

'I'm ever so grateful to you for offering me the job, but you know as well as I do that Tom's the right person for the job. He's the one who has worked towards it. It's what he's dreamed about for years. Tom wasn't working his butt off for me; he was doing it for you and the good of the department.'

'And all the things I said earlier were correct,' said Sir Wilfred. 'You're dedicated, ruthless, and considerate and you get what you want. That's what it takes to be a good Director.'

She mulled that one over for a moment and Tom could see she was going to use what he had just said against Sir Wilfred. Her lips tightened and she frowned ever so slightly. Tom just sat still and waited.

'In that case, Sir Wilfred, I do not accept your offer.'

'What!' he bellowed. 'But you can't.'

'You said I get what I want and what I want is for my husband to be the new Director. He could do as good a job as I could, if not better in some ways and I would like you to offer him the job.' She took a breath and carried on. 'To be quite honest, I don't want the job, I never did. It carries too much responsibility and Tom knows all too well about responsibility. While I've worked here over the past few weeks Tom has been caring for two twin children and two babies, yes with some help, but he has learnt what it means to give up what's important, to care about the real things in life. He would make a valuable Director and one who would lead the department with a firm hand, yet faithfully and with determination. I beg you, please give Tom the job. Besides, I'm pregnant!'

Earlier that morning Tom had been reading Scarlett's book on pregnancy and that in the first few weeks, the mother's emotions are all over the place. The plea she had just made was worthy of a political election speech. She cried as she sat back down again and leant her head against Tom's shoulder. The Board members all muttered to each other and to Sir Wilfred who seemed quite shocked but in control. After a few moments deliberation he asked them all to settle down.

'Well, Scarlett, I must say I'm disappointed that you cannot accept my offer, but understand fully your position. On behalf of myself and these gentlemen present, I offer you and Tom our warmest congratulations. I am left with no alternative but to offer you, Tom, the job of Customer Service Director. As Scarlett says, you would make a valuable Director and we'd be proud to have you on the team. What do you say?'

All eyes were on Tom and he felt nervous. All the decisions he had made and thoughts he had had over the past weeks flew around in his head and he wondered if what he was about to say would be the right thing to do. Scarlett nudged him gently and gave him a curious look. Tom stood up and faced the Board.

'I have done a lot of thinking while I've been away from Thornes even though I have been surrounded by screaming babies and meddling toddlers. I have had a chance to take stock of my life and to find out what was important to me. My years at Thornes have been fruitful and I've learnt a lot from you and your expertise and I thank you all so much. All of you are aware that I've spent the past three years working towards this job which is why you will all be very surprised when I say – I resign.'

Scarlett was the first to jump to her feet, quickly followed by Sir Wilfred.

'But my dear boy, you can't? I need you.'

Scarlett grabbed Tom's shoulders and turned him towards her. 'Tom, what are you doing? Are you angry with me for being offered the job? If you are, then I'm sorry. You've got to take this; you can't be so stubborn. This was your dream!'

Tom cupped his hands around her face and said, 'I'm not angry with you, in fact I want you to have the job. My dream has changed but I don't have to wait anymore to get it.'

'What do you mean?'

'Just wait. I'll explain later.' Tom walked up to Sir Wilfred and faced the Board. 'I'm sorry to spring this on you but if there's one thing I've learnt it's that I'd rather be a valuable father than a valuable Director. I love my family and I want to be there for them far more than I ever have been. Being a Director would mean I'd see even less of them and that's not good for anyone. I don't want to come to work every day and see glum faces around me as people try to appease others and argue their views. I want to make people smile and that's what I intend to do.'

Sir Wilfred looked angry as he considered what Tom had said and then his face relaxed. 'Well, it seems like you've made up your mind, Tom. I don't feel I can stand in your way of your dreams, so I accept your resignation and wish you all the best for the future whatever it may hold.' His last words were sincere.

'Thank you, Sir.'

'However, you do leave me in a sticky situation, Farrow.'

'Oh, what's that, Sir?'

'We don't have anyone to fill the position of Director, do we?'

He stared at Tom with wide eyes. It was obvious he was expecting Tom to decide who would make a good candidate for the job and there was only one person Tom had in mind. He picked up the handset on

Sir Wilfred's phone and dialled Craig's mobile number. Tom knew he would be dancing away over in the boardroom and that his mobile would be turned on. He answered it.

'Craig, this is Tom. Please come over to the meeting room and bring Howard in with you. Yes, now please.' Tom replaced the handset. 'They'll be here in a moment.'

Howard and Craig came in looking as though they had just left the house. Even at a party, these two kept themselves smart and ready for work. They were reliable, trustworthy and workaholics. Tom just knew that the one he wouldn't choose to be the new Director would not take it personally, as he would be promoted anyway.

'Sir Wilfred, you know Craig Spanner and Howard Sprat.'

'I do. Very good boys indeed.'

'Yes, well, if you and the Board would trust my judgement, I would like you to offer Craig my old job of Head of Department and Howard the job of Director of Customer Services.'

The two of them looked surprised but pleasantly so.

Tom continued. 'Craig has worked with me for four years and has been a good manager. He is very well liked by the staff and he can keep his head when others are losing theirs. Howard here, in my opinion, is the obvious choice for Director. Howard has shown his past managerial skills to be second to none. He is forever implementing new ideas and he can have anything done for you at the drop of a hat. He is worthy of the job and the two of them make as good a team as Scarlett and I ever did. You would be doing yourselves a great injustice if you didn't offer them the jobs.' Tom stared at Sir Wilfred. 'What do you say?'

Sir Wilfred stared back and nodded. 'I'm going to miss you, Farrow.'

'And I you, sir.'

He looked across the boardroom at Howard and Craig who both seemed to be standing at attention waiting for their orders.

'Well, what do you say, boys? Do you want the jobs?'

'Yes, sir!' they both replied military fashion.

Sir Wilfred put out his arm, Tom did likewise, and they shook hands. 'I envy you, Tom, I really do.'

'Don't envy me, sir.' Tom winked at Charlene. 'Just enjoy yourself.'

All the Board members rose from their seats to congratulate Howard and Craig. Scarlett stormed around the table towards Tom. Tom could see she was angry.

'A word, please.'

She took his arm and dragged him out of the room into the corridor. On the way out Tom gave Howard and Craig the thumbs up.

'What have you done? Are you insane?' she barked.

'Let me explain.'

'Explain? You'd better, buster. I have worked my backside off for you and I want to know what dream you have now that has made you give up your job just after I refused mine. Well? And wipe that ridiculous grin off your face, I don't like it.'

Tom couldn't wipe the grin off. It was permanent. Tom slowly reached into his jacket pocket and withdrew a door key on a silver chain.

'This was my dream, but it's now reality.'

'What are you talking about, Tom. It's a key.'

'No ordinary key. It's our key to freedom.'

She said nothing for a moment and before she opened her mouth, Tom put his finger to it.

'Come on. Let's go and I'll show you.'

Tom took her hand and led her down the corridor. Just as they were about to go outside, Howard and Craig burst into the corridor and shouted after them.

'Hey, Tom! You're the best, mate!' cried Howard.

'Yeah, mate, thanks a million!' shouted Craig.

'You're welcome. You owe me a pint and lunch though.'

'It's a small price to pay for a very large gift,' replied Howard.

Tom wished them good luck and waved goodbye.

It was pitch dark as Tom stopped the car at the side of the road. Scarlett was getting anxious and hungry so Tom quickly hopped out of the car and ran around to her door. Tom tossed her a scarf. 'Here, put this over your eyes.'

'What for?'

'It's a surprise. Trust me. You do trust me, don't you?'

'Of course, you're just making me nervous.'

Tom helped her out of the car, walked her onto the pavement, and faced her away from the road.

'Okay, now stay here a minute while I go and open the door.'

'Open what door?'

'It's the surprise.' Tom ran to the door, opened it, and checked that the lights were working before turning them off again and running back to her. 'Okay, you can remove the scarf.'

She took it off and blinked her eyes to try to get some light in them. 'I can't see too much seeing as you've left the lights off, but I can tell it's a shop front.'

Her voice was lacking enthusiasm.

'This is no ordinary shop front. Wait here.'

Tom ran inside the shop and switched on all the lights. He watched for her reaction as she took in the sign above the shop. Her mouth opened wide before turning into a huge smile.

'Do you like it?' Tom asked from the doorway.

Her gaze focused on the sky-blue neon lights shining brightly above her. 'Farrow's Barrow', she read aloud. Then a short pause. 'It's perfect.'

Tom joined her on the pavement and put his arms around her.

'It's incredible,' she said. 'What made you buy it?'

'Well, it's leased actually. The insurance money from the painting came in handy for the deposit.'

She thumped him on his chest. 'Don't be facetious, Tom. Tell me.'

'Well, this is the sweet shop I always came to as a child to spend my pocket money and it holds so many happy memories for me, and I'm sure for a lot of other people too. It's also were I bought those dodgy gum packets and when I returned a few days later to give the owner an earful I found it closed down. I couldn't let the shop close. The old man who used to run this shop died a couple of years ago. He was so kind and gentle. He would go out of his way to get you whatever you wanted, nothing was any trouble for him, and the kids adored him. Before the twins and Jasper arrived, I never knew there was anything more important than my work. After looking after them for a while, my priorities began to change. I guess it all changed at Nick's funeral. The thought of the kids not growing up with a father made me fearful of Alex's future. Okay, so I'm alive, but if I carried on at Thornes, he may grow up hardly ever seeing me or knowing me. I knew something had to give and so when I saw this place up for lease I jumped at it. It'll be ours to care for, Alex can be with me as I work, and what could be more satisfying than seeing smiles on the faces of children as they buy their sweets. I can't think of a job that's more rewarding.'

Scarlett kissed him and Tom felt the cold of her tears as they fell down her cheeks.

'I love you, Tom Farrow.'

'And I love you. So do you want to see inside?'

'You bet.'

They walked inside and Scarlett shut the door. 'Got any stock in yet?'

'Yep!'

'Have you any strawberry shrimps?'

'Boxes of them.'

Alex's Christening was great. Everyone was invited. George had a seat of honour as Godfather, but Tom still thought he was happier because he was sitting next to Isidora – the love of his life. It would take him a while to get used to the idea of the two of them together. Sam managed to find a girl to bring with him. Apparently, he had promised to buy her the outfit she was wearing if she kissed him in front of everyone. Judging by the lack of material on it Tom reckoned he got off lightly. Maud sat in the choir stalls, but she still felt part of the family. Howard and Craig sat like two Wall Street bankers behind Sir Wilfred and Charlene. They made a handsome couple in a strange sort of way. Jackie sat towards the back of the congregation. She didn't want any of the children to disrupt the service, but as it happened, they sat quietly throughout. Geri and Paulo watched from the foyer not wishing to intrude. The Vicar was very gentle with Alex as he paraded him down the body of the church after he had christened him. Alex cooed at all the strange faces that peered at him and even managed to release a noisy burp as John finished off with a short prayer of thanksgiving.

Afterwards everyone returned to the Farrow's house for a light lunch. It was fun to entertain. They hadn't done it since Alex had been born so it was nice to have the opportunity to see all their friends together under one roof. During dessert, Sir Wilfred felt obliged to thank Scarlett and Tom for their hospitality and he wished them well for the new baby and their new venture with the shop. He was a kind man and someone Tom could look up to and respect. The kind of person Tom wanted to be to Alex.

As everyone left Tom handed them all a little parcel of sweets containing a business card for 'Farrow's Barrow'. Well, he needed to drum up custom somehow. Scarlett shut the door, turned, leant against it, and sighed. 'I'll get Alex and put him down to bed then I'll do the clearing up.'

'Don't worry, Maud put him down before she left and I'll do the tidying up later. Come and sit down.'

She sat next to Tom at the foot of the stairs.

'Tom. Are you sure you're doing the right thing?'

'I can honestly say this is the one decision I have made that I am one hundred per cent positive about. Yes, I am doing the right thing.

I'm not just doing it for me; I'm doing it for all of us.'

'Good! I'm glad I have you back. So, what now?'

'Let's just enjoy the peace and quiet now that we've got the house to ourselves again.'

'And just what have you got in mind?'

He cuddled up to her and laid his head against hers.

'Well, seeing as I have to take it apart how about one last race around Monaco?'

Scarlett lifted her head and smiled as she began to stand up. Tom knew what she was thinking.

'On one condition,' she said turning on the bottom step.

'What?'

'That I get the blue car.'

'But that's the faster one.'

'I know,' she replied as she ran up the stairs.

'That's not fair, said Tom. 'I want the blue one. Scarlett! Scarlett!'

Tom chased his wife up the stairs knowing he'd let her win. Not out of chivalry, but out of love for the most beautiful woman in his life.

Printed in Great Britain
by Amazon

80517158R00176